MW01115995

LAW FIRM GROWTH ACCELERATOR

THE PROVEN FRAMEWORK FOR MULTIPLYING
YOUR IMPACT, PROFIT, AND FREEDOM

BILL HAUSER & ANDREW STICKEL

LAW FIRM GROWTH ACCELERATOR
The Proven Framework for Multiplying Your Impact, Profit, and Freedom

Copyright © 2024. Bill Hauser & Andrew Stickel. All rights reserved. No part of this publication may be reproduced, distributed, or transmitted in any form or by any means, including photocopying, recording, or other electronic or mechanical methods, without the prior written permission of the publisher, except in the case of brief quotations embodied in critical reviews and certain other noncommercial uses permitted by copyright law.

For permission requests, speaking inquiries, and bulk order purchase options, email marketing@smbteam.com.

SMBteam.com
Scribe: Greta Meyers
Editing by Lori Lynn | Lori Lynn Enterprises
Book Design by Transcendent Publishing | transcendentpublishing.com

ISBN: 979-8-9906867-3-1

Disclaimer: The authors make no guarantees concerning the level of success you may experience by following the advice and strategies contained in this book, and you accept the risk that results will differ for each individual. The testimonials and examples provided in this book show exceptional results, which may not apply to the average reader and are not intended to represent or guarantee that you will achieve the same or similar results.

Printed in the United States of America.

DEDICATION

For Chelsie, whose belief in me has been unwavering. Your support is invaluable. To Malayla, Aubrey, and Mason—you are my constant motivation to pursue excellence, showing me daily what's truly important in life.

—A.S.

This book is dedicated to the four most important women in my life. My beautiful and supportive wife Emily for giving me the freedom to be my truest self. My mom, who taught me self-belief. My daughter Camille for giving me purpose. And, my dog Jade for being the best dog on planet Earth. With these four ladies in my life, I can never go wrong.

—B.H.

TABLE OF CONTENTS

FOREWORD

I had the pleasure of meeting Bill Hauser and Andy Stickel a few years ago. At that point, my partners and I, along with our amazing team, had built our law firm, Dudley DeBosier, into a sizable practice with over 60 attorneys across the state of Louisiana. We had also bought an advertising agency, CJ Advertising, which represented over 50 law firms across the country. Additionally, I had been doing consulting for over a decade, working with 200+ law firms from all over on how to build their practice. I had seen a lot of incredible firms, and I had been around some amazing people in the legal space. In spite of all that I had seen and been around, the first time that I joined Bill, Andy, and the SMB Team on one of their webinars, I thought to myself, "This is different."

I was struck by the energy, the community, and the culture of the hundreds of law firms that the SMB Team was helping. I was impressed with the practical, tangible advice that was being given by the speakers. They were making firms better. They were helping firms grow. They weren't doing it for just a few firms, but hundreds. I was immediately a fan. From that point on, whenever Bill or Andy reaches out and asks me to be a part of anything they are doing, I am in. So it is an honor for me to write the introduction to this book.

If you want to grow your law firm or if you want to make changes to your law firm, you don't have to do it alone. You shouldn't do it alone. You are foolish if you try to do it alone. There is a quote by Charlie "Tremendous" Jones, a former motivational speaker, that says, "You will be the same person in five years as you are today except for the people you meet and the books you read." I believe that you will have the same law firm in five years that you have today, except for the coaches you work with and the books you read. Bill and Andy are those coaches, and this is one of those books that will change your firm for the better.

It may seem like you have all the time in the world to build your ideal firm. It may feel like there is no rush to make things happen. The truth is that time flies by quickly. The truth is that we don't have that much time to create a great firm. This book will save you time. There are no shortcuts, but it will save you the time of having to figure out things on your own. I highly encourage you to read this great book, read it slowly, take notes, and apply it. You and your firm will be better off for it.

—Chad Dudley, Esq.
Partner, Dudley DeBosier Injury Lawyers

INTRODUCTION

"Do not wait: the time will never be 'just right.' Start where you stand, and work whatever tools you may have at your command, and better tools will be found as you go along."

—Napoleon Hill

This isn't what he'd pictured.

John started his law firm because he had a vision. Full of inspiration and hope, he imagined himself descending the steps outside the courthouse in the wake of his beaming client, brimming with excitement about their hard-earned victory. Met with a bank of microphones thrust in his face from eager reporters, he would be fully prepared with his statement. In those early days, he was convinced he was going to change the world by fighting injustice and sticking up for people who couldn't defend themselves.

Along the way, John's plan was to secure financial success. His bank account—strike that, *accounts*—would be a cornucopia of abundance. He visualized taking his family on exotic vacations, maybe buying a second home where he could make memories by the lakeshore or on the ski slopes. The financial security he earned would free up his time, enabling him to coach his kids' sports teams. He'd treat his wife to romantic getaways to Bora Bora or Tahiti.

And his clients! They would be so happy. So happy, in fact, they would *insist* that their friends hire him. They'd leave glowing five-star reviews online and send him handwritten, heartfelt letters about how he'd changed their lives. In his large, well-designed office, those cards would be prominently displayed, reminding him and everyone else that his success as a lawyer was causing a ripple effect of justice won.

His vision of running a law firm meant making an impact. It meant wealth. It meant freedom.

But that's not his reality.

Ten years in, and John is working on a Saturday afternoon instead of cheering on his daughter at her soccer game. He hasn't taken a real vacation since he started the firm. How could he? His employees can't be trusted to run the firm in his absence—they're good enough to not get fired, but that's about it.

Every time he goes to court, he knows there will be three fires to put out by the time he gets back to the office. He still has to be involved in all aspects of running his business, which is exhausting. The 60-hour workweeks aren't doing his physique any favors either—he's definitely not waking up early to hit the gym after a late night work session fueled by KFC and M&Ms.

And so much for the romantic getaways. John's wife complains that he works too much, even as he tries to explain how much stress he's under. He fires back, "Do you think I *want* to work 16-hour days or nights or weekends? Do you think I *want* to take every client that comes along because I'm so stressed out there won't be another one?" He feels like the strain is making him a crappy spouse, parent, friend … human.

When he walks out of the courthouse, he doesn't feel like a justice warrior. He feels constant, low-level anxiety. He often wonders, *Am I even making an impact?* He reassures himself that he is, but he knows his commitment to his clients comes at the expense of missing quality time with his family.

There's financial stress too. Over the years, the source of that stress has evolved but never gone away. In the beginning, he wasn't even sure if his firm would be profitable at the end of the month. Then, he knew profit would come, but he didn't know how much. Often, he had no idea where his next case would come from.

Later, his firm's profit eventually increased but then plateaued. He finally got beyond the plateau but only by working 80-hour weeks—and he began to realize that it only put him at a slightly higher plateau. There's also a nagging suspicion in the back of his mind that he's probably missing out on cases that would be a perfect fit because he's too busy working on cases that that he has **no choice** but to take. He's relying almost entirely on word-of-mouth referrals just to stay afloat.

His law firm's growth has stagnated. It feels like he has nothing real to show for all his years of work. Where's his legacy?

If he stopped working with clients today, his firm would be worth $0, because he's the one doing all the work.

What's especially aggravating are the billboards and social media ads he sees from the new lawyer in town. Even though this hotshot has only been working for a third of the time that John has and isn't nearly as good, he's still stealing John's cases. And there's only one reason. He's good at marketing.

The only solution John can think of is to go back to the way things were when he first started the firm. He continues to grind, grind, grind, even though he knows it's untenable. His wife sees it. His friends see it. His kids feel it. He's heading toward burnout.

He thinks, *Maybe I'll just stay small. It's complicated enough already. Why would I ever grow my law firm? Why would I ever invest in more marketing, bring on more clients, or hire more people, when it's already so stressful?* He resigns himself to just *work harder, work harder, work harder.*

What, if anything, can be done to take him back to the fantasy that started him down this path in the first place? He went all in on his vision of owning a law firm, burning the ships that would have enabled him to do anything else. But his dream life still feels miles away.

Why is the gap between his expectations and reality so far off?

What Law School Doesn't Teach

Here's the thing. John knows how to be a great lawyer. He can build the perfect case and meticulously pick apart any argument from the opposing counsel. Critical thinking and legal analysis are his forte. That's what he learned in law school and he's only improved with practice. As a lawyer, he's nailing it.

But that's led to some unforeseen consequences. The one thing he won't sacrifice is client results. He's not going to let just anyone take on his cases. *He* has to handle his casework. Unfortunately, since he also has to run all other aspects of the firm, he's completely overwhelmed. He *would* delegate responsibilities if he could. After all, he doesn't want to be a "jack of all trades." But when he puts up a job ad, he only gets mediocre candidates. Mediocre hires do mediocre work. After hiring someone new, John thinks, *I could have saved myself money and time and produced better results if I had just done it all myself.* And that's what keeps him doing everything on his own with a small team of employees who are just good enough to keep the doors open but can't be trusted to run the ship without him.

The truth is, law school teaches people how to practice law, not how to hire or manage people. Not how to get clients. Not how to cast vision or set quarterly goals or figure out how to make a profit. Not one of John's brilliant professors ever taught him a lick of any of that stuff.

John can't find his way out, and it's not his fault.

No one taught him how to run a business. Most law schools train lawyers to work for government agencies or big law firms. They're not trying to create entrepreneurs.

John realized early on that getting hired at a firm where his hours of hard work were making the partners rich wasn't what he wanted, so he branched out on his own. Now he's living an exhausting reality, rather than the dream life he'd envisioned.

He *could* figure it out, if he found the right advisor. But he doesn't know who to trust. In the meantime, he feels paralyzed, not knowing what next step to take.

Law Firm Growth Accelerator

In the early days of running our businesses, we were frustrated too. We got ripped off by bogus agencies. We hired mediocre employees who did stupid things. (Ever had an employee show up higher than Snoop Dogg at 9 a.m.? We have.) We had to learn the hard way how to forecast, budget, and increase revenue.

And we know the pain—deeply, personally—of not knowing whether or not you're going to turn a profit or leave a legacy. We also know that John's dream life is possible. *Your dream life is possible.* We've seen it happen—not just in a few fortunate law firms, but consistently for *hundreds* of law firm owners.

At the time of this writing, about 400 law firms are actively using our coaching and marketing services. **Over the last two years, our average law firm client grew their annual revenues by 81%.** This is based on data reported directly from our clients. Compare that to the average *5%* growth rate of a law firm in the U.S., according to IBIS World[1], and that means our clients are growing 16 times faster than the average

---

[1] Claire O'Connor, Law Firms in the US, IBISWorld, July 2017, https://my.ibisworld.com/us/en/industry/54111

law firm. These firms are across 14 practice areas, range in revenue from small to large and are in both high- and low-competition markets.

Through trial and error, working with thousands of law firms, and mentorship from the most successful law firm owners and business minds in the world, our company, SMB Team, discovered there are only four pillars that must be in place for a law firm owner to grow their revenues, profits, and freedom—while having a bigger impact on their clients' lives.

When you master these four pillars, your revenue increases, which leads to profit and freedom increasing, which leads to the ultimate goal of becoming a Freedom Entrepreneur and living the life you had envisioned at the beginning of your career.

What are these four pillars?

1. Lead Generation
2. Intake
3. Self-Managing Team
4. Profits

The graphic below illustrates our Law Firm Growth Acceleration model with lead generation at the base of the triangle and profits at the peak. When you master the four pillars, you create more positive *impact* on your clients' lives. More *freedom* for you as you empower a high-performing team. More *money* for your firm, your family, and your employees. Do you think you could master four more things if it meant more time, freedom, and money? If it meant you would finally get to live the life of your dreams?

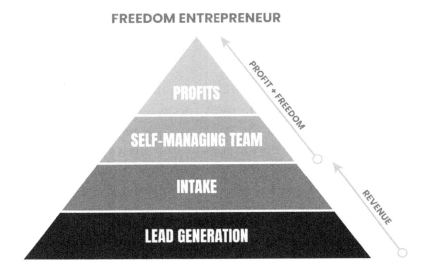

Lead Generation

The first thing you need is quality, consistent lead generation that doesn't depend on you shaking hands and kissing babies. Leads are like gasoline for your law firm's growth plan. With an empty tank of gas, your law firm will not grow. You need an abundance of leads—so many leads that you can pick and choose the perfect-fit cases you want. Most importantly, your lead generation should work without your personal time input.

Intake

Second, you need an intake system to turn those leads into signed clients. And, yes, your intake system should work without you personally hopping on the phone. If you get tons of leads but don't have a system to turn them into clients, your marketing efforts are pointless. You might as well not even generate leads, right? And, if every lead has to talk to you, get ready for a brain hemorrhage.

Self-Managing Team

Once you get your lead generation and intake handled, you will increase your active caseload and gross revenues. To handle your new abundance of clients, you need a self-managing team of rockstar employees. You don't get freedom without a team of A-players running your law firm—without you—helping your clients get the results that they need, using processes you put in place. Only with a team can your law firm be run like a well-oiled machine, giving you more freedom to step away. This requires a scalable hiring system and team management system.

Profits

Finally, you need to make sure that you're making a profit. If your revenue goes up but your *expenses* increase faster than your revenue, then you're not helping your firm, your employees, or yourself. Profit is not a selfish thing. If you don't have a profitable business model, you can't help anybody. You can't hire remarkable employees to give your clients stellar results. You can't invest in marketing. You can't pay your employees more money. And on top of that, you can't give yourself and your family the life that you've been dreaming of. Profitability is both where we *begin* in charting a path toward growth, and where we *end* as we confirm your arrival at Freedom Entrepreneur.

The Law Firm Growth Accelerator is the path to the life of freedom most attorneys envision at the beginning of their careers. If you master the four pillars, which are laid out in detail in the pages of this book, you will know *with absolute certainty* what to do at every stage of your law firm's growth journey. We leave no stone unturned.

You will know *precisely* how to allocate your budget once you are making more revenue.

You will discover the specific dollar amount to invest in marketing, where to focus your marketing efforts depending on your current stage of growth, what results you can expect, as well as how to make the most of that investment.

You will find step-by-step guidance in setting up an intake system that will ensure you sign up a high percentage of right-fit cases from your new lead sources. You will learn how to *replace* yourself from the intake process with highly trained intake specialists who use well-crafted inbound phone call scripts.

You will uncover a multi-year blueprint on how to hire the right roles, at the right time, and know how much to pay them so that they can run your law firm on autopilot, *with or without you*.

This blueprint spells out exactly how to command high profits in your law firm, no matter how many people you hire, how much you spend on marketing, or how much time you take off.

Our goal is for you to know with absolute certainty that a specific dollar amount will be deposited, net, into your take-home bank account every single month.

It's not only possible, it's within reach. And it can happen for you.

The Four Problems Hindering Growth

Here's how it works. The Law Firm Growth Acceleration model works backward from the four major problems that prevent law firm owners from growing their firms. You're probably familiar with many of these.

1. Insufficient lead generation, i.e. struggling to find qualified, new potential clients.
2. Ineffective intake, i.e. you don't have a honed process to turn potential clients into signed cases.
3. Micromanaging organizational structure, i.e. you as the owner have to be involved in every part of your firm's activity. (No vacations for you.)
4. Low or unpredictable profit margins, i.e. you can't count on your firm's profitability.

SMB Team worked backward from those four problems and invented a new way to help scale a law firm through our numbers-based goal-setting model. Cutting-edge digital marketing to create lead abundance. Sales and intake scripting, training, and systems to turn "right fit" leads into signed clients. Virtual assistant solutions to handle the repetitive tasks in your firm. Strategies to attract A-players, hire a self-managing team, and create bullet-proof systems for your firm, all while maintaining high profits.

We are the only company in the legal industry solving all of these problems under one umbrella, and in this book, you will learn our most powerful battle-tested strategies.

Your Marching Orders

In this book, we're going to teach you how to address each one of those four problems and create a profound transformation in your law firm and life.

Part 1: Plan Your Profit

In Part 1, we focus on planning your Profit. We teach you how to reverse-engineer your vision into a profitable, long-term, value-focused business plan. You'll learn how to think like a business owner and get clarity on your firm's specific growth goals and purpose. We're also going to call out any mental hang-ups that may be holding you back from pursuing rapid growth.

Once you've got your own mindset right, we teach you about the Lawyer Legacy Staircase™, so you know precisely how you'll need to evolve your identity to guide your firm toward each level of growth. In Chapters 3, 4, and 5, we get down to brass tacks: you learn how to write a Vivid Vision, project your annual growth, and identify and roll out your quarterly goals. We'll also teach you what Key Performance Indicators (KPIs) to watch like a hawk, so you're making decisions strategically, and you'll learn the 20/40/10 budget allocation rule.

Part 2: Growing Your Firm

In Part 2, we focus on growing your firm through lead abundance and intake. First, we'll give you a high-level overview of marketing strategy and fundamentals, so that you know how to evaluate the efficacy of whatever marketing firm you may choose to hire. Then it's time for more brass tacks.

Chapter 7 teaches you the strategies for *Demand Marketing* to amplify your lead abundance through an effective page-one Google strategy and SEO. In Chapter 8, we tackle the world of social media, teaching you strategies to effectively build your *Awareness Marketing*—including simple proven strategies on how to record killer videos.

The end of Part 2 will shift our attention to intake and sales, the next level up in the pyramid. Chapter 9 gives you specific strategies to level up your intake system and secure more *right fit* clients, so that you're not dependent on taking whatever nightmare client walks in the door.

Part 3: Self-Managing Team

Part 3 focuses on building and leading a team of rock stars. Because—holy crap—now that you have all these new signed cases, what do you do? You have to hire, delegate, and replace yourself in the casework. You'll learn how to attract and recruit the best of the best, and we'll even tell you what to pay them. Then—and this is key—we'll explain how to *lead* these all-stars so that they deliver their best.

Finally, we'll teach you strategies to WOW your clients, so that they refer their friends, write your five-star reviews, and continue fanning the flame of your rapidly growing firm. When put all together, your new lead abundance, strong intake system, and your self-managing team of rock stars will help lead you to the profitability targets you mapped out to begin with.

The Ultimate Goal

This book is going to teach you how to produce world-class client results, without requiring your personal investment of time. (No more 16-hour workdays!) It's going to teach you to create a legal results-producing system and team that you can put your stamp of approval on. (No more putting out fires every time you get back to the office!) It will provide you with a proven system to attract lawyers who—believe it or not—will handle your cases *even better than you,* lawyers you would be proud to introduce your clients to as their new representation. (Now you can book your tickets to Bora Bora!) In short, it will help you evolve from a lawyer to a business owner to a freedom entrepreneur.

This book isn't just another law firm book with vague principles about "how you need a vision" and so on. We're giving you nuts and bolts. Proven strategies with proof to back up every one. We're not going to prompt you to look within and reflect. We're going to prescribe clear steps to take, based on math and statistical success.

And this book isn't about incremental growth either. If you want to grow your law firm slowly, by 5 or 10%, year over year—don't read this book. This book is for people who want to grow their law firm, profit, and personal freedom by 100% or more. We're making the claim with this book that these principles will help you *double* every one of those things—so, if you're growth-minded, you're in the right place.

Why Did We Write This Book?

First, let's call out the elephant in the room. This is a book for lawyers, but neither one of us is a lawyer. Why should you listen to us about how to run a law firm?

Here's why … Aside from the fact that we are friends with and students of some of the smartest law firm owners and business builders in the world, a law firm is first and foremost a service business. Your product happens to be legal services. Our products happen to be marketing, coaching, and virtual assistant services.

We grew our own business (SMB Team) from 0 to over 100 full-time employees, $25.8M in annual collected revenue, and a $100M valuation in just 6 years. All self-made. Due to the impact SMB Team has on its clients and employees (and a 915% three-year growth rate), INC 5000 ranked SMB Team in the top 730 fastest-growing companies in the entire United States in 2022 and 2023 (#729 and #641 respectively) and the #1 fastest growing non-software company in the legal industry two years in a row.

We've both run multiple successful service businesses and found that every single business grows and dies for the same reasons. At the end of the day, the principles are the same.

Although we're not lawyers, every single strategy in this book is one that we have personally used and had success with. We've also taught these principles to hundreds of lawyers who have also had enormous success, as our earlier statistics testify.

Maybe that brings up a new misgiving for you since we're professional marketers. Did we write this book just to sell you on our own programs and get you to give SMB Team money? Is this just one big marketing shill?

Well, obviously, we're not going to turn away qualified clients who like this book and recognize the ways we can help. If SMB Team gets new business from people reading this book and buying into the strategies we share, we'd consider that a major plus. But that's not our main motivation for writing this. You'll see what we mean in later chapters. We literally give away all of our secrets, so you can do them yourself.

We wrote this book because we've seen the success of these principles and we want to spread the good news. In fact, this book is us drinking our own Kool-Aid®. As you'll read later in the book, one of the strategies we recommend for your marketing is to prove you can help people by actually helping them. In this book, we set out to actually help you! We're holding nothing back. In fact, we've included a number of additional free resources that you can link to for even deeper training in key areas.

Why would we do that?

Why is the key word.

Each one of us has a deep, personal *why* for investing the time we have into these pages, which goes far beyond making sales.

BILL HAUSER NARRATES

I'll share more about this in Chapter 1, but for me, my "why" in life is driven by wanting to help people avoid the financial ruin my family experienced. My dad ran his own paving company but didn't have the knowledge to turn his business into a self-managing company.

My dad broke his back for my mom and me. And, despite his decades of hard work, our family went bankrupt in 2008. My life was upended in the years after that.

In every law firm owner I see, I see a picture of my dad. I see someone who is an artist at what they do, an expert, someone who loves serving clients. But I also recognize the tragedy they could experience if they don't get clarity on how to run their law firms like a business. The horrible years following my family's bankruptcy and turmoil is a reality that's too close for comfort—especially if business owners don't recognize that they need to be *more* than an expert in their craft. They also need to know how to effectively run a business.

I have a vision to transform the state of the legal industry so that every firm we help becomes recession-proof and self-managing. So more families like mine are spared the heartache I went through as a result of a business failure. So I can help people—and their families—succeed, thrive, and experience their best lives.

That's why, when I started SMB Team, it didn't ever feel like enough to just offer marketing services. I felt compelled to offer coaching too. Everything I learned that was helping me strengthen my own business, I wanted to pass on.

In fact, that's why I sought out Andy's company to merge with. Andy and I were both primarily running marketing companies, but we were *also* both running coaching programs. And for some reason, we were also the only two people in the entire legal industry with over 400 YouTube videos educating lawyers for free.

Andy and I shared some weird spiritual connection. How else to explain why we were both doing lawyer marketing, coaching, and making hundreds of free law firm growth videos for free on YouTube?

We knew lawyers didn't just need another marketing agency. Lawyers needed a path to learn marketing and business. They needed to be able to get off the hamster wheel of constantly churning through so-called marketing gurus. Hiring one after another, and after thousands of dollars spent with no real return on investment, they think, *Well, that didn't work.*

As insiders in the marketing world, we know that most marketing firms want you to become dependent on them so that you never leave. Andy and I both felt the opposite. We wanted our clients to become so good at marketing and management that they *wouldn't* need us anymore. Because then, they would be recession-proof! They would have built a business that ensured financial stability and a positive impact for everyone they came into contact with.

For me, this book is a continuation of my personal mission to help business owners run profitable, successful businesses so that their firms and their families become financially secure, capable of impacting the world for good.

ANDY STICKEL NARRATES

Why did *I* write this book? Because I was inspired by another book, *Extreme Ownership,* by Jocko Willink and Leif Babin.

I didn't use to take "extreme ownership" over my clients' success. When I was early in my years running a marketing firm, we would get our clients lots of leads, but they didn't know what to do with them—they weren't turning those leads into signed clients. Even when they managed to secure clients, I would see that they weren't running their firms properly. They were great lawyers, but had no idea how to run a business.

For a long time, I just complained about that. "This is so annoying. We're doing such a good job getting them leads, but they suck at turning them into profit."

But then it was worse than annoying. Because even if they were the ones that sucked, we were the ones that got fired.

After reading *Extreme Ownership,* I took a hard look at myself. There's a quote in the book that especially resonated with me: "Leaders must own everything in their world. There is no one else to blame." I said, "What if I took responsibility for my clients' results, instead of blaming them? What opportunities can I find to help them level up?"

My new attitude changed the game completely. I started making coaching videos for my clients to train them on areas of the business where I saw they could shore things up. I started being way more proactive in getting my clients resources. And it worked. Our clients began experiencing way more success and my marketing firm took off.

Then—ironically—I had the opportunity to relieve myself of responsibility altogether. Right before Bill and I merged our companies, I was offered $9M for my business. I could have just walked away and retired early. The moment felt like a crossroads. I wondered, *Do I just take the money? Or do I merge with Bill and finish what I started to serve my clients?*

The crossroads gave me the clarity to identify the mission I wanted to live for. I wanted to help an entire industry. I wanted to finish what I started. I wanted to do that because—as Bill implied—it's not just about helping lawyers. It means helping everyone the lawyers touch. Their families, their clients, their employees, and so on. We had the potential to make an impact on *all* those people, if we even helped just one law firm expand their reach.

I want that ripple effect.

Apply Everything You Learn and This Could Happen

When we joined forces, our missions and our effectiveness at helping our clients grew exponentially. Before meeting Bill, Andy was able to build his company from $0 to $4M per year in revenue. In nine years, he achieved that growth *just* by using the marketing principles in the book. When it came to management, vision, or planning, he was just winging it. He never set quarterly goals or made a budget. *Just* using the marketing principles in Part 2, the company grew to a four million revenue within a decade.

Before meeting Andy, Bill grew his company from zero to $4.8M in annual revenue in just four years (about three times faster than Andy). He did that by using the management *and* marketing principles in this book—this shows how much faster growth can happen when you apply *multiple* principles from this book.

When we joined forces in 2022, we went from $8.8M in combined revenues to *over $14M in one year*. Our companies did $25.8M in collected revenues. By the end of 2024, we are projected to do $51M in revenues and will have an enterprise value of $158M.

Is our company perfect? No. While we still have *so much* to improve on, this level of growth only comes because of the array of transformational services we offer our clients and the fact that a low percentage of law firms who work with us leave.

We don't share this to brag. We share this to show you these principles work to grow your revenues, your client happiness and your net worth simultaneously. We've lived them. We live *by* them. This same multiplier effect can happen for *you* if you apply all that you learn from this book.

And if there's still any doubt about why we do what we do, this message from one of our clients epitomizes our "why":

> *Bill and Andy,*
>
> *You have been a godsend to my business and to my personal life.*
>
> *I used to struggle to pay my two employees and even myself on a consistent basis.*

It was a miracle that a case settled for almost the exact amount I needed to invest to join. I prayed with tears that night and asked God to make sure you were the real deal. You were definitely the real deal.

Since joining with SMB Team, I now have 11 employees. I purchased a million-dollar home on a golf course and paid cash for my Tesla.

SMB Team changed my life, and I will be forever grateful.

—Deidra

That's why we do what we do.

Let's Hit the Gas

If you've been looking for the key to get you unstuck, this is it. These strategies are proven not only by us but also by our hundreds of successful clients. They've been informed by some of the best business minds out there. Since we weren't born to families of successful entrepreneurs, the two of us spend over half a million dollars per year just on coaches, consultants, and mentors—to get answers.

We've learned from many of the brilliant people we've had the luxury of being able to interview on our podcast (some of whom we're now close friends with), like Mike Morse, Glen Lerner, Andrew Finkelstein, Morris Bart, Alexander Shunnarah, Dan Newlin, Rex Parris, Chad Dudley, and more. These are some of the most successful, highest revenue-grossing law firm owners in the country, and they've shared the lessons they learned from their mistakes with us.

All of that, we're passing on to you.

Enough of the hype. Let's put the rubber to the road and start the process of turning your vision into reality. We're going to start with the top of the Law Firm Growth Accelerator: Profit. By helping you envision where you want to go, you'll be able to correctly build the foundation of Lead Generation, then Intake, then a Self-Managing Team. By the end of Part 1, you'll know precisely how much your firm stands to make in the next three years, how to implement annual and quarterly goals, and how to read your numbers to track your progress.

Let's get you more profit, more freedom, and greater impact. It begins by helping you build the law firm that you set out to build in the first place.

The life that you want is within reach!

PART 1

PLAN YOUR PROFIT

*Identify Where You Want to Go and Learn How to
Reverse Engineer Your Dreams into Reality*

FREEDOM ENTREPRENEUR

PROFITS

SELF-MANAGING TEAM

THE ABYSS

INTAKE

LEAD GENERATION

PROFIT + FREEDOM

REVENUE

CHAPTER 1

YOUR COMPASS POINT

WHERE ARE YOU GOING AND WHY?

"Hard choices, easy life. Easy choices, hard life."

—Jerzy Gregorek

BILL HAUSER NARRATES

The first time I had any idea my family was in financial trouble was the day I stumbled across my mom's suicide note ... and then my dad's almost-attempt.

I had come home from high school and walked into my computer room, planning to start a video gaming session. But the desk area wasn't clear. A piece of paper had fallen out of a folder from the filing cabinet and landed next to the desk. I picked it up, planning to stick it back in its folder, and close the drawer. That's when I recognized my mom's handwriting.

She had written down information about her assets, where they could be located, and who they should be given to. Then I read the words that stopped my entire being: "After I kill myself."

At first, I thought it was a joke. My brain hurtled full throttle toward denial. *How was this possible?* Did my mother—the role model of my life—really feel broken enough to make her want to kill herself? Was she in such despair to the point she felt it was necessary to write a list of her assets in a suicide note? That one piece of paper and all it represented made me question everything about reality.

Thankfully, my mom didn't harm herself. I confronted her about it. She made it seem like it wasn't real—or at least, wasn't serious. But when I pressed my parents for more information, I found out what that note *did* represent. My parents were experiencing financial issues. Serious ones.

Catastrophic ones.

They tried to assure me they would turn things around. After all, Dad was the best paving contractor in Media, Pennsylvania. He'd always had a small staff, keeping the business lean. They'd experienced plenty of ups and downs with the business before. "This is no big deal," they told me.

But these financial issues *were* a big deal—and they were at the root of every horrific experience I encountered in the years that followed.

These financial issues were the reason I parked my truck away from our house, so the bank wouldn't see it when they drove up to our house to repossess it. That didn't matter. The bank eventually repossessed my truck anyway.

These financial issues were at the root of Dad's affair, too, which I discovered during a weekend trip with my buddies to our family's mountain house in the Poconos. My dad told me a real estate investor lady would be there that weekend— "to help me with investments." She stayed late that Friday. Then, she stayed the night. The next morning, I needed to get the keys to the truck off my dad's dresser so my friends and I could go to a dirt bike race. When I opened the door to the bedroom, I saw my dad—naked—lying down on the bed next to the woman.

These financial issues were at the root of my parents' marriage ending and the two years of silence between my dad and me. After I returned home from the weekend at the cabin, I told my mom what I had seen, despite my dad telling me to keep it between us. Within minutes, my mom threw all my dad's clothes out onto the front lawn.

These financial issues were behind all of our assets getting repossessed, every one of the business's fleet of paving trucks getting repossessed, our family declaring bankruptcy, and the short sale of our house.

And they were at the root of my dad's near suicide. He finally broke the silence and called me in a panicky rage, ranting on the phone about how everything that happened with our family was my fault because I'd told my mom. "If you had just been a man and not told her, then our whole family would still be together!" His voice got louder and higher, like

5

a roller coaster about to dive, and then suddenly, the phone went dead.

Later, I was told that when he hung up on me, he was holding a gun to his head and was considering taking his own life. Instead, he had ended up shooting every round in that gun out into the woods behind the house.

There were a lot of factors that contributed to those scenarios. But my interpretation—both then and now—was that they were all mainly rooted in their financial issues. It was the financial stress that seemed to cause my parents' marriage to unravel. It was the business failing that led to the bankruptcy and the humiliating financial losses. It was the financial issues that were behind both of them contemplating suicide.

Why bother sharing all this? Why open a book about growing your law firm with trauma from my childhood? Because this story has directly informed everything that follows.

Because of these experiences, I've made it my life's mission to ensure *no one* else has to go through the pain my family experienced due to a flawed business. Andy and I have set out to help as many law firm owners as possible build their own recession-proof businesses—as we build our own. Every bit of research, every strategy, every investment I've made in my own learning, which I've passed on to you in this book, comes from that mission.

I've made it my life's mission to ensure *no one* else has to go through the pain my family experienced due to flawed financial planning.

The mistakes that led to my family business crumbling—in fact, Andy and I encounter those same mistakes nearly every day in our work helping lawyers grow their law firms.

Luckily, these mistakes are caused by "false beliefs" which can be corrected—as long as you're willing to shift your mindset.

Wrong, Wrong, Wrong

The Law Firm Growth Accelerator model will take you on a journey from stagnancy to growth, from scarcity to abundance, from feeling overwhelmed by your firm to functioning from a place of freedom. It will also ask you to evolve your identity from lawyer to business owner, to freedom entrepreneur—something we'll talk much more about in Chapter 2.

But before *any of that can happen,* you need to get your belief system right. It is impossible for you to evolve as a leader or for your firm to grow with the wrong belief system.

Here's why. Your beliefs determine your actions—and a set of wrong beliefs can set your business up for failure. Many business owners like my dad have faulty beliefs, and they're some of the most common false assumptions made by owners of law firms. Ironically, all of these assumptions are rooted in good intentions, with the intent of maximizing your effectiveness as a lawyer. The only problem is, they're bad data— and they can actually do more harm than good. So, what are those faulty beliefs?

1. **Staying small is the answer.** Many business owners think, "If I keep my team small and just stay at my current size, life will be easier, and I'll have less stress and

7

overhead." But if your law firm stays small, everything will depend on *you* and you won't have the staff to pick up the slack when you're gone—giving you no freedom. The reality is, *everything* is hard. Staying small doesn't make running a business easy. It creates its own challenges. Big is hard, small is hard. It's hard to be broke, and it's hard to be rich (Although—being rich gives you the capital to solve your "hard" problems). If you learn how to build a business that runs without you, then building a bigger team will make your life *much* easier.

2. **Average marketing and word-of-mouth will get the job done.** My dad had *one* main form of marketing for his company: yellow page ads. When the recession hit, people were more reluctant to spend money. The only way they would spend money is if there was a clear differentiating factor favoring the business they wanted to spend money with—a point that is usually communicated through good marketing. My dad's average newspaper ads didn't give people a clear and compelling reason to choose his paving company over all the others in his market. Therefore, his company was viewed as a commodity. So many law firms compete on generic things like "years of experience." Law firms who want to crush it in the future must know how to become omnipresent and build a differentiated value proposition and brand.

3. **If I'm great at lawyering, I'll have a great business.** Wrong. My dad was great at paving, construction, and hardscaping. That didn't guarantee him business success. This is a common assumption among lawyers

too—but there is *no* correlation between being great at your job and getting paid for it. If you don't believe that, type your law firm's keywords into Google and see what comes up on the first page. Do the best attorneys come up, or the best marketers? If your prospective clients don't know that you're amazing at your job, they're going to go with whatever law firm *markets* itself as being amazing at the job. Being a great lawyer—or a great contractor—does not guarantee you will build a recession-proof business.

4. **Nobody can do _____ better than me.** My dad thought he was the only one who could do sales consultations. I understand why. It's because he was so good at sales. As a result, he didn't bother training anyone on his team to do sales. When the recession hit, he was trying to run *all* aspects of the business while navigating a ton of economic stress. Guess what happened to his "expertise" as a salesman? It fell by the wayside when he was trying to juggle everything else too. All the paving companies I remember that succeeded through the recession had expert salespeople whose *only* job was to close deals. This same thing applies to running a law firm. You think you're the only one who can run your cases or handle intake. Eventually, that will become the weakness of your business—the areas in which you are the best. There are 8 billion people on Earth. Someone can do it better than you.

5. **Eighty-hour workweeks are normal.** My dad easily worked 80-hour weeks. He broke his back for us. The problem was, it made him less effective as a

strategic leader. It was the business owners who *didn't* burn themselves out with 80-hour workweeks who were able to focus on strategies that enabled them to successfully navigate the recession. That's true, no matter what industry you're in. Twenty years from now, the only people who remember that you worked late are your loved ones. Time does not equal value. Spend your time on higher value things and you will be able to spend less time working *in* your business.

6. **You should hire people who are not as smart as you.** Wrong again. My dad always was the smartest person in the room. But when problems came up that he didn't know how to handle, no one else did either. The companies with bigger teams and a ton of smart people on staff had the resources and brainpower to weather the economic challenges. You need people smarter than you at intake, marketing, and especially the legal work on your team, in order to feel real freedom.

None of these false beliefs will cut it in a marketplace as competitive as the one we're in right now. While I love my dad with all of my heart and I know how hard he worked for us, my dad did not position himself to run a business that worked well with his life. Instead, the business ran *his* life, and when the business fell apart, his life did too.

The way you design your business will determine the design of your life.

Do you want more freedom, more success, less anxiety, better clients, and more money?

Do you want to be in a position where your business won't be rocked by one speed bump, one emergency, one pandemic, one economic recession?

All those benefits come when you intentionally design your business, take steps to bring your dream life into fruition, and—first and foremost—*make the mindset shift to think like a business owner instead of a lawyer.* We know this because we've guided hundreds of law firms into greater freedom, greater prosperity, and more satisfying work.

So, how do you make the mindset shift? We're about to break it down.

The Lawyer Legacy Staircase

Law schools are great at teaching you how to think like a lawyer. They are *terrible* at teaching you how to run a business. The hard fact is that being a lawyer has nothing to do with running a successful and thriving business. In fact, much of what they teach in law school is the opposite of what you need to know to run a business.

They don't teach you marketing or sales or how to hire people. They don't teach you how to manage people. They are preparing you to be *employees*, grinding away to make other law firm owners rich or work for the government. Your years in law school did not teach you how to be a leader or anything about psychology. Yet, all those skills are necessary for any business owner. There's a good chance you weren't even aware that you were likely going to *be* a business owner.

This is why you need a mindset shift, from thinking like a lawyer to thinking like a business owner. If you want more profit, freedom, and impact, your firm needs to scale up. That requires you to evolve your identity into thinking differently than you have before.

Now, here's the good news. You've *already* evolved your identity from law student to lawyer. And, if you're reading this book, you've most likely made another massive leap— from lawyer to solo practitioner. You *know* how to climb this staircase.

But going further with your firm requires you to go even further with yourself, starting with your mindset. You're going to need to climb higher from small business manager to law firm CEO to law firm *owner*—where the firm runs itself. And at the *top* of this staircase is your dream life. It's where wealth, impact, and freedom reside. It's the place where you have fully evolved into a freedom entrepreneur and can leave a lasting legacy—for your family, your firm, and your broader community. That's why we title this journey the "Lawyer Legacy Staircase." We're going to discuss this much more in Chapter 2.

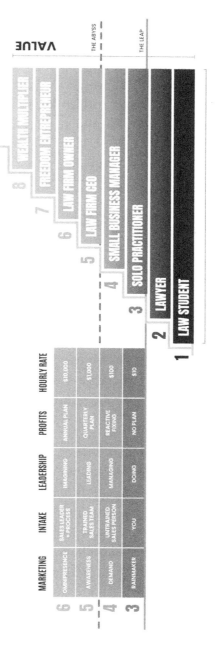

The climb leads to incredible benefits—but it's not an easy one. And, as any Navy SEAL will tell you, the biggest obstacle to doing hard things is your own mindset. You need to want this bad enough to do the work required to get there. You also need to kill the *old* beliefs that are currently hindering your ability to take on the challenge of this staircase.

That's why—no offense—we think you need a brain transplant.

You Need a Brain Transplant

Being a good lawyer is *not enough* to run a successful law firm. Too many lawyers believe the opposite—and it's killing their business.

The first step to changing your brain is to become goal-obsessed. Becoming goal-obsessed starts with learning the art of auto-suggestion, otherwise known as self-suggestion. The best way to learn auto-suggestion is to start writing down your goals every day.

It sounds simple, but after writing down my goals every single day for the past eight years, I can tell you it's amazingly powerful. A 1953 Harvard study known as "The Harvard Study on Goals" studied the outcomes of Harvard MBA students who wrote down their goals (3%), versus students who had goals but didn't write them down (13%), versus students who did not admit to having goals at all (84%). The difference was stark and instructive.

"Ten years later, it was discovered that the 13% who had non-written goals earned on average twice as much as the 84% who did not have goals at all. The 3% who had written goals outperformed everyone altogether by earning 10 times as much as all of the other 97% combined."[2]

Why did the MBA students who had written down their goals so far surpass the others? Because, once they had their goals written down, they were able to take the next step and do whatever it took to achieve those goals.

If every law firm owner took the time to write down exactly how much revenue they wanted to generate, exactly how many employees they wanted, exactly how much profit they wanted, and exactly how much free time they wanted, the legal industry would be a radically different place. Most lawyers would be reaching their business goals.

Instead, they stumble into their current revenue levels and get stuck where they are, just getting by. They did well on one criminal defense case and decided to specialize in criminal law. Or they saw another lawyer win a big settlement from a personal injury case and thought, "Yeah, I'll go for those cases." No planning, no vision, no clue about how their

---

[2] Dugan, Jerry. "The Surprising Truth About A Famous Goals Research Study |." Beyondtherut (blog). December 15, 2022. https://beyondtherut.com/goals-research-harvard-yale-goals-study/#:~:text=Weekly%20Progress%20Reports-,The%20Famous%20Harvard%20(or%20Yale)%20Goals%20Research%20Study,than%20those%20who%20didn't.

decision might play out in the marketplace. In other words, no *business* mindset.

Magic Johnson, the great basketball player, was a speaker at our Relentless Lawyer Bootcamp, an event attended by 900 lawyers. He spoke about how, at the end of his basketball career, he abandoned the basketball player part of his identity to embrace becoming a business owner and investor. Essentially, he gave himself a brain transplant by completely changing his mindset. He even changed his name to reflect his new identity, going by *Earvin "Magic" Johnson* instead of just Magic Johnson.

Earvin Magic Johnson figured out how to do in business what he had done on the basketball court. *Dominate.* At our summit, he shared about how his deal selling inner-city Starbucks stores back to Howard Schultz crushed the money he made in basketball. "That was the moment when everybody said, 'He now has a track record of success.' Now, instead of me chasing the deals, the deals were chasing me. My phone started ringing off the hook. Everybody wanted to invest with me. I went from millions to now playing in the *billions*."

Earvin Magic Johnson's mental shift was, "I'm a business owner." These days, his personal net worth is now in the ballpark of $620M.

This is the same shift that you, a lawyer reading this book, need to make. Let go of being a lawyer and learn to be a leader. A *business* leader.

> **Tell yourself, "I'm a business owner first and that business happens to be a law firm. And, oh yeah, I *happen* to be a lawyer."**

This is the exact opposite of what most lawyers think. They think they are a lawyer first and a business owner second. But that's not a recipe for success, it's a blueprint for failure. At best, it's a recipe for mediocrity.

This book is not intended to convince you to adopt our goals or anyone else's goals. Maybe you want to build a big law firm with a thousand people on staff and dominate your market. Or maybe you want to work less and spend more time with your kids. Either of these options, or countless others, are equally valid and *equally possible*.

This book is about convincing you to figure out exactly what you want. Design the law firm and life of your dreams, then work backward from that clear endpoint to make it come true.

Pick Your Dream Life

It's time to think like a kid writing a letter to Santa Claus. What *do* you want? Answering the questions highlighted in each next section of this chapter helps you sketch out your compass point. In the next few chapters, you're going to be plugging in specific numbers for the "Profit" part of the Law Firm Growth Accelerator triangle. It's the pinnacle of the framework, shaped like an arrow. Think of it as the point of your compass, showing you where you want to go. All of your profit numbers will be informed by your answers to the questions we're about to have you brainstorm.

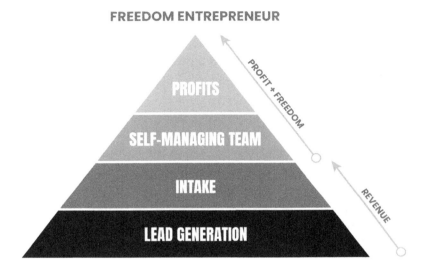

Check out the directional arrows along the side. That's what you *gain* as you implement the Law Firm Growth Accelerator. First revenue, then more freedom and more profit. At the apex of that mountain, you get the life for yourself and your family that others only dream of. We call that becoming a Freedom Entrepreneur. You own your time, your businesses work for you—without you—making you financially free. Essentially, you have the freedom to do whatever you want.

Only 1% of entrepreneurs will ever experience this level of freedom. However, there's a proven path to becoming a Freedom Entrepreneur. Are you willing to do what 99% of business owners are unwilling to do to achieve this freedom? If so, the rest of this book will show you how.

Starting … *now.*

Where Do You Want to Go?

Your most important task as a law firm owner is defining where your firm is going. In Chapter 3, we're going to give you a thorough step-by-step process that you can use to capture and articulate the direction of your firm to your team. We call this your Vivid Vision. Your job as leader is to set the tone and direction of the entire company, starting with your own clarity on where you want to go.

Too vague? We'll narrow it down for you. After working with hundreds of law firms, we've found that 99% of lawyers are aiming for some variation of the following three outcomes in mind, either consciously or unconsciously.

1. **Cashing in.** You want to *sell* your law firm for $_____ in _____ years. (Fill in the amount and the years that suit you.)

2. **Self-Management and Profit.** You want to make $_____ per year for _____ years from your law firm while having _____ free days per year (Again, fill in the amounts and the years you desire.)

3. **Domination.** You don't care about money or time. You just want to scale your firm up, dominate your market, and bury your competition.

Most lawyers are focused on outcomes one and two, but we believe all lawyers have at least a little bit of three in them (some have a *lot*) because most lawyers are competitive in their bones. Whether you've chosen outcomes one, two, *or* three, the rest of our book is going to show you the exact steps to take to make that happen.

Consider those three outcomes and pick the version that appeals to you. Be specific about time and money. Decide exactly how big you want to be. Be as detailed as you can. Write it down.

Now, *visualize* that outcome. You might want to sell your firm for a $100M. Great! To *visualize* that goal, mentally rehearse the day you receive that $100M check.

What does the check feel like? Where are you standing when you grasp it? What does the room look like? What are you wearing? What are you tasting? Are you getting an adrenaline surge? Are the corners of your mouth tugging to the side in an uncontrollable grin? Are you laughing? What emotion are you experiencing as you accept that obscene amount of money? What does it feel like to then tell your family they never have to work again? Play that scenario over in your mind from start to finish. Rehearse it. Live it.

That's what visualization is.

We bring up athletes as examples because their competitive lives are all about achieving winning outcomes. Michael Phelps, the Olympic champion swimmer, once said in an interview that the difference between him and his competitors was that he *visualized* his winning performances. He didn't just set a goal of winning—he *saw* himself surge ahead of the other swimmers, touch the finish wall first, achieve victory, and stand on the podium to receive his medal. He mentally rehearsed the experience. He *visualized*. He put himself in that mental space of winning and achieving his desired outcome.

What worked for him can work for you if you do the same. Rehearse your outcome. *Visualize* it to make it real. Identify and visualize. That's the first step in solving for *where* you want to go.

BILL HAUSER NARRATES

Why Do You Want to Go There?

What's your WHY? The answer to this question must be an emotional one. If it isn't, you're much less likely to succeed.

Steve Jobs, legendary Apple founder and CEO, said, "If you don't love what you do, you're going to give up." Without a strong WHY, when things get tough (they will) and they don't go the way you plan (they won't), it's going to be a lot easier to say something like, "This isn't worth it. I'm done."

I am extremely passionate about my WHY for SMB Team because it's connected to some of the worst pain in my life. Here's what I've written down for my WHY: "Fueled by the pain of my parents' bankruptcy, divorce, and their near-suicides during the 2008 recession, I (Bill Hauser) REFUSE to let people and businesses feel the same pain that I felt. My mission is to create a company that is recession-proof and that allows our team to do what they love. In that process, we help our clients build the same security in their own companies."

I *must* reach my vision, and I have deep, personal reasons for feeling compelled to do so. It's no accident that SMB Team has done as well as it has in just six years. A huge reason we've been so successful is that I had an incredibly strong emotional attachment to my goals. That's incentivized me to do whatever I needed to do to reach those goals. The same will be true for you when you identify your WHY.

A lot of people, including lawyers and business owners, approach their goals in life backward. They start with the "what" and the "how" and leave the WHY until the end. Their "what" might be winning cases. Their "how" is being an effective lawyer. Their WHY is—well, who knows? Making a living? Paying the bills?

Those are not emotional motivators. Reverse that order. Start with the WHY, *then* go to "what" and "how."

In spite of all the pain my family went through, I consider it a blessing. It gave me my WHY.

If you don't have a similar blessing in your own life, think about what you want to give back to your family. That can be your WHY. Or, you may be passionate about serving the clients in your market. You may want to become a divorce lawyer so you can prevent families from feeling the pain that you went through when your own parents got divorced. Maybe you want to ride your motorcycle on the Pacific Coast Highway whenever you want to. That can be your emotional reason. You might want to make your practice so successful that you have the time and energy to get on those two wheels and feel the wind on your face as you zip along the beach.

There are *personal* WHYs, like finding time for your passions. And there are *external* WHYs, like helping homeless people get fair treatment in the legal system. At the intersection of these two WHYs—the personal and external—you find someone unstoppable. You find someone passionate, determined, and absolutely hell-bent on realizing their goals for the future.

The strongest leaders on the planet are crystal clear on their WHY. They know exactly what they want and why they want it, and they figure out the how based on the WHY.

Consider, for example, what happens when people try to quit smoking when they have a non-emotional reason versus an emotional one.

1. **Cost to my wallet.** I'm a smoker and I just figured out how much money I spend *each year* on smoking. That's too much money going down the drain. I'm going to quit smoking.

2. **Cost to my family.** I'm a smoker and I just figured out that my life expectancy is greatly reduced by my habit. This means it's likely my kids are going to grow up without a father. That's unacceptable. I'm going to quit smoking.

In the first scenario, the smoker has a good economic reason to kick his habit. It's practical but non-emotional. In the second scenario, the smoker has a strong *emotional* reason to kick his habit. Which do you think is going to lead to success?

What's the equivalent, for you, of your kids growing up without their father?

I spoke with an attorney who told me, that when he was a kid, his father was never around to coach his little league team. Now he has a son, and he sees the same pattern in their relationship. He works long hours and can't find the time to be with his son in a meaningful way.

I told him we were going to help him. We were going to show him how to increase his revenue so he could put a team in place at his firm that he could afford, which would give him time to coach his own son's little league team. We were going to teach him to delegate. We were going to show him how to make his law practice help him be a better father.

Your passion cannot be all about your selfish needs. You must connect to your internal purpose—your personal mission. Money, at the end of the day, is just a pile of green paper or some digits on your banking app. Money must *lead* to something. It must allow you to reach your mission, to realize your passion.

Whatever you use to motivate yourself, make it strong and emotional. Without a clear WHY, you're more likely to give up. Think of your WHY as your insurance policy against giving up. It will be the single most important thing that will make you stick with your plans and your personal mission through the hard times.

Share Your Purpose

Your personal mission is only part of the equation here. It's the most important part *for you*, but you also need an external purpose. Why? Because there is no reason for other people to spend their working lives laboring for *your* dream life. They need more than that.

Your personal mission should be known to everyone in your firm. Be open about the goals you are striving for. In addition, be very clear about your *external purpose.* Everyone should know WHY they are working at your firm, what change in the market you are striving for, and what outcome will be considered a success.

Take a firm that specializes in personal injury cases. The owner of that firm might have a personal experience with an insurance company that would not pay on a claim. She became a lawyer to prevent that sort of thing from happening to others. That's her personal mission and it's solid.

But that's not enough for the rest of the firm. They can't be there to make her feel better. The *external purpose* for the firm is to go after insurance companies that take advantage of injured people. The firm sticks up for the little guy, the person without a lot of resources to fight the fraud. That's the sort of *external purpose* the rest of the firm can get behind.

Everyone on our team at SMB knows Bill's personal mission to ensure no other families have to go through what he went through. He's very open about it. They also all understand the *external purpose* for SMB, which is to help other firms build a law practice that is strong enough to be recession proof. We exist to help lawyers build the long-term firm of their dreams.

ANDY STICKEL NARRATES

Now, Do You Believe It?

One of our mentors taught us a ridiculous amount about business and motivation, and he's explained that what you believe will lead to the action you choose to take. If your beliefs are clouded by anxiety, you are not going to act. But if you are in a state of *anticipation*, you will take positive action.

Your beliefs directly inform the actions you choose to take.

If the payoff is huge and *you believe it can actually happen,* then you're going to take all the actions necessary to realize your dreams.

Perfect example to illustrate this: I bribe my daughter Aubrey all the time to help her stay in a mindset of anticipation while she's playing soccer. I'll say, "Listen—if your team shuts out this game, I'll buy you ice cream." Something along those lines. For some reason, she plays so much better when she's anticipating that ice cream. She goes out and she reverse engineers that shut out. She runs faster, jumps higher, plays harder, and even when she's tired, she'll put in extra effort. None of that would happen if she had a mindset of anxiety, where she's worried about how well the other team might play. That promise of mint chocolate chip is her favorable outcome and with that mindset of anticipation, she plays her heart out.

It's the same with your law firm. I see lawyers adopt a mindset of anxiety all the time. They're in a market competing against a firm with more money and clients. The anxious law firm owners tell themselves, "I can't compete with that." But the *successful* law firm owners choose a mindset of anticipation. They say, "I can compete with them. I'm going to get creative. I'm going to do what Bill and Andy tell me to do and make a killing in this market."

Robert T. Kiyosaki, in his book *Rich Dad, Poor Dad,* tells a similar story about mindset. He says poor people look at a desirable thing like an exotic vacation or a beautiful house and think, "I'll never be able to afford that." Rich people, on the other hand, ask, "*How* can I afford that?" They frame the situation in such a way that they fill their mind with anticipation instead of anxiety. That's why they become rich. Instead of saying *can't,* they ask *how?*

Take a look at your personal vision. Consider your internal and external purpose. How do you feel about the reality of making those happen?

If your thoughts fill with words like "can't," reframe your assumptions! Ask yourself *how* you can compete with those big spenders. By anticipating the possibility of a favorable outcome, you will be much more likely to *achieve* a favorable outcome. You'll be motivated to take positive actions to move closer to your goal.

The great thing about this approach is that your initial stats don't have anything to do with your ability to achieve success. You could be a mid-size firm or a small firm. It's irrelevant.

All you need to start is clarity on your vision and the *belief* that you can compete with bigger firms. That belief leads to action. You start coming up with solutions. You start investing in SEO or making videos to post on YouTube. Or you go to local events or sponsor podcasts or do TV ads or paste your picture on the sides of buses.

Your head and your attitude will be in a place where good things start happening. A mindset of anticipation means you take positive actions to move closer to your goals.

Here's a quote from our mentor Myron Golden. "Whatever you believe about a future-based outcome, whether it is positive or negative, is made up." Read that quote again. The future hasn't happened yet. Do you believe your firm will fail? That's an idea you have for the future which you've made up in your head. Do you believe you're going to 2X your firm's revenue over the next year? Great! Hasn't happened yet. Beliefs are not facts.

But beliefs can and *will* direct your actions and your life. Beliefs may not *equal* outcomes, but they sure point you in the right direction. That's why my kid turns into Mia Hamm when she's thinking about ice cream after a shutout.

Given that, why would you give a single ounce of energy to a belief that doesn't serve you at the highest level? And why *wouldn't* you give all your energy to a belief that could lead to your best outcome?

Ditch the anxiety. Choose a mindset of anticipation. Ice cream's right around the corner. Now, play your heart out.

Why Aren't You Already Doing This?

If we were to ask a group of people at one of our conferences, "How many of you want to be in the best shape of your lives?" every hand would go up.

So, why aren't they *already* in the best shape of their lives? They know what to do. Eat less, move more. It's simple. They could write that down. They could make it their vision.

Yet few actually do it.

It's the same with your law firm. You know what to do. You wrote down your vision. You know your internal and external purpose. In the chapters that come, you're going to get more and more clarity about what steps to take next.

Are you going to do it? Many law firm owners don't.

Why?

There are four main reasons why law firm owners don't do what it takes to improve their position in the marketplace and move closer to their goals. Let's look at each one.

Lack of Belief

This one is simple. You don't believe in your vision. You don't believe improving your position in the marketplace is possible. You have decided to take the *facts* of your current circumstances and interpret them as *limitations*.

Maybe you've tried some strategies in the past that didn't work. Maybe you think the pain of growing will be greater than the reward. You might think running a bigger law firm is going to be a living hell. You won't be able to manage all those people and you don't want to give up your case work.

If you have any of these thoughts, you will never act.

In a way, the problem here is not so much a lack of belief as it is believing the wrong thing.

You are *going* to have a belief of some kind. Why not believe in something that can improve your life? Why not believe in your vision?

Your interpretation of the facts is holding you back.

> **Current facts are not limitations. They are, instead, information you can use. They are guides to help you attain the next level of success.**

The lack of belief in their vision is the number one reason lawyers don't improve their lives. Don't let this happen to you. Believe in your vision.

"I Don't Know How"

Another limiting belief that will prevent you from taking action is "I don't know how." But here's a secret. *No one knows how.*

At least not at first. If you think you must have vast and precise knowledge to achieve your vision, you need to check your assumptions.

Nobody learns to swim by sitting in a conference, listening to a swimmer describe the process. It won't happen. You also don't learn to swim by sitting in a chair reading *Swimming for Dummies*. The way to learn how to swim is to get in the water and *swim*. You flap your arms around and kick your legs and gasp for breath and think you're going to die by drowning and then you figure it out. You learn how to swim.

We were never ready to put on events when we started. How did we learn? By putting on events. At first, these events weren't very successful. That didn't matter, not in the long run. We *learned*. We jumped out of the plane and built our parachutes on the way down.

Can you guess how we learned to get on the phone and make sales? We got on the phone and tried to sell things to people.

Amazing trial lawyers don't emerge fully formed when they come out of law school. They get great by trying cases. It's a sure bet that you're a better lawyer now than you were five years ago. Why is that? Because you've been doing the work. You learn how to try cases by trying cases.

So don't think you can't reach your vision because you don't have the knowledge, aren't good with computers, have never managed people, or don't know what to do with big sums of money. We're going to give you some instructions about all of that, but you're actually going to learn how to do it by getting your hands on computers, managing people, and dealing with large sums of money.

You're not going to learn these things right away. On the contrary, you will make mistakes. Everyone does. That's how you learn! That's part of the process. The way to hire the right people is by hiring the wrong people and learning from that.

The way to find out what works in marketing is by learning what doesn't work in marketing.

That's why, for example, we might put up 10 ads in various media. Eight of them won't work. But two of them will. We learned something by doing that. We learned which ads work. Not because we were marketing geniuses who were smart enough to know the two successful ads ahead of time. Rather, it was because we put up 10 ads to see what *would* work.

Everyone learns by *doing*. If you aren't doing, you're most likely not learning. Change your *identity* from being a passive agent to being an active agent.

> **If you think you must have vast and precise knowledge to achieve your vision, you need to check your assumptions. You learn by doing.**

Lack of Investment and Focus

Why else would you not take yourself to the proverbial gym and do the work to grow your law firm? Lack of investment and focus. We're not talking here about investing in real estate or crypto or any of the other crap that lawyers seem to flock to whenever they hear the word *investing*. What we *are* talking about is investing in yourself, your vision. Law firm owners often fail to make the critical investments in themselves.

Lawyers need to invest in three main areas for their business to grow and thrive. No lawyer looking to achieve greater success should skimp on any of these.

1. **Money.** Your law firm will grow in direct proportion to how much you invest in marketing, payroll, and yourself.

2. **Time.** Your law firm will grow as you invest the time to learn what you need from going to workshops and conferences or from a relationship with a mentor.

3. **Focus.** Lawyers often get distracted by other investments like the stock market or real estate when they need to focus on the best asset they have—their own law firm.

Neglecting any of these can be a killer for your law firm. The main reason for not investing in any of these areas is fear. Lawyers are afraid of investing in themselves.

Say you're making $500K a year right now. And let's say you want to be making $2M next year. You look at your budget and figure you need to spend 20% on advertising. This is where a lot of lawyers will freak out because 20% of $2M is $400K. They think, *That's 80% of my current earnings! I can't afford that!* So, they stop investing in themselves.

In Chapter 3, we'll go into greater detail about budgeting when we explain something we call the 20/40/10 rule, which will make a lot of this clearer. For now, just understand that budgeting worries don't have to stop you from investing in yourself.

Too many lawyers, once they've set their goals, won't spend the money, hire the people, or acquire the knowledge necessary to get there. That's a lack of investment.

People often say that buying a house is the most important investment they make. However, in reality, the place where you put your effort, time, and money—into your law firm—is where you spend most of your awake hours. It's where you create and grow your money and what you own. Surprisingly, many law firm owners don't view it this way.

When you put your effort, time, and money into your law firm, you're not just making money but building genuine wealth. Why? Because you can *sell* your law firm for a lot more money compared to what you earn each year—anywhere from *five* to *fifteen* times more, depending on what you do. Nothing else can give you such a return on investment.

Stick to your vision. Don't take your eyes off your vision until you have achieved it. And stay focused. Your own law firm will bring you a much greater ROI than any other investment you could possibly come up with.

Unwillingness to Delegate

You'll get a pretty clear picture of your level of freedom as a business owner—or your lack thereof—using something we call the vacation test.

Here's how the vacation test works. Imagine you took a vacation to a remote location, without access to phone or internet. How long could your law firm run itself before all wheels fall off?

A. One month—or longer. My team has got it!

B. One week

C. One day

D. Who am I kidding? The wheels have already fallen off!

Don't feel bad—most of our clients are somewhere in the range of B, C, or D when we start work with them. Some don't even want to engage the vacation test and wave it off. "I don't even like taking vacation anyway!" We're going to hold ourselves back from coughing "yeah, right" under our breath and say, for the sake of argument, that the vacation test isn't particularly relevant for you.

In that case, let's change it to the hospital test. What if you got sick and ended up in the hospital, unable to work?

This happened to a client of ours. She got Covid and had to be in the hospital for two weeks. Thankfully, we had helped her build her staff out to be self-managing, so her absence didn't impact the daily activity of the firm—but if it had happened before our work with her, the effects would have been catastrophic.

If you got hurt, or very ill—if your absence wasn't optional, like a vacation, but required because your body wouldn't give you any alternative—how long could your firm go without you? Would anything quickly break in your business?

Case work? Intake? Marketing? All of the above?

Whatever your answer, that is the weak point (or points) in your firm. Those are the areas where you should be hiring. Now.

Unwillingness to delegate is the fourth Achilles' heel that prevents law firm owners from taking action toward their dream life. Maybe you believe no one can do case work as good as you do. (You're probably wrong.) Or maybe you think your marketing prowess is second to none and can't be done by anyone else. (Again, probably wrong.)

Everything can be delegated. And, ultimately, everything should. Yes, we said *should*. Make this a part of your brain transplant. You *should* delegate all tasks in your firm. We're going to discuss this much more in Chapter 2 when we explain the Lawyer Legacy Staircase, but understand this: it is *impossible* to scale your firm, get more profit, or achieve greater freedom in your life so long as everything depends on you. Growth requires delegation.

Start first by delegating everything you suck at to others. Then delegate things you're okay at. After all that's underway, delegate your strengths.

Why would you do this? Simple. Because scaling up means you need to operate less like a lawyer, and more like a business owner.

You are no longer a lawyer. You are a business owner. And successful business owners delegate as much as they can.

Don't take our word for it. Look around. Successful real estate moguls don't sell real estate. They hire people to sell real estate. Successful auto execs don't spend their time on the assembly line. They hire people to build cars. Someone with a successful chain of restaurants doesn't cook. They hire chefs to do that. We could go on, but the principle is sound. To be successful, you need to delegate as much as you can.

How do you start? How do you know, for example, what you suck at? Easy. Take a personality test. That will show you where your strengths and weaknesses are.

Quick-Hitting Hack: Scan the QR code below for three excellent tools that will help you delegate everything you suck at.

(You'll find all the other bonuses from the book here or you can go to **yourdreamlawfirm.com**.)

- **Personality Assessment Test:** To know your areas of deficiency, personality assessments are the best way to gain self-awareness. For example, if you're a low-detail person and you never have anyone spell that out for you, you'll spend your whole life doing high-detail work, thinking, *I've got to get better at this.* No, you don't. You need to delegate. A personality assessment can spell out the fact that you'll never be a high-detail person—so don't waste years of your life getting good at a weakness someone else could do better than you. Two tests that we find absolutely indispensable are the DiSC® Assessment and Kolbe A™ Index.

- **Activity Audit:** Look at your calendar for the last 30, 60, 90 days. Make a list of all the stuff you hate doing. These are the tasks someone else can do better than you. Combine this with your personality assessment and the things that would break if you took a vacation, and you have your not-to-do list. This is the opposite of what most people have, which is a to-do

---

list. A not-to-do list are the things in your firm you will no longer be doing. They are the items you will be delegating.

- **Hourly Rate Diagram:** This is where you figure out the highest-value tasks in a law firm. What is of higher value, answering a phone call from a client or designing your phone call answering process? Is it putting out a client fire or is it creating a better client experience process, so a fire doesn't pop up? In both cases, it should be clear that the higher-value task is the latter of the two. Identify an approximate hourly rate for all the different tasks in your law firm. Then, remove yourself from the low-value tasks and concentrate on the processes that *govern* those tasks.

**Scan this QR Code
to Unlock This Bonus**

Performing these kinds of assessments can be extremely powerful. A client named Peter used to specialize in bankruptcy. One year, instead of handling another bankruptcy, he did a market analysis to determine the demand for bankruptcy representation in his market. This "high-value" task revealed there was very little demand for bankruptcy cases, so he switched to estate planning, which his research showed was a high-value niche in his area. He increased his revenue by $120K per month in *one month*.

How did he find the time to do the market research that increased his income? By delegating. He hired someone to handle his calls, so he had the free time to think about his business.

Personality tests, activity audits, and hourly rate diagrams are amazingly powerful tools. Use them to help you assess yourself and your business. They will get you closer to your vision. They will help you on the road to success. And—critically—they will show you where you need to delegate!

ANDY STICKEL NARRATES

Keep Your Eyes on the Prize

There's one lesson I repeat to my kids repeatedly, hoping they will internalize it and live it. "Whether you think you can or you think you can't, you're right."

This year, my son made me one of those Father's Day books. You know the kind I mean. It's full of statements like, "This is my Dad's favorite food," or "This is my Dad's favorite color," and then the kid draws a picture and tries to spell out a word. It's cute. In the book my son gave me, there was a page that said, "This is my Dad's favorite quote." He'd written: "Whether you think you can or you think you can't, you're right."

Holy crap. They actually *do* listen.

We hope you're listening as well. This is an important lesson. As important for a 70-year-old as it is for a 7-year-old.

Everything in life is a mindset. What we've tried to do in this chapter is convince you that your mindset does not have to be an accident or some random idea you picked up somewhere.

You can change it. You can set yourself up for success by changing your beliefs!

> **If you believe in where you're going—if you *see* that the payoff is clear and irresistible and has purpose embedded in it—you will jump through any struggle, any adversity. You will do whatever it takes to make that payoff happen.**

Everybody has the same number of hours in the day. Remember, the thing that separates successful people from unsuccessful people is that successful people don't say, "I can't do that." They say, "*How* can I do that?"

How can you increase your revenue? How can you get more clients? How can you build a more prominent law firm?

Good news! We're going to give you the answers to *all of those questions* in the chapters to come. But you still need to actually take action. You still need to cultivate a mindset of anticipation. You still need to remember that fundamental mindset shift. You are a business owner, not a lawyer. We're going to teach you, step-by-step, how to evolve your identity as we discuss the Lawyer Legacy Staircase in greater depth in Chapter 2.

Chapter 1 | Takeaways

1. In order to climb the Lawyer Legacy Staircase and scale up your firm, you need a brain transplant. Think of yourself from now on as a business owner, not a lawyer.

2. Identify your personal goals for where you want to take your law firm. Be specific about the details.

    a. **Cashing In**. Sell your law firm for how much, and by when?

    b. **Self-Management and Profit**. How much, how many free days, how soon?

    c. **Domination**. Dominate your market. What will that look like?

3. Identify your internal purpose (the emotional reason you want to fulfill your goals) and your external purpose (the WHY that will motivate your team to execute).

4. Think critically about your mindset. Are you functioning from a place of anxiety or anticipation? How can you move yourself to anticipation by visualizing the dream?

5. Get honest with yourself. Are you guilty of any of the four reasons lawyers tend not to take action in the direction of their dreams? Which ones? Why? What could you do to remove those barriers for yourself so that you can start reverse engineering your dream life?

CHAPTER 2

THE LAWYER LEGACY STAIRCASE

EVOLVE YOUR IDENTITY AND SCALE UP YOUR FIRM

"If you don't know where you are going,
you'll end up someplace else."

—Yogi Berra

ANDY STICKEL NARRATES

"'When I hit year 40, I'm retiring. I'm done.'"

The speaker on the other end of the line was a new client, David Buckley. He was quoting his wife, and his chuckle did not quite disguise his desperation.

He went on to explain their situation. "My law firm has been making around 400 grand a year for the last 30 years. And my wife and I have enjoyed a comfortable lifestyle when we add in her income as an oncology nurse—but we can't sustain that lifestyle *without* her income. She's been a nurse for

37 years and she's retiring in three. We either downsize our lifestyle, or I have to figure out a way to make more money."

"The fact that you've called me makes me think you want to try door number two," I said.

"I like our lifestyle," David admitted. "If there's a way to retool my law firm to make more money, I want to make it happen."

David didn't realize it at the time, but his desire to retool his law firm had prompted him to start climbing the Lawyer Legacy Staircase. What is the Lawyer Legacy Staircase? It's a representation of the journey every law firm owner must navigate. The first step starts with becoming a law student, and the next major step happens after passing the bar, getting hired at a firm, and becoming a lawyer. Step 3 occurs by taking the leap into self-employment, practicing law as a solo practitioner. From there, the stairway escalates into higher levels of leadership, which means higher levels of growth, profit, and freedom.

LAWYER LEGACY STAIRCASE

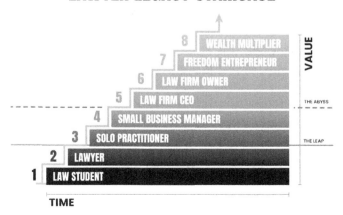

So where was David? David was on Step 3, functioning as a Solo Practitioner. Technically, he owned his own business, but it wasn't functioning as a business—it was more of a job. Without his constant activity, the business would fail. And David had been on that step a long time. He had kept himself on a plateau of law firm stagnancy for his entire career and was functioning as a rainmaker. In other words, he was the owner *and* the business. He was the one who had to make it rain. He took most of the cases. He relied on word of mouth to get new clients. He hired helpers based on a gut feeling and told them what to do.

He didn't push for more growth because he didn't want to deal with the added complexities that would be required to scale up. And the firm's revenue had stayed static at approximately $400K per year, for decades.

Now, faced with the loss of his wife's income, David realized he was going to have to start running his law firm differently if he wanted to make more money. That's when he made the critical mindset shift we coached you through in the last chapter. He started asking, "*How* do I do this?" In his online searches, he came across one of my ads. He joined a webinar, and now he was here, on the phone with me, after purchasing my program.

I started talking with David about what he would need to do to scale up his business. After we began implementing a marketing program for him, David found his way to Bill. (This was before Bill and I merged our companies into one.) Through our two programs, David learned how to hire the right people and hold them accountable, so he could delegate his casework, intake, and all the other processes that had kept him doing busy work for 30 years.

This opened up time for him to work *on* the business, instead of *in* the business. He was able to focus more on strategy and processes and implement marketing campaigns that brought the right clients through his door.

David had climbed several key steps on the Lawyer Legacy Staircase. From Solo Practitioner to Small Business Manager, to Law Firm CEO, to Law Firm *Owner.* He had even managed to cross "The Abyss," which required him to take the plunge of investing according to *where he was going,* not with the funds he already had. He had to spend more on marketing, endure heightened stress for a season, and put in more of his time to develop a self-managing team. He evolved his identity from managing his law firm like a lawyer to leading it like a business owner.

By applying these new strategies, David scaled up. In fact, he scaled *way* up.

David's wife has retired and there's been no lifestyle downsizing required for either of them. This year, he's on track to do close to four *million* in revenue. When he called to tell me that, he was literally crying with happiness—it was such a weight off his shoulders.

So, how'd he do it? He pushed his belief demons aside. He started taking action toward the *next* phase of growth in his law firm. You can do the same.

Most lawyers we work with are somewhere between Steps 3 and 6 on the Lawyer Legacy Staircase. You've made the leap from working at someone else's firm as a Lawyer (Step 2) to being a Solo Practitioner (Step 3), and maybe you've even taken the next step to being a Small Business Manager (Step 4). But crossing The Abyss smoothly to get to Steps 5 and 6 is an area where you could use some coaching. That's what we're here for.

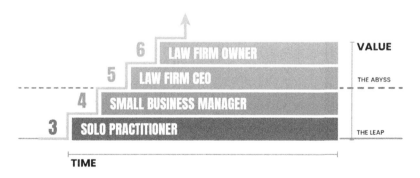

In order to become a Freedom Entrepreneur and make your dream life happen, you need to (A) recognize where you're at, so that you can (B) learn how to create a plan to get yourself to the next step and reach your growth goals.

Evolving Your Identity from Solo Practitioner to Law Firm Owner

So, where are you at? If you're reading this book, we can say pretty confidently that you've climbed beyond Steps 1 and 2:

1. Law Student
2. Lawyer

You began this climb when you set your sights on the legal profession by becoming a law student. Getting into law school, pushing your way through late-night study sessions, memorizing briefs, and doing mock trials. Then, you took another major step. You graduated! You studied and passed the bar. You applied to various firms. Then, you found one to hire you and you started practicing law for real. Anyone who has made it to Step 2 has already put in an enormous amount of work and effort.

If you made the leap to Step 3, you get even more bragging rights. You went from working for someone else to working for yourself. This is often the scariest and most difficult step on the entire staircase—and if you've taken it, you've already achieved a huge and courageous step.

But now, like David, you're looking to climb higher. You want to know how to build this thing—so that you lead a firm working for you, instead of you working your tail off for the firm. In this chapter, we're going to examine closely the steps of growth you need to guide your law firm through as it scales up into greater and greater success:

3. **Solo Practitioner**
4. **Small Business Manager**
5. **Law Firm CEO**
6. **Law Firm Owner**

We're going to walk you through the characteristics of each of these steps in the categories of marketing, intake, leadership, profit, and the approximate hourly rate of your tasks. In doing so, you'll be able to size up your scale, evolve your identity, and identify your next move to pursue your vision.

Here's a preview, and we'll break this graphic down step by step as we go through the chapter:

LAWYER LEGACY STAIRCASE

Step 3: Solo Practitioner

LEAD GENERATION	INTAKE	SELF-MANAGING TEAM	PROFITS	HOURLY RATE
RAINMAKER	YOU	DOING	NO PLAN	$10

As a solo practitioner, you function as a *rainmaker*. In other words, if you want money—*you've* got to make it rain—yourself. That's your entire **marketing** approach. In fact, you rely on word of mouth and your own sheer hustle to get new clients. You create the opportunities, do the work, and get the job done.

You're the one doing all your client **intake**. *You* take all calls, respond to every new inquiry, handle all your own cases, and answer every client question.

You're not **leading** a team, you're leading yourself and maybe 1-2 helpers. In other words, your form of leadership as a solo practitioner is to *do almost everything yourself.*

As far as **profit** goes—you're winging it. There's *no plan*. Your overhead is low, since you have so few employees and you also can't predict what you're going to make or where your next client is going to come from. You're busting your tail and hoping for the best.

Unfortunately, this means you're doing low-level tasks—the kind that could be compensated at an **hourly rate of** *$10*. You're taking calls that, in larger firms, are handled by a Virtual Assistant. You're trying to render graphics that could be designed for cheap by a freelancer on Fiverr. And all of this is taking a great deal of your *time*.

Most lawyers who run their own firms start out as solo practitioners—and that's no small thing. Of every 100 lawyers out there, 80 choose to remain as employees in someone else's firm. Only 20% of lawyers make the brave leap to becoming solo practitioners. So, if you're in rainmaker mode, you should feel good about it! Without rain, crops die. The rain you're making keeps you and your firm alive. It's crucial. When we say you're operating as a rainmaker, we mean it in a positive sense.

But there's a drawback to being your firm's rainmaker. In our experience, we have seen roughly 80% of law firm owners never escape being a solo—so everyone's doing it. It isn't scalable. And, the hard truth is the person who does the most work makes the least money. If you're taking all the calls and typing all the documents and personally handling cases, you are limiting your growth. You can't work 24 hours a day, and even if you could, that would still be a limiting factor that would cap your growth.

We haven't yet shown you the labels for the X- and Y-axis on our Lawyer Legacy Staircase, but it's time you had a chance to view them. The X-axis signifies your *time*. The Y-axis signifies your *value*. In other words, if you spend your time doing low-value stuff, you'll have to spend more time working *in* your law firm. But as your revenue, profit, and value goes up—in other words, as you start doing tasks worth a much higher hourly rate—you tend to have more freedom with your time along the way.

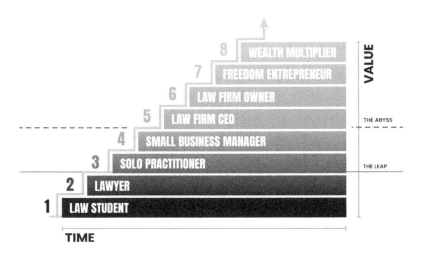

As a Solo Practitioner, you have more freedom with your time than when you were working for someone else—but not much. Given that everything depends on you, you feel significant stress and have unpredictable profits. The stress and the demands are so intense, in fact, you might doubt whether or not you should have made the leap at all.

In order to evolve your identity and move your firm to the next step, you need to think differently. See if this sounds like you: "I'm the only one who can answer the phones. I'm the only one who can do the casework. I'm the only one who can talk to clients."

Those sorts of thoughts will keep you stuck on the Solo Practitioner step.

When David Buckley began working with us, everything in his firm depended on him. Every client had David's personal number. Every phone call needed to be fielded by him. He took the lead on every case. And that bottleneck was constraining his firm's growth.

Your profit as a Solo Practitioner is limited because you're constrained by your own mind and muscles. If *you* don't physically work, you don't get paid. And for the most part, this is where every single law firm owner begins, unless you inherited a firm. You started up your practice, you put your last name on the sign, and without realizing it, you made yourself the business.

If *you* are the primary relationship with clients, *you* are the intake, and *you* are the case management. Therefore, *you* are the bottleneck.

We would caution all Solo Practitioners to beware the "fatal assumption," a phrase coined by Michael Gerber, author of *The E-Myth Revisited,* which is the top entrepreneur book ever written. Michael is now a friend of Bill's. When we interviewed Michael for our event, The Law Firm Expansion Summit, he unpacked the idea of the fatal assumption.

"Just because you understand the technical work of a business," says Michael, "that doesn't mean you understand the business that does technical work. In other words, just because you understand lawyering, that doesn't mean you understand how to run a *business* that *produces* legal outcomes."

Law firm owners still on the Solo Practitioner step often fall guilty to this fatal assumption, but there's no correlation between being a good lawyer and getting paid for it.

However, there's a direct correlation between being great at running a law firm and getting paid for it.

Another common characteristic of this phase that impedes growth is relying on word of mouth as your main marketing strategy. You might even brag about it. "We're a 'word-of-mouth' firm." But because you rely so heavily on word of mouth, you can't choose the type of cases you want. You've designed a practice based on whoever the heck randomly decides to call you. And since you're not flooded with leads, you take whatever case walks in the door, even if they're a-hole clients or outside your specialty. You take any client—because you need them! The result is scarcity rather than abundance.

"Word of mouth" is a trap—there's no way it can scale. Sure, it may cover your survival needs and you may get your 20% margins. But then what? You go for 10, 20 years, and then die on the limitations of the word-of-mouth trap. You're 100% dependent on other people, which means that you have no control over your destiny.

But in that case—how *do* you scale your marketing? Asking questions like these causes you to hit your head on the ceiling of complexity, which is low when you're a Solo Practitioner. The ceiling of complexity is a concept Bill learned from his coach, Dan Sullivan. It describes the limits you impose on yourself because you don't know any better. You've operated this way, in some cases, for a decade or more. No one's ever taught you what to do. You fall back into your comfort zone, doing things the way you've always done them.

However, to graduate to the next step, Small Business Manager, you've got to learn new concepts and skills to operate in a different way. In other words, you need to raise that ceiling of complexity and give yourself room to grow. After all, if you continue to do what you've always done, you'll get what you've always gotten.

Climbing this staircase *will* require you to step out of your comfort zone—which can be difficult because the Solo Practitioner step feels very comfortable. But is it *really* that comfortable? You can't escape your business. You can't even go on vacation without things falling apart because it all depends on you. There's scarcity instead of abundance, and there's pressure instead of freedom. Where's the comfort in any of that?

It's those drawbacks that cause people like David Buckley to ask, "What's beyond this?"

Step: 3 Solo Practitioner

- *Marketing.* You make it rain, relying on word–of–mouth referrals and your own hustle.

- *Intake.* You handle all aspects of intake: inquiries, calls, client emails, scheduling—everything.

- *Leadership.* You are working hard for yourself and your clients. You *are* the business.

- *Profit.* It's anyone's guess! You're busting your tail and hoping for the best. Revenue and profit are limited by your own ability to work.

- *Hourly Rate.* You're doing the kind of tasks worth $10 an hour.

Step 4: Small Business Manager

LEAD GENERATION	INTAKE	SELF-MANAGING TEAM	PROFITS	HOURLY RATE
DEMAND	UNTRAINED SALES PERSON	MANAGING	REACTIVE FIXING	$100

This fourth step is a very big and admirable leap: from Solo Practitioner to Small Business Manager. Why are we calling you a small business *manager* instead of a small business *owner*? Well, a manager works *in* the business. An owner works *on* the business or has someone else running the business. At Step 4, you're still working *in* the business.

At Step 3, as a Solo, you were only working hard for your clients. Now, in Step 4, you're working hard for your clients and a small team of people—usually three to 19 employees. In our experience, we've seen about 15% of law firm owners ever get past the solo stage and to this size of a team. Roughly 80% of your time is spent practicing law by necessity, and 20% is as a reactive manager. At this phase, you still have a job. You're receiving compensation as a result of the time you put in, and you still have client problems that funnel up to you. Heck, at Step 4, you have all kinds of problems funneling up to you.

You've made a strategic and very important shift in your **marketing,** however, which might even be what first prompted you to start hiring more people. Rather than relying exclusively on word-of-mouth referrals, you found at least one scalable lead generation system—in other words, a source for leads that can increase as your firm grows. The most effective, scalable lead generation method for firms at this phase is called *Demand Marketing*.

Demand Marketing is your strategy to show up online for clients who are "in demand" for you. It's what happens when a client types "San Diego accident lawyer" into Google and your firm is the first name that pops up in the results. In Demand Marketing, you have set yourself up to *meet* the customer's demand, specifically through your Google strategy. Typically, that strategy involves getting yourself on page one through ads first, and later on, via search engine optimization—a strategy we'll discuss much more in Chapter 7. When your firm has one scalable lead generation strategy, you've successfully moved up to Step 4. When doing Demand Marketing, you are always asking yourself, "How do I get my law firm *known* to clients in demand for the most profitable services I provide?"

This marketing shift can cause *significant* growth. Mark Reel is a law firm owner in southern California and a multi-year client of ours. In the two years since working with us, he went from making $125K per year to making $8M per year. He launched himself from Rainmaker marketing to Demand Marketing, and in doing so, moved himself up many steps on the Lawyer Legacy Staircase. Mark Reel told us that 65% of his growth came from leads who found his firm off page one of Google.

If you're scratching your head, thinking, *I'm going to need some help to do all this*, then you've hit on another characteristic of a Small Business Manager. You start hiring employees. Unfortunately, during this phase, what you really hire are "helpers"—employees with less experience.

With all the new leads that you're generating through Demand Marketing, you can't handle **intake** exclusively anymore. Your lead volume will become high enough that you will have to remove yourself from any form of early-stage intake, also known as "qualifying intake."

In other words, you may still get on the phone with a pre-qualified client of a certain case value, but only after someone else in your firm—someone you've hired—has collected the potential client's name, email, pertinent case details, etc. and determined that they are a qualified client. You no longer handle any early-stage intake. Sounds nice, doesn't it? The problem is this—when you're in the Small Business Manager phase, you typically hire an untrained salesperson, which we'll fix in the next step.

Guess what else is nice? When you start generating leads from people searching for your law firm, you start getting the exact types of cases that you want. You start getting more phone calls with "right fit" clients. You're able to say "No" to some of the unappealing word-of-mouth cases that you got in the past because you're getting more of the cases that you want on a consistent basis.

As far as **leadership** goes, you're now personally *managing* a small team. This requires quite a bit of your energy and focus because most of your team at this stage has less expertise than you do. You hesitate to delegate—which is why being a Small Business Manager still requires quite a lot of your time—since getting your less experienced team up to speed involves a lot of micromanagement. In future steps, you'll have a leadership team to manage your employees. And, eventually, you'll have more profit to reinvest in hiring rock stars that don't need to be micromanaged. But, not yet.

At this stage, you're now more consistently making a **profit.** All those new leads through Demand Marketing have helped ensure a steady stream of clients coming your way. But you're doing a lot of *reactive profit fixing* as you discover that expenses in one area are draining profit, or that you need to charge more per case to remain profitable. You still don't have a pro-active profit plan, but you're getting close.

Still, you've delegated more lower-value tasks and are now operating at an **hourly rate** of around *$100.* That's because your take-home money still mostly comes from you doing your job as a lawyer, handling most of the casework and managing your small team, with some marketing strategy mixed in.

Most lawyers stop at Step 4. But if you want to continue scaling up, you have an important decision to make. Getting to Step 5 requires that you invest in infrastructure, marketing, your knowledge, and hiring highly qualified team members. Taking that plunge is the only way to move toward the lifestyle you dream of—but it also means crossing The Abyss.

Step 4: Small Business Manager

- *Marketing.* You build your first scalable lead generation strategy, typically by shifting into Demand Marketing with a strong Google page-one strategy.

- *Intake.* You now have an untrained salesperson filtering through leads and handling your pre-qualifying intake conversations.

- *Leadership.* You're reactively managing your clients and a small team of 3-19 employees. You spend 80% of your time practicing law by necessity, and 20% of your time putting out fires. You delegate a bit more and therefore focus on slightly higher-value actions.

- *Profit.* Profit is made through reactive fixes. There's more revenue coming in, but also more expenses. You're constantly discovering issues that need to be fixed, such as with your cash flow, pricing, or lowering expenses.

- *Hourly Rate.* You're now working at an hourly rate of around $100—because most of your work now is lawyering. You still have "a job," in addition to managing your team.

Between Steps 4 and 5: The Abyss

Here's the bad news. If you want to scale from Step 4 to Step 5, you need to overhaul your practice. Is it worth the overhaul? In a word, YES. Step 5 is where you start gaining some serious freedom and scalable profits—in our experience, only 2% of lawyers ever get here.

To truly have freedom from your firm, you need to fix your foundation. Your foundation consists of your systems and your team. If everyone is doing things their own way, then doubling the size of your firm is going to cause a lot of headaches. The first step to fixing your foundation is to get clear on and document the core systems of your law firm. Then, you need to have your team follow those systems or hire better, more expensive people.

With a better team, you can delegate all casework and intake. You can also start delegating authority rather than tasks for the first time—like making someone in charge of a whole department of your firm (like intake, case management or marketing).

The problem is that rebuilding your systems and then trying to enforce them on a team that's used to doing things their own way is hard. Hiring A-players is expensive. You're going to need more revenue to pay for these A-players. Therefore, you also need to expand your marketing strategy which will cost even more money. You may need to fire some members of your current team—maybe even most of them—which will cause stress. And, giving up nearly all of your casework can cause an identity crisis.

Welcome to The Abyss.

Do you want to cross The Abyss? Profits will temporarily plummet. Stress is going to increase. You'll become increasingly aware of everything you don't know how to do. You'll find that you're working a lot harder while making less money. Sometimes, you're making *no* money. In fact, sometimes you're even in the red—not because you're not a great lawyer, but because you're not a great business owner. You have to invest in your own knowledge to successfully make that identity shift from being a lawyer/manager to being a CEO. That's hard!

Maybe worst of all, in The Abyss, you'll realize the team you have isn't the right team. Many of the people who were with you when you started up the firm aren't hanging so well with the new momentum you generated from your new marketing, even though they feel like family. There's Glenda, who always shows up a half hour late and tries to smooth it over by showing you pictures of her puppy. Sean, whose slowness to learn is offset by his wide-eyed eagerness. Harry, the crotchety old guard who agreed to come out of retirement to help you get the firm off the ground but complains about every new change. You know, those guys? Those guys are starting to seriously buckle under the speed you're moving now.

Your own bandwidth as a manager is also wearing thin. You've tried promoting some of your employees to manage the others, but in several cases, it's not going well. Several "managers" don't know how to solve problems without your involvement, which sort of defeats the purpose of them being managers. Lloyd for instance—he's always underfoot, asking you questions and tattling on his team members about various ways they're underperforming, when it's *his* job to get them performing well!

Alone in your office, late at night, you must face the inevitable. It's time to rebuild your team. If you hope to successfully cross The Abyss, your firm must undergo a "team rebuild." Letting people do things their own way is not going to cut it anymore. You need a high-performing team. Glenda, Sean, Harry, and Lloyd—they all need to be given clear expectations for their roles. After a month or two of coaching, those who do not meet your expectations should be fired and replaced with A-players. You can't turn a C-player into an A-player. You can try, but it's going to waste you a ton of time.

When SMB Team was making this shift, we went through this process and only kept a single remarkable employee from our first batch of employees. The people who helped us get to $1.5M were not able to meet our expectations of running a $10M business, and that's true for most firms.

Some of those we helped transition out of the business we helped find new jobs at smaller companies with great recommendation letters. Others started their own business and succeeded.

Call it harsh. It is what it is. Our coach Cameron Herold always tells us, "Half of your employees can't survive one doubling of a business. Another half won't survive two doublings." If your team can't develop fast enough in line with your growth, they have to go. Fast-growing companies are really personal development organizations. All people in a fast-growing business must develop themselves as fast as the business grows.

If your team feels like a family, that's not a good thing. That usually means that everyone is doing things their own way.

And, it means you're accepting mediocrity because they're "part of the family." Championship-winning teams are not families. They are teams with clear roles and responsibilities.

Family vibes are holding you back from scaling your firm.

When you had between five and ten employees, you couldn't afford to fire anyone—especially because you were maxed out already from trying to do everything in the firm. Now that your firm is growing fast, you can't afford to *keep* underperformers.

Letting go of people who have been with you since Day 1 is arguably the hardest part of crossing The Abyss. It's very difficult—but 100% necessary. And one thought that might make this move a tiny bit easier to stomach. You can trust your employees will land on their feet after learning a lot under your roof.

Failing to make these shifts decisively can cause some people to remain in The Abyss for years and years. Some people never get out of it, and some people will take a U-turn and say, "Right, I've tried it. Step 5 is not for me. I'm going to downsize and go back to being a Sole Practitioner."

But here's the good news. Here's the promise of this book: when you know what to do and how to do it, *crossing The Abyss is not that difficult*. This book is going to spell out exactly what you need to do to make this shift as quick and painless as possible.

If you choose to cross The Abyss as a law firm, then congratulations! You've now graduated to Step 5, Law Firm CEO.

Step 5: Law Firm CEO

LEAD GENERATION	INTAKE	SELF-MANAGING TEAM	PROFITS	HOURLY RATE
AWARENESS	TRAINED SALES TEAM	LEADING	QUARTERLY PLAN	$1,000

As a Law Firm CEO, you've now gotten to the point where things are clicking and you start gaining some serious freedom and scalable profits. Growth is happening fast. You're climbing out of The Abyss! You should congratulate yourself because so few lawyers ever get here. This is where you have a leadership team to manage your employees, you practice law by choice (not by necessity), and you can take a month off and have your firm run itself.

One big reason for that growth is the fact that you now have multiple lead generation systems that can scale, all working simultaneously. This is typically when you layer *Awareness Marketing* on top of your Demand Marketing.

Awareness Marketing means you are making people *aware* of your law firm—often, people who don't even need your services yet. You do this by embracing social media or other cost-effective awareness marketing channels. Doing so enables you to build a relationship with your audience who will start to feel as though they know, like, and trust you. This has been a key strategy for SMB Team, using our vast library of online content to expand our visibility, brand, and client relationships.

Awareness Marketing requires that you build a brand. You're not waiting for people to type your name or services into a Google search box. As lucrative as Demand Marketing can be (and—to be clear, we still recommend you *maintain* your Demand Marketing as you move onto Step 5), it eventually will reach a limit in terms of its audience. You need Awareness Marketing to take you into the next tier of growth and revenue.

Maybe this seems counter-intuitive. Why would you want people who don't need your services to become aware of you? Here's why: because some of those people will need your services in the future. And if they already know, like, and trust you because they've been following your useful social media content for over a year, they are going to think of you before they type anything into Google.

That's because you've made a brand they know and recognize. They are aware of you. This awareness builds trust before they've even met you or called you. We're going to teach you a truckload more about Awareness Marketing in Chapter 8.

Now, there are issues with all this. When you start embracing social media marketing, you're going to get a higher percentage of unqualified leads. One reason for this is that social media is overrun with bots that try to mimic human behavior. Bots will click on things and engage with posts just to try to appear more human in order to fool Facebook.

Also, many people may accidentally click on your ads and submit their information when they're simply trying to close the lead form. Even people who intend to submit their information may click your ad in the midst of a mindless scroll and then immediately forget they ever intended to engage with you. There's also a very large population of people who intentionally opt in, but don't answer calls from numbers they don't recognize, meaning even a good lead from a real human could produce nothing for your firm.

The point is, you'll get plenty of leads in Awareness Marketing that end up being no damn good. That's why, in Step 5, you level up your **intake** with an improved system and a *trained sales team*. With an improved intake system in place and a trained sales team, your ROI is going to rise significantly. Many law firm owners look at their percentage of "bad leads" from social media and conclude that Awareness Marketing is no good. But the growth-minded law firm CEO looks at all those leads and figures, "Hey … there must be something to this Awareness Marketing! My lead volume is exploding!"

It's *worth* figuring out a system to sort through the bad leads. Let us tell you why. Our business partner, Ethen Ostroff, solved this problem when his firm signed 1,924 new cases in his first 18 months leading the firm. The kicker? Those new cases came from approximately *24K* leads. In other words, 92% of those leads were bad. But because of his stellar intake system, his average cost per case was shockingly low: only $259 per case. If you get to a place like Ethen Ostroff where 92% of your leads are "bad," that's actually a benefit, because that's when most firms quit! If you stay in the game, you'll outlast the competition and scoop up the good leads. We'll unpack Ethen's intake methods more in Chapter 9.

Regarding **leadership,** as the CEO of your law firm, you're still somewhat involved in the business, but you function more as a *leader* than a manager. Less of your time is spent in the day-to-day of the law firm, and more of it focuses on large-impact decisions. Your firm starts functioning as a team of teams, with you focusing on getting systems in place and training excellent managers to lead their direct reports. You will find that you are spending most or all your time on team building, management, and brand maintenance. In fact, you will be doing very little, if any, hands-on lawyering.

Eventually, your goal is to fully *replace* yourself in all aspects of the business, at which point you'll be able to function as an owner in Step 6. That's the goal in continuing to proactively grow your business. You're building greater profitability for your firm, and greater personal freedom for yourself.

Speaking of **profit,** there's now a high level of predictability with your revenue. You've been able to map out *quarterly plans* for your profits. Thanks to your high lead volume, staying on top of your KPIs (more on that in Chapter 4), and your high-performing team, you are able to predict and strategize with a high level of accuracy on your quarterly profit.

In terms of your **hourly rate,** you're working less and only doing tasks that command a high level of value—around *$1K* per hour, doing high-level strategic thinking and leadership. Yes, you heard us. You're finally *working less.* It's now possible for you to imagine taking a *real* vacation because your firm can run without you, thanks to your highly capable, self-managing team.

Feel weird? This is exactly what's supposed to happen. You are leading your firm like a CEO rather than a lawyer. And as a result, you've now got a multi-million dollar law firm that is scalable and sellable.

Also, you're ready to step up to 6: Law Firm *Owner.* Compared to what you went through to cross from Step 4 to Step 5, this next step is a breeze.

Step 5: Law Firm CEO

- *Marketing.* On top of your Demand Marketing, you layer on another scalable lead generation strategy. Typically, Awareness Marketing.

- *Intake.* Intake is handled by a trained sales team, using a refined intake process.

- *Leadership.* You function as your firm's leader, overseeing managers who direct teams. You only personally take on the cases you want.

- *Profit.* With greater predictability over your revenue and KPIs, you now have quarterly plans and can make decisions on expected future income.

- *Hourly Rate.* You're working less and doing tasks at a value of $1K/hr.

Step 6: Law Firm Owner

LEAD GENERATION	INTAKE	SELF-MANAGING TEAM	PROFITS	HOURLY RATE
OMNIPRESENCE	SALES LEADER + PROCESS	IMAGINING	ANNUAL PLAN	$10,000

Why is a Law Firm CEO different from a Law Firm Owner? What's the distinction?

It's the same distinction between an NFL Head Coach and an NFL Team Owner. The head coach shows up to every practice, every game, every training camp. The owner gets to choose where and when he or she shows up. Moving from Step 5 to Step 6 means you, as a law firm *owner,* have officially graduated to a place where you have a self-managing business.

How is that possible? In fact, it's easy—once you have a self-managing firm and self-managing cash flow. When you've made it to Step 6, your firm receives cash flow as a result of something you built, not your personal time input.

You are no longer the CEO of your firm. Instead, you hire a CEO or COO to be in charge of all operations of your firm. You also up-level your leadership team to an executive team. Whereas your leadership team included members of your team who were promoted from within, an executive team is built by finding and recruiting the best people in your industry who have already scaled big businesses in accordance with your future goals.

You now have complete freedom from the day-to-day operations of your firm. You are the owner of a business, not the doer of a business. And, because you're replaceable, your law firm is now worth something and can be sold for over 8-figures.

Best of all, you are now a "beginner business scaler." You've scaled one business, and now you can do it quickly with another business. This allows for duplication.

So, let's get a closer look at the inner workings of a firm that has successfully made it to this stage of growth.

Your **marketing** is *omnipresent*—thanks to your willingness to spend more than you've ever spent on marketing because you're so confident of the return you'll get. In other words, your firm is *everywhere*. You're on page one of Google. You're all over social media. When people think of your law firm's category, you're the first firm that comes to mind. You have completely blanketed the marketing landscape and far outstrip the competition in visibility.

Thankfully, you have a stellar **intake** team to handle all those incoming leads. You don't even touch intake anymore. It's all handled by your *sales leader, trained sales team, and honed intake system*. These are high-performing professionals who can handle intake from beginning to end, ensuring your firm only works with its ideal, right fit clients, providing them with a smooth and seamless experience, and enabling consistent communication across the law firm.

Your **leadership** model is that of chief visionary. Your main job now is *imagining*. Where does the firm go next? Who might you want to recruit? What firm might you want to buy? You have stellar leaders in place who can function as CEO, CFO, and COO. They're running the firm. As owner, you get to imagine all the new places you might go.

Your **profit** is now predictable, and you hit or exceed your targets every quarter. You have systems in place that enable you to confidently achieve every aspect of your annual plan. Whereas you may have been operating with an annual plan on the previous steps, there were many variants as you scaled up. As a result, you never knew how the chips would fall. Now, things are much more predictable. You know precisely what your firm will make this year. As a result, you can continue to invest aggressively in marketing, staff, and getting answers.

Your **hourly rate** as a Law Firm Owner is somewhere in the ballpark of *$10K*. In other words, one hour of your time spent imagining and thinking big could lead to profits that equal $10K down the road. If this seems hard to believe, consider the fact that when you have successfully arrived as a Law Firm Owner, your firm will be worth at least $10M. Yes, you heard that right. Ten *million*. This is an achievable goal for all law firms, and it is what we believe every law firm *should* be striving for.

The good news is that this is the easiest transition of all because of the groundwork you established when taking the last three steps! By the time you climb to Step 6, you have removed yourself from the day-to-day lawyering your firm performs. You've transitioned to a role where you're mainly sharing the firm's vision and coaching members of your team. You tell people what the vision is, and they figure out how to make it happen.

Warren Buffet once said in an interview that his job is super simple. He picks the right managers and allocates capital.[3] He is a resource allocator. He invests in the right people, and he

---

[3] Haigh, Marilyn. 2019. "Warren Buffett on Managing People: Find the '.400 Hitters' and Don't Tell Them How to Swing." CNBC, February 13, 2019. https://www.cnbc.com/2019/02/13/warren-buffett-on-managing-find-the-point400-hitters-and-then-dont-tell-them-how-to-swing.html.

invests his money in the right places. This has made him one of the richest people on the planet.

And—this is crucial—he doesn't do any of the work himself.

Every lawyer should take a lesson from his example. To be truly successful, you need to stop being a lawyer and, instead, be the vision and allocator of resources for your firm.

Step 6: Law Firm Owner

- *Marketing.* You have now achieved omnipresence in your core practice area(s). Your entire market associates you as the go-to choice for an attorney.

- *Intake.* Intake is led by a sales team leader, conducted by a trained sales team, and uses a highly developed system and process.

- *Leadership.* You function as Chief Imagination Officer—meaning you've removed yourself from the day-to-day functioning of the firm and instead lead as visionary.

- *Profit.* Revenue is at an all-time high. You have systems in place that make your profits predictable, enabling you to confidently achieve every aspect of your annual plan. You hit or exceed your targets every quarter and can aggressively invest in new staff, marketing, and opportunities.

- *Hourly Rate.* An hour of your investment now stands to produce $10K in new profits.

Your Climb Beyond Step 6

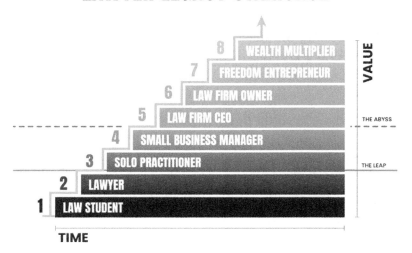

LAWYER LEGACY STAIRCASE

You began this journey in law school. You continued your journey by becoming a lawyer. Then, you made your first scary leap into running your own firm as a solo practitioner.

That's where you began—and that's where many firms stay, as a small solo act. Small Business Statistics found that out of every 10 small businesses, eight have only one employee.[4] But you don't have to stay there.

Every lawyer–turned–business–owner can climb this staircase to Step 4, as a Small Business Manager. Then to Step 5, as a

---

[4] Main, Kelly. 2022. "Small Business Statistics Of 2023." Forbes Advisor, December 7, 2022. https://www.forbes.com/advisor/business/small-business-statistics/.

Law Firm CEO. Then to Step 6: Law Firm Owner. Beginning that climb simply requires that you push your belief demons aside and start taking action toward the next phase of growth in your law firm.

What's beyond Step 6? That's where the dreams get *really* big—and that's when Law Firm Owners tend to get *really* rich.

Step 7 means you either optimize for freedom or start expanding by buying other firms or businesses. Once you've learned how to scale one business, you realize that you now understand how to scale any number of businesses. Take David Buckley, for instance, the lawyer whose story opened this chapter. Not only did he grow his firm's revenue from $400K to $4M within a few years by climbing this staircase, but he just sent us a text to let us know he's started acquiring other Personal Injury firms. He has now graduated to Step 7. He's an *expansion* entrepreneur, otherwise known as a *freedom* entrepreneur. His firm manages itself, allowing him the freedom to explore new opportunities as a business owner or simply spend time with his wife in their early years of semi-retirement.

As a Freedom Entrepreneur, you can duplicate your scaling model across different markets and practice areas, mergers, and acquisitions. You can also pursue geographic expansion.

At this point, you can build multi-million dollar businesses in under one year.

You also have a self-multiplying business and cash flow with your law firm. Your law firm doesn't just self-manage without you, it grows without you. This is where you start getting a really high enterprise value for your law firm, where you can sell your law firm for $50M–$100M. This is where you become rich in time and money.

What's Step 8? Step 8 may as well be Step Infinity because the sky's the limit. Step 8 is when you become a Wealth Multiplier—this is where you leave your legacy on the world. You are now managing money. You're no longer managing businesses at all. You're trading money for businesses. You're buying businesses, doing investments, investing in real estate, you're an angel investor, and so on. At this point, you go from rich to *wealthy*.

It's not uncommon for big law firm owners to own other businesses that are completely unrelated to law. For instance, when we interviewed Bill Mattar, the owner of the largest law firm in New York state and a popular internet personality, he told us that he doesn't just run the largest law firm in his state. He owns *eight* different businesses. He is a lawyer, who became a law firm owner, who became an expansion entrepreneur, who is now a Wealth Multiplier.

Now, you don't *have* to climb those last two steps. Once you arrive at Step 6, you can choose to autopilot and profit your law firm as-is. But for some of you, that won't be enough. You're going to want to take all the battle scars you earned from scaling your firm, then reapply that knowledge somewhere else for a result that's even bigger, faster, and more beautiful. This is exactly what happened to us when we partnered with Attorney Assistant. We were able to take everything we learned in scaling SMB Team, roll out all the lessons we describe in the following chapters, and then watch the business take off. We don't even run the business. We have an exceptional CEO who runs it, Ethen Ostroff.

However high you choose to climb, remember that each of these steps represents a success for you. Each step is an accomplishment. The important thing to remember is that each next step is *more successful* than the one preceding it. As you climb upwards from Step 3, you move from trading your *time* to get results, to trading your *money* to get results. Have other people run your firm, produce a profit, and build a commercially profitable enterprise that works without you.

Ultimately, you want to get to a place with your firm where your investment of time is completely optional. That's what will get you greater profit, impact, and freedom.

Now, you might be thinking something like, "Wow! This all sounds amazing! I think I'll tuck all this information away in my subconscious and maybe someday I'll use it to be more successful."

Don't do this! Don't wallflower while your life passes you by. Remember, you don't learn from *in*action. You learn *in* action. Commit to your vision and then start doing things. Fail fast! Then move on. Change is scary, but it's necessary for any positive evolution of your life.

One of our mentors, Myron Golden, sometimes likes to bust out a little parable in his mentoring conversations with us.

He'll say, "I talked to a forklift driver the other day. He told me he had 30 years of experience driving a forklift. I told him, 'No you don't. You have *one* year of experience driving a forklift, and you've repeated it 30 times.'"

We think of that quote when we meet law firm owners who are in the place where David Buckley started out. They've learned to do one thing really well—but they got stuck there. They do the same thing every day over and over and over again. They never get out of the forklift.

How do you get unstuck? How do you generate the inertia you need to take the first step beyond where you've gotten so comfortable? You *commit* to change. That's why we're going to end this chapter by talking you through the four C's of initiating change.

The Four C's of Initiating Change

The most important thing you can do to reach success is to *make the decision* to move on to the next step *now*. Most law firm owners never make that decision. They think they can't grow their law firm to the next level because they lack one or more of the four C's necessary for initiating change.

- **Commitment.** I can't *commit* to taking my law firm to the next level until I know I'm capable of doing it successfully.

- **Courage.** I can't grow my law firm to the next level until I have the *courage* to risk my current level of success.

- **Capability.** I can't grow my law firm to the next level until I have the *capability* to hire the right people.

- **Confidence.** I can't grow my law firm to the next level until I have the *confidence* to spend more on marketing.

We learned about the four C's from Dan Sullivan in his book, *The Four C's Formula*. Here is his diagram:

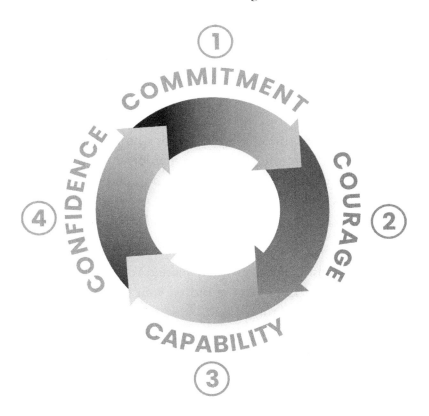

This diagram demonstrates a simple truth. You must commit *first*. That's all you need to begin. Courage, capability, and confidence only grow as a *result* of first taking the step of commitment. In the case of running your law firm, that might look like you committing to hire an associate attorney, or investing in a Google Ads campaign.

How do you get from commitment to *courage*? Dan has a few insights on that. He says, "Fear is wetting your pants. Courage is doing what you set out to do with wet pants."[5]

Do it with wet pants. That's courage!

Once you've *committed* and found the *courage* to do the damn thing, then force that commitment by taking a step. You now have a sense of what that will entail for your hiring, marketing, and delegating, so pick one of those areas to start working on. Whatever it is, it's going to prove to you that you have the *capability* to render change, because you will be doing things you never had to do before! That's huge. "Hey, I just spent a ton of money on advertising even though I was scared to do it. And look! I doubled my quality clients."

What does this do? It gives you *confidence*. You feel like a rock star! You *are* a rock star! You've moved your firm a major step forward on the road to success.

And guess what that does for you? It moves you to the *next level* of commitment, whether it's hiring or delegating or whatever you need to do.

---

[5] Sullivan, Dan. n.d. "Courage: The Key to Confidence." https://resources. strategiccoach.com/the-multiplier-mindset-blog/courage-the-key-to-confidence-2.

The cycle repeats. You go to your new commitment and then on through courage, capability, and confidence all over again. Each time, you level up.

Each time, you discover new courage, capabilities, and confidence. It's a non-stop loop that never has to end, and it's a beautiful thing.

All of this will require taking a risk, and sometimes, people want to avoid risk. But really, there's no such thing as a no-risk option. In fact, often the things that we associate with being the "safe option" can come back to bite us. For example, in 2007, everyone thought the "no risk" investment option was real estate, only to get hit by underwater mortgages during the Great Recession. Getting into your car is a risk. Even staying at home is a risk! You can't avoid risk entirely, so it's best to *understand* risk. Understanding risk can enable you to successfully navigate your next step. Shaan Puri, from the *My First Million* podcast, taught us a lot about how to view risk productively.

The number one risk that lawyers are afraid of is failure. "What if I do it and it doesn't work?" In that case, you achieve our favorite kind of risk: the one that ends in failure. Yes, failure! We have learned so much more from our failures than our successes. Failure sounds scary—but is it, really? True, when you fail, you typically lose a little bit of time and a little bit of money. But what do you gain? You gain experiences. You gain relationships. You gain skills. In other words, you gain courage, capability, and confidence that you'll use to do even better next time.

Even if you lose money with a "failure," you still end up gaining a lot. Take Andy, for instance. He's started around 15 businesses that didn't make him any money, but he doesn't consider those failures. They still moved him forward. In fact, one failure led him to meet someone who became his close friend and, nearly ten years later, his business partner in a new venture. In 2023, that venture made around $4M in revenue! That was the fruit that grew out of failure. Despite everyone being afraid of failure, it isn't nearly as bad as the alternative: mediocrity.

When you choose to remain comfortable and never step out in risk, you choose mediocrity. Living in mediocrity means you have something that's not bad enough to fail, but it's not good enough to be great. And in our opinion, mediocrity is worse than failure because mediocrity robs you of your most precious resource—your *time*. In the instance of failure, you still get the lessons out of it. You still grow in courage, capability, and confidence. Then you can take those skills and try something else. But you get none of that when you stay comfortable. You just stay stuck.

Here's the *worst* thing you can do: attempt to avoid all risk. If you're never willing to risk a single dollar, or a new hire, or a marketing campaign—you're putting your dreams at risk. You're putting your *future self* at risk, because you're not daring to become the person that you could be, or to build the business that could do something great.

The best risk is a calculated risk—and that's the one you take on when you step out in commitment. You set your eyes on a goal and you commit to it, even though you know it's risky.

But because you've got your eyes wide open to the risk, you research the heck out of it. Best-case scenario, you succeed. Worst-case scenario, you "just" grow in courage, capability, and confidence, ready to take on the next commitment.

So, have courage. Make that first commitment. Yes, it's a risk. But even if it fails, you grow in profound ways and escape the trap of mediocrity. One of the reasons we wrote this book is so that you can risk with your eyes wide open, fully equipped to optimize your likelihood of success.

And guess what? You've already taken a big risk and journeyed through these four C's! When you started your law firm, you made a *commitment*, and you followed through on it. You hung out a shingle and started taking clients. This took *courage*. It forced you to become more *capable,* and that made you more *confident*. This is no different. It's exactly what you've already done.

Here's a great, big, fat tip for you: the easiest way to move to the next level of growth is to find somebody who's already done it and get them to show you how. A good mentor will help you commit, move forward with courage, and develop your capability and confidence by sharing their own experiences with you. In fact, one of the wisest steps you could take to *commit* to growth is by hiring a mentor! Follow the advice in this Ken Schramm quote: "Smart people learn from their mistakes. Wise people learn from the mistakes of others."

You *need* mentors to guide you to the next level. It's a classic step on the Hero's Journey! Luke Skywalker had Obi-Wan Kenobi and Yoda. "The Karate Kid," a.k.a. Daniel LaRusso, learns martial arts and important life lessons from Mr. Miyagi. Frodo Baggins from *The Lord of the Rings* is mentored by Gandalf, who guides him on his quest to destroy the One Ring. And it's not just fictional heroes who need mentors. Tony Robbins had Jim Rohn. Michael Jordan had Dean Smith and Phil Jackson. Mentors are, quite literally, a game changer.

If you want to climb this Lawyer Legacy Staircase, find a mentor who's already climbed a similar one. Pay them to show you how to follow their lead. Learning from their wisdom will be the easiest way to understand what you need to do to get to the next level and how.

The problem is that most lawyers go through just one cycle of the four C's and stop there. They take one step and then get comfortable in stasis. It took commitment to get there. It took courage. They gained capability and confidence—but did not repeat the cycle.

Don't be like those lawyers. Be like David Buckley. When he texted us recently to let us know he just acquired another PI firm, he added, "Everything is possible when you *commit to change and surround yourself with the people who encourage and support you.*" (Our emphasis.)

David Buckley and countless others are living the future that can await you when you choose to do the hard work of evolving your identity and putting in the effort to climb this staircase. It's no small task, but it's entirely possible.

Commit to the next step, then take *one* action in that direction. Success is achieved through identifying a good strategy and then committing to action. You are always *one* strategy, *one* delegation, or *one* mentor away from your next stage of growth. Essentially, those all boil down to *one* action. SMB Team took a critical step up our own staircase when we took the *one* action of moving into Demand Marketing. The only thing that changed was that we launched Google ad campaigns. That was it. Then, we took another major step by expanding to Awareness Marketing, launching a Meta ads campaign on Facebook. One strategy. Each of those steps brought in millions more in revenue, allowing us to hire more and better people, and helping us evolve as leaders because we could afford to invest in great coaches.

What's the *one* action you need to take next?

We're going to show you the way. You need a proven goal-attainment model to reach the phase of growth you want to hit. Blind ambition never works, as we have tried to demonstrate here.

On the other hand, ambition combined with a proven roadmap to achieving that ambition *always* works. As Zig Ziglar said, "You don't have to be great to start, but you have to start to be great." That said, let's talk about the roadmap you need to execute your plan.

Chapter 2 | Takeaways

1. Identify your current step on the Lawyer Legacy Staircase:

   a. *Step 3, Solo Practitioner.* You're the one making it rain. You're a solo act and you do everything. You are surviving, but profit is unpredictable and you rely solely on word of mouth to get referrals. You are not in a place where you could sell your firm or even leave it for a month and expect it to be intact when you get back.

b. *Step 4, Small Business Manager.* You've shifted your marketing to a Demand approach (page one of Google and SEO) and the increased number of leads means you also need to hire additional employees. You shift from doing everything to managing a small team of employees, most of whom know less than you. Revenue is more steady, but overall profit is wobbly and requires your reactive fixes to ensure the firm stays in the black.

c. *Step 5, Law Firm CEO.* You've now shifted into doing Awareness Marketing (building awareness in a customer base that isn't yet looking for you, usually through social media) and realize you need a better system and better team to handle all the new leads. The challenge of making this transition is called The Abyss. Once you've crossed The Abyss, you function as a CEO, leading high-performing managers of a high-performing team. You're now delegating all tasks except for vision, strategy, and executive leadership tasks.

d. *Step 6, Law Firm Owner.* You now function less like an NFL Head Coach, and more like a Team Owner. The firm can easily run without you, which frees you up to imagine the next big direction you might choose to take. The firm has blanketed the marketing landscape with an omnipresent effect.

Your profits are clearly mapped out in an annual plan.

2. The Four C's of initiating change begins with commitment. Then comes courage (do it with wet pants), capability, and confidence. How committed are you to taking the necessary action toward your dream life you identified in Chapter 1? What could you do to increase your level of commitment?

3. What *one* action do you take to start the scaling process? As you read the following chapters, consider what one strategy, delegation, or mentor you want to take action in to get the ball rolling.

CHAPTER 3

PLANNING YOUR LAW FIRM GROWTH STRATEGY

TURNING YOUR VISION INTO REALITY

If you fail to plan, you are planning to fail.

—Benjamin Franklin

BILL HAUSER NARRATES

"Dude, what the heck?!" my roommate asked as I got back from the bathroom. "You're like the guy from *Beautiful Mind*." He pointed at my computer screen. "What is this crap?"

He was staring at the Excel spreadsheet I'd been working on. It was a 10-year plan for the business I hadn't started yet, with every single year's revenues mapped out for the next decade.

Was it crazy? Maybe it was crazy. Before I started SMB team, I refused to make one single sale until I felt crystal clear on my vision for where I wanted to take the company. I had seen what had happened when my family's business operated without a plan: The uncertainty. The constant guessing. The embarrassing questions to our accountant—"Hey, did we have a good year, or not?"—as though my mom and dad had no idea about whether or not their entire past year of work was profitable. As a teenager observing all this, I was mentally taking notes. Later, when we went through bankruptcy, the demise of my parents' business and marriage both seemed related to a lack of planning.

That wasn't going to be my story. As a 26-year-old, I was thinking about quitting my sales job at Yellowpages.com to start my own marketing company—but not until I had created the Excel spreadsheet to end all spreadsheets. I asked myself something along the lines of, *If I had no limits on my abilities, a windstorm of cash, and could attract anyone to my team that I wanted—what would be true for me?* (Later, I would read the book *Vivid Vision* and would discover that this question is part of a specific process to generate a comprehensive vision. The book changed my life—no surprise, given how obsessed I was with vision from the start!) I had answered that question for Year 1, Year 2, Year 3, and so on, all the way up to Year 10. Every year was mapped out with incredible detail.

My roommate stared from the document back to me, incredulous, waiting for answers. "Maybe it's a little extreme," I said, shrugging.

"You think?" he asked.

I laughed off his comments. Within a few weeks, I quit my job. I planned to live off of my bonus check from Yellowpages.com while I got my company off the ground.

But then that Excel spreadsheet stayed dormant for the next eight months. I was massively insecure my plan wouldn't actually take off—I didn't *believe* my vision was possible. I hid my insecurity behind busyness, telling myself, "I've got to get my vendors in place. I've got to set up my accounting software. I've got to build these relationships. I can't reach out to clients until I have a website." I didn't make a single sale.

Then, I finally ran out of money. It was the best thing that could have happened. I got down to the last couple thousand dollars in my bank account and said to myself, "Enough of this planning crap. I need to go out and sell something."

In my first month of actually trying to get sales, I landed eight lawyer clients. *Oh my gosh—this is AMAZING,* I thought. Fast forward six years and SMB Team had become a multi-eight-figure business with 100 full-time W-2 employees.

What happened between that first sale and the $25.8M+ a year in revenue that we're doing now? What created that change?

If I were to boil it down, I would say the lion's share of our success started with that clear plan. I committed to that plan and determined that I would execute on that plan every year. Then, I pumped money and time and effort into learning what I didn't know. I read around 100 (no exaggeration) books on business personal development.

I started interviewing people like Verne Harnish, author of *Scaling Up*; Gino Wickman, the author of *Traction;* and Michael Gerber, author of *E-Myth*. I found a coach, Cameron Herold, who grew the revenue for 1-800-GOT-JUNK from zero to $100M in five years. Most of these interviews are now on my YouTube channel. And I started putting together information about what worked and what didn't work with scaling a business.

As I was getting answers from all these amazing thought leaders, I realized that my 10-year plan—as comprehensive as I'd tried to make it—hadn't provided me with everything my company needed. There were still a few key pieces we needed to get in place. I didn't have a vision. In fact, I didn't even really know *how* to form a clear vision. I didn't have a true annual plan with clear budget projections. I didn't have clear key performance indicators (KPIs) to help me evaluate our numbers.

But we got all those things. We started figuring them out. And now we're going to explain each one to help *you* scale up at the pace you want.

Most lawyers simply stumble into the business aspects of their firm—they learn enough to keep the lights on and pay their few employees, with the hope they'll make enough to keep lawyering. It's similar to the mentality I saw in my parents. In our first two chapters, we explained why you need to start thinking of yourself as a *business owner* first, instead of a lawyer.

Now, we're going to get into the nuts and bolts of making your vision for your law firm a reality. The prescription is this:

- Turn your dream life into a Vivid Vision. (We'll explain what that is in a second.)

- Turn the Vivid Vision into an annual plan.

- Base your annual plan's budget on the 20/40/10 rule.

- Guide your 20/40/10 budget according to the 5 KPIs.

- Use the 5 KPIs to create your 90-day Quarterly Boulders.

BOOM! That's how you build the law firm of your dreams. Well—that, and the stuff we're going to share in the rest of this book.

We're going to tackle the first few bullets in this chapter, and the last two in the next chapter. Think of this business growth plan as a funnel:

At the top of the funnel is your Vivid Vision. It's wide and big and imaginative. Then, you get more specific, mapping out your annual plan. The funnel gets more narrow and more specific still as you get into the five KPIs, your key performance indicators. And finally, you get into the nitty gritty specifics that will make it all happen within your particular context, with the Quarterly Boulders.

Let's talk through each one.

Vivid Vision

Can you actually see what someone says, physically? No. You can't see what someone says with your eyes, but you can through your mind's eye. A Vivid Vision is a chance for you to take everything that you see in *your* mind's eye about the future of your law firm and transfer it to as many other people's minds as humanly possible.

If your vision stays in your head, it's dead. But if your vision is shared, clear, documented, and regularly referred to, then people will start seeing what you're saying. In his book, *Vivid Vision,* my coach Cameron Herold teaches ambitious entrepreneurs how to take what's in their head and make it public.

A Vivid Vision is a three- to six-page PDF document that breaks down every big-picture three-year reality that you see in your head. It answers the question: *If you had no limitations, a windstorm of cash, and could retain*

every key hire, how would your law firm look and feel three years from today?

Here's how to start putting it together, according to Cameron Herold. First, start with that question. If your limitations weren't real, you had a windstorm of cash, and you could attract any A-player to work with your firm, what would be true three years from today? With that in mind, answer the following questions:

1. How much profit and revenue will your firm be generating?
2. How many staff will you have?
3. How many active cases will you have, of what case types?
4. What is your marketing budget?
5. How will your law firm look and feel when your law firm's goals are reached?
6. How will you and the team feel when those goals are reached?
7. What values will your team operate by to get to this three-year vision?

Once you've answered those questions, you'll write a draft that vividly describes all of those responses in a document of six pages or fewer. And that's the Vivid Vision—essentially, a snapshot of everything your firm is about and plans to achieve.

Quick-Hitting Hack: This list of questions may prompt you to think of a different question: "*How* do I determine my annual growth rate? I don't know how much I'm going to make next year! And definitely not how much I'm going to make in three years." The question implies the information is going to come from some external source. Not so! That information comes from *your decision.* YOU are the one to decide how fast you want to grow, how big you want to get, and what your profit margins are going to be! Once you make the decision, you work backward to reverse engineer it into a reality. No external source is going to give you the data from your vision. It comes from you thinking big and having fun!

Still hungry for something more concrete? Make it simple: 2X. At SMB Team, we assume we're going to double our revenue every year, and we base our Vivid Vision on that assumption. If you're not sure where to start, that could be a good jumping-off point.

To be clear, the Vivid Vision is not a mission statement we're talking about or generic goals that never get done. Most companies have mission statements, but how many people can actually remember them? Not many. They're forgettable.

On the other hand, a Vivid Vision is a clear picture of your mission *acted out.* These are not core value platitudes hung in a frame in the workplace bathroom. It's what your company lives and dies on. It's the core-value-driven world of your firm's future. It provides a picture of what your firm will feel like when you experience the results of goals reached.

Quick-Hitting Hack: For more about creating your Vivid Vision, read Cameron Herold's book on the subject, *Vivid Vision*. If you want to read through SMB Team's Vivid Vision as an example, check it out here.

(You'll find all the other bonuses from the book here or you can go to **yourdreamlawfirm.com**.)

Scan this QR Code to Unlock This Bonus

Vivid Vision: DON'Ts

A few tips to optimize your experience spinning this incredible Vivid Vision into existence:

- When you're writing your firm's Vivid Vision, don't worry (yet) about the *how.* Don't worry about how you're going to get it done. That comes later.

- Seriously, don't forecast or do any math equations.

- Don't do detailed analysis, either.

- And no typing! Handwriting allows for more creativity, enables you to easily draw, helps you connect with

nature without a computer, and eliminates the temptation of computer distractions.[6]

- Also, don't bother bringing a ton of people to brainstorm with you. Your Vivid Vision is not a democracy.
It doesn't have to appeal to everyone. It might even
repel some people. In fact, the clearer your Vision is, the
clearer it will be to you down the road who *should* and
shouldn't be on your team.

- Finally, don't make this about your personal goals,
take-home pay, or thoughts about your quality of life.
We had you reflect on your dream life in Chapter 1
because it's a critical element of your commitment to
grow your law firm—and you can create your own
private personal Vivid Vision. However, leave those *personal* considerations out of your law firm's Vivid Vision,
since it will be shared with your employees. They won't
be motivated by details about your take-home pay—
but they *will* be motivated by the target revenue for
the firm since that will impact *their* take-home pay. The
Vivid Vision is the blueprint for the law firm that will
allow your personal goals to take place but needs to be
relevant for the law firm as a whole.

[6] Jones, Alexandra Mae. 2020. "New study suggests handwriting engages the brain more than typing." CTV News. October 4, 2020. https://www.google.com/url?q=https://www.ctvnews.ca/health/new-study-suggests-handwriting-engages-the-brain-more-than-typing-1.5132542?cache%3Dlxaherxk&sa=D&source=docs&ust=1693848731085457&usg=AOvVaw2jZp3SHeBP4WCGwGvylPxJ.

Vivid Vision: DO's

- Do get yourself *away* from the environment where you work 24/7.

- In fact, get yourself outdoors: not a parking lot, or the adjacent park where you can see your firm's building. Get somewhere you can feel free.

- Use your imagination! Seriously. This is a time to let yourself think big.

- Consider that essential question: *If you had no limitations, a windstorm of cash, and could retain every key hire, how would your law firm look and feel three years from today?*

- Now, consider that future reality in terms of your firm's purpose, core values, culture, marketing efforts, customer experience, financial targets, and so on.

- When you take all those imaginings and finally put them into a cohesive document, you should have somewhere between four to six pages.

Your Vivid Vision does not require team members' buy-in. *You* decide the Vision. You don't need other people's buy-in to create it. You just … create it! Then, you find people who are attracted to it. You'll also probably find out who is repelled by it. That's a good thing—that means the Vivid Vision is accomplishing one of its two main purposes.

How to Use Your Vivid Vision

What are the two main purposes of a Vivid Vision?

A) To keep your team excited about where the firm is going, and to hold them accountable to their contributions toward that vision. For that reason, you should embed it into your quarterly review process.

And B) to attract the *right* people to your team and repel the *wrong* people away from it. For that reason, you should embed the Vivid Vision into your recruiting process. Use it between your first and second interviews. Send the candidate the Vivid Vision, ask them to read it, and then make a 30- to 60-second video explaining how they intend to make that vision come true. If they don't return that video to you, they should no longer be considered in your hiring process. You want people to self-select in, or self-select out.

A Vivid Vision should keep your team excited about where the firm is going, and to hold them accountable to their contributions toward that vision. It should also attract the *right* people to your team and repel the *wrong* people away from it.

When going through the process of forming and rolling out your Vivid Vision, expect to screw it up. Expect to make mistakes. Then, learn from those mistakes and get better. In fact, in our coaching program, we call the first year of implementing this system, the "ROAP Year," which stands for Roll Out And Practice. It means you're going to roll it out, make mistakes, learn from your mistakes, and roll it out again. You'll make more mistakes, but each time you're getting better, and eventually, you figure it out. That growth will probably take about a year.

Everyone wants an overnight solution—but real growth takes time. Think of how long it took you to become a lawyer! We're recommending a fundamentally new way of thinking, new operating procedures, and new habits. It will take time for you to adapt and hone your processes to incorporate all of this. But—to quote Myron Golden again—"You can't rush the washing machine. In order for the clothes to get clean, they've got to go through all the cycles."

Some people love the imaginative brainstorming of the Vivid Vision phase. They're the ones who get lost in sunsets and love to do things like hike without a map. Others geek out over enormous Excel spreadsheets. They're the ones who are itching to make this practical and are starting to wonder, *When are we going to get to the HOW?*

Right now.

Annual Plan

Okay, you've got your big, beautiful Vivid Vision down and you've made it available to everyone on your team. Good job.

Now, you're going to *reverse engineer* that Vivid Vision, so that it becomes your reality. Here's how you do it:

- Break the three-year vision into a year-by-year execution plan: Year 1, Year 2, Year 3. This is your **annual execution plan.** We're going to explain how to set this up and how to align your budget accordingly.

- Within each annual execution plan, identify five key numbers to help you track your progress, also known

as your **five key performance indicators (KPIs).**
We'll explain these in the next chapter.

- You also identify your **"quarterly boulders"** which
we'll discuss more in the next chapter. Basically, these
are the big milestones you're looking to hit every quarter, which will help you stay on track toward the Vivid
Vision.

Let's say that your Vivid Vision is to "10X" your law firm
within three years. In order to hit that, you need to double
your law firm (2X) within the first year and 5X the firm
by the end of the second year. Ideally, that will give you the
momentum you need to 10X it by the end of Year 3 to
achieve your Vivid Vision.

So, you've gotten three years mapped out and have committed to double your firm within a year. Now, you have to break
down your targets for Year 1. In your annual execution plan,
you're going to have a spreadsheet that lists horizontally what
your revenues will be for every single month. Within twelve
months, those revenues should gradually scale up until you've
successfully hit your goal and doubled your revenue.

Between month 1 and month 12, you've mapped out revenue
targets that will successfully double your firm and help you
hit that Year 1 goal—if you stay on track.

Are you scratching your head, wondering how you're going
to hit those monthly revenues? As part of your annual execution plan, you also need to identify *what* percent of your revenue is going to come from *which* type of cases. In other words,
you need to identify your **ideal case buckets**.

Quick-Hitting Hack: If you don't have the budget to hire a full-time CFO, consider a fractional CFO to help you create your annual plan and analyze your law firm's financial health. While SMB Team offers this service, there are many other options available as well.

Ideal Case Buckets: Revenue Targets

Here's how this works. Let's say you run a personal injury firm. You've decided you want to target car accidents, workers' comp, and construction accidents. You're looking ahead to three months, where your revenue target is $480K. You can typically expect the following **average case value (ACV)** from each category:

- Car accidents: $8K fee/case

- Workers' comp: $8K fee/case

- Construction: $20K fee/case

How are you going to hit $480K? You decide you want twelve construction cases, which is going to net $240K in fees. The remaining $240K, you're going to divide between the other two categories. That means you need to get 15 car accidents ($120K), and 15 workers' comp cases ($120K). You've identified your ideal case buckets.

There's only one problem. Even though you've got a lot of traction in workers' comp and car accidents, you're currently only pulling in a few construction cases per month. Given that construction is your highest value case bucket, you need to seriously step up your game in that category.

Can you see where we're going? You now have the information you need to form a *marketing* strategy. With your marketing budget, you need to majorly target *construction* personal injury cases.

"But wait," you might be asking—"how much do I spend on marketing? In fact, how much do I spend on anything? I've got my revenue targets figured out—but what about my budget?"

Great question.

Budget Categories: The 20/40/10 Rule

Stating the obvious here, your annual plan should also include budget categories. You need to know how you're going to *make* money, and you also need a plan for how you're going to *spend* money. Good news! We're going to make this really easy for you.

First, identify how much you want to make. Let's say your goal revenue is $1M. Then, you want to spend according to the following rule, basing the percentages on your target revenue:

The 20/40/10 Rule

- 20% goes to your marketing budget
- 40% goes to payroll
- 10% goes to getting answers by investing in professional development for yourself and your team
- The remaining 30% should cover your fixed costs and include your net profit

Don't freak out—we're going to explain how this works. To start with, you'll scale up to these percentages gradually. For example, if you want to make one million this year, you'd budget $200K for marketing, which is $16,666 per month on average. However, the spend would look more like this:

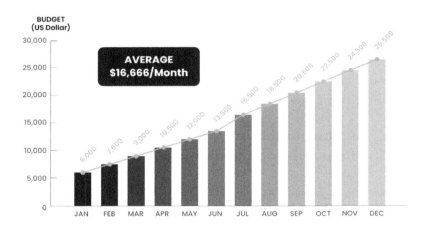

You'll take a similar scaled approach in all three categories. These three powerful variables—marketing, staff, and getting answers—have *everything* to do with how fast you grow your firm. You may not yet be sold on the percentages we just listed, but you're about to become a believer.

The First 20% Goes to Marketing

If you're serious about wanting to grow your law firm fast, you need to be spending 20% of your future gross revenues on marketing. This is not popular advice. If you ever heard of the "Profit First" model, this is the opposite. This is a proven model for rapid growth.

What's included in your marketing spend? That includes your online ad spend, offline advertising spend, marketing vendors or freelancers, and full-time in-house marketing staff.

Most attorneys tend to be skeptical of that number. That's because most law firms currently spend a measly *2%* of their gross revenues on marketing. Actually—to be exact—IBIS World puts the average marketing spending by U.S. law firms between *0.8* and *1.6%* of gross revenue.[7]

Want to know the average annual growth rate of all those average firms? Between 0.5% and 1.4%, year-over-year growth. That's *funny*, isn't it?

The amount that lawyers spend on marketing is almost identical to their annual growth rate.

If you think that's a coincidence, you're kidding yourself. Tiny investments in marketing have a direct correlation to piddly, pathetic, puny growth. If you want to become average, study the averages. We're speaking ironically, obviously. But in many cases, that's exactly what lawyers do. They call their lawyer friend at a different firm and ask, "Hey, what are you spending on marketing?" As though *that's* the data they should be basing their own marketing spending on. That's like taking financial advice from someone who's regularly broke.

No, no, no.

If you want to phone a friend, your first question should be, "How fast is your law firm growing?" If they respond and

---

[7] Claire O'Connor, Law Firms in the US, IBISWorld, July 2017, https://my.ibisworld.com/us/en/industry/54111

tell you they're not growing at all, then *don't* ask them, "How much are you spending on marketing?"

If you want to *grow*, you need to pay attention to what the law firms with a fast annual growth rate are doing. We've had the privilege of interviewing lawyers like Alexander Shunnarah, the largest personal injury lawyer in all of Alabama, who has over 3,000 billboards. We've also been able to interview Morris Bart, who runs a law firm with over 400 employees and does multiple nine figures a year in revenue. We've interviewed Darryl Isaacs, who runs the biggest law firm in the central U.S., and Mike Morse, the biggest in Michigan. We've interviewed *a lot* of the biggest lawyers in the United States.

How much do you think those law firms are spending on marketing?

Anywhere from *19 to 35%* of their current gross revenues on marketing. If you just wet your pants a little, we understand.

Here's the point: the conventional wisdom on how much you should spend on marketing is probably wrong. You should be spending somewhere around 20% of your gross annual revenue on your marketing.

Like we said before—if you really want to commit to fast growth—you should base that 20% investment number on your *target* annual revenue, not your *current* annual revenue. Spend your money on where you're going. Multiply every month's *target* revenues by 20%, and that creates your marketing expense for that corresponding month.

You just wrote down a three-year vision, right? If you *knew for sure* you were going to reach that vision, would you spend more on marketing? If you *knew for sure* you would bring in $100K/month in new revenue, would you spend $20K/month on marketing? Would you hire more people? Would you invest in getting answers via your personal development?

"If I knew *for sure*—then, yes. But Bill and Andy … I don't know for sure!"

When lawyers are reluctant to make these investments, it's usually because they don't fully believe in the vision. In some cases—not in *your* case, because you've read the book up to this point, but in *some* cases—law firm owners don't even have a vision in the first place. But if you have the vision, and you *believe* the vision is true, and you know that marketing and payroll are the two biggest expenses that will get you to that vision—then, muster up your courage.

Wait, never mind, courage doesn't come first. Get ready to *commit*.

20% of your gross revenue goes to marketing.

> **Quick-Hitting Hack:** Unless your firm is already flooded with leads, most law firm growth starts with an increase in marketing aggression. Marketing is the inception of growth. However, if you're convinced that you don't have the money to do this (first of all, check that assumption—no one has money; you earn money by getting more clients), then expect to invest that 20% with your *time*. You need to spend 20% of your gross revenue or 20% of your time acquiring new cases. Ideally, you're doing both. If you can't level up your investment to that degree, it's unlikely you will scale your firm at the rate you want. You can pay for your marketing with your money or your time. Pick one.

The Next 40% Goes to Payroll

Budget category number two is payroll. Payroll gets 40% of your annual gross revenue. Why? Because you can't do it all yourself. If you want to scale fast, you need to delegate tasks to A-players. When you increase lead volume, you need people to answer your phones instead of you. You need other lawyers to handle your cases instead of you. You need people to do marketing, instead of you.

How do you do that? You spend money on payroll.

What's included in payroll? Any full-time employee, except those working full time in your marketing department, as they are counted toward your 20% marketing budget. The most successful law firms spend 20% on attorney payroll and 20% on non-attorney payroll. Non-attorney payroll can include your support staff or full-time intake staff—anything that's not an attorney.

Of the 20% you spend on non-attorney payroll, we advise spending about 7.5% on your intake team and 12.5% on support staff.

The biggest hurdle to *not* increasing your payroll spending is … Want to guess? … Not believing you'll get a return on that investment. You probably have some B and C players on your team, currently. If you're not getting a good return from your current team, of course you would be hesitant to hire more people. You assume you're going to get more of the same. (This is why we warned you about team rebuild in Chapter 2.)

The good news is this book intends to show you how to hold your team accountable and demand high performance, rather than just giving everyone participation trophies for choosing to take your money in the form of a salary. (Hiring and managing top performers will be the focus of Chapters 10 and 11.)

Holding your team accountable is not something you need to feel guilty for. It's a requirement for growth.

The healthiest of all law firms run at a $250K **revenue per employee ratio.** That's a good rule of thumb. One employee per $250K of revenue. If we're talking about a firm that brings in around $1M per year, a *healthy* firm has four full-time employees.

$1M revenue/4 employees = $250K revenue per employee

Now, is that typically what we see? No. *Average* firms (there's that ugly word again) run between $120K and $200K per employee, depending on their practice area. If your firm makes $1M in revenue and you have six employees who are telling you another employee is needed—that's a sign your systems are broken, current employees may be working at low efficiency, or you have B-players. Before hiring another one, there are several steps you can take to evaluate and improve the efficiency of your current team.

In Part 3 of this book, we'll talk about specific steps you can take to help your employees function at a high efficiency level. Until then, we'll give you a preview of what's to come. Consider the following questions to evaluate your team's efficiency. (This is by no means an exhaustive list!)

- Does your team have the proper training they need to perform the duties assigned?

- What automations could be implemented to make the team more effective?

- Is the right person performing the right task?

- What key performance indicators (KPIs) are in place to measure labor efficiency?

- Does your team have the right tools to complete the job efficiently?

- Have you set the proper expectations of what you expect your team to accomplish?

- Are you providing your team with the freedom to explore more efficient solutions to problems? (HINT: A-players should be able to self-solve, provided they're given the autonomy and trust to do so.)

Certainly, there are low-margin law firms and higher-margin law firms, so take those numbers with a grain of salt. Still, knowing this principle is important as you scale and hire people. If you think you'd need to hire a ton of people to get your revenues up, chances are you don't have A-players, you're not managing your people very well or they don't have the skills and motivation they need to succeed.

Quick-Hitting Hack: When you're scaling your law firm, your revenue per employee will dip temporarily—especially during The Abyss. That's to be expected. Never limit hiring someone because your revenue per employee is too low when you're looking to grow rapidly. However, if you recognize that you have too many employees for your revenue size because some of your employees are low performers, consider replacing those underperformers on your team and keeping your payroll at the same level. This is called a "Team Rebuild."

If you suspect your current employees aren't achieving the numbers they could be—or if they're doing excellent work, but your average case value isn't what it should be—this is a moment to pause. Make a mental note to dig into some of the content on effective management or increasing your case value when we discuss it later in the book.

Of your 40% investment in payroll, the most successful law firms spend 20% on non-attorney payroll, and 20% on attorney payroll.

World-class PI firms are bringing in $1M *per lawyer*. In other practice areas, that number should be over $500K (closer to $700K). What would that mean for a world-class PI firm making $2M per year? They've got two top-notch lawyers. You might be thinking that's pretty atypical. True! A lot of law firms need more than one lawyer to bring in these amounts of revenue and that's a sign that they're either not managed well or don't have the skills or motivation to excel in their job. That's why Part 3 of this book focuses on how to lead a self-managing team of rock stars.

How do you figure out your 40% number? When you were figuring out your marketing budget, you multiplied each month's target revenue by 20%. You're going to do the same thing with payroll: take your target gross revenue number, multiply it by 40%, and that's what you're spending on payroll for each month throughout the year. This will allow you to project out your hiring needs throughout the year.

Quick-Hitting Hack: Figuring out these percentages will look slightly different, depending on whether you're considering a *cash*-based budget or a *projection*-based budget. For instance, a personal injury lawyer doesn't collect cash up front. They get paid when their client gets paid, which might be eight months to two years after they sign up for a case. We recommend you create two separate annual plans. One on a *cash collected* basis, and another on a *projected case value* basis. If that personal injury lawyer expects an average auto accident case to be worth $8K in fees to her firm, that average case value informs the *projected* version of the annual plan. On the *cash collected* version, you would put that dollar amount into *next* year's annual plan, when those fees are likely to be collected.

The *cash collected* annual plan refers to cash in hand. The *projected case value* refers to your predictions of how much cash you will eventually have in hand.

Just like with your marketing budget, the most *committed* lawyers spend on their future revenue projections. They look at where their future revenues are and spend accordingly.

And yes, this might mean going into debt for a time, if necessary. You don't *have* to do that—you could choose to run your budget percentages based on your cash in hand. That might feel less risky, but there's still an opportunity cost. When you operate based on what you currently have, you run the risk of never taking the leap. If you don't have the revenues right now, how will you get additional cases unless you spend money on marketing and payroll? Most times, you're gambling, hoping that cases will *somehow* come in and *somehow* pay for your marketing next year.

But if you've done the work we've recommended—form the Vivid Vision, build the annual plan, identify your revenue targets—then you know where you're going. You can *commit*, spend money now, get lines of credit in place, and spend to where you're going rather than spending based on where you're at.

10%: Getting Answers

The last 10% of your budget should be spent on getting answers to your business growth problems via personal development, for both you and your staff—but only up to when you hit $5M in revenue. That means you should spend no more than $500K per year on personal development. This includes coaches, mentors, consultants, and education.

The two of us collectively spend $600K per year on SMB Team's personal development. It's the most important thing we invest in. Here are just a few examples of how we've spent some of that money—along with the ROI of those investments.

- When we wanted to learn how to do virtual events, we joined two masterminds and hired three of the best people in the virtual event space to learn how to hold our own events. These cost us $200K—not a small price tag. But their guidance resulted in *over $10M* as our ROI. Great deal!

- When we built a sales team, we hired three consultants to help. That investment led to another $10M ROI.

- To learn how to scale the SMB Team to 100 employees required a lot of leadership development. We hired Cameron Herold for $50K per year for three years and another CEO of a $500M company at $100K per year to provide one-on-one coaching. The amount of time we saved by learning from these two individuals' mistakes is worth tens of millions of dollars on its own.

- We've participated in 15 other business masterminds and coaching programs. The collective wisdom from those experiences resulted in us reaching our goals six years in a row and building a company worth over $100M. Once again—great deal!

Now, could we have done this on our own, with no guidance? Maybe! We could've hunted down people and convinced them to meet with us for free. But that would've required our time. When you're growing fast, the last thing you want to do is waste time.

Still not convinced the investment is worth it? We've mentioned the names of a number of world-class lawyers that we've had the honor to interview in this chapter. These business owners have *prioritized* personal development. They do one-on-one coaching. They do group coaching. They go to educational seminars. Most importantly, *all* of them are part of Mastermind groups, meeting with other growth-minded attorneys to strategize on growth opportunities for their firms. The most successful attorneys form high-level masterminds on their own and spend money to be a part of others. They look at mastermind groups as the *highest* value use of their time. That's how the *highest-grossing revenue* lawyers invest their time and money.

And, unfortunately, if you aren't a big-name lawyer yet—then other big-name lawyers won't want to meet with you. So, until you get there, we suggest you pay to play.

The *highest-grossing revenue* lawyers view mastermind groups as the *highest* value use of their time.

Quick-Hitting Hack: A quick rundown of personal development opportunities ...

- *Masterminds* are small groups of growth-minded business owners that meet (usually quarterly) to strategize, share best practices, and discuss growth opportunities for each member's business. Andy and Bill have found the more money you pay, the more elite the group you get to meet with. In Napoleon Hill's book *Think and Grow Rich*, this is key.

- *Educational seminars* are one-sided learning opportunities where someone teaches you a ton of information, either online or in person.

- *Interactive group workshops* provide you with a framework and guide you through implementing it, allowing you time to create a customized plan for your firm in a group setting.

- *One-on-one coaching* is an ongoing relationship where you meet with a personal coach 1–4 times per month and work through individualized problems. This is the highest level of accountability.

- *Consulting* is where you hire someone (usually on a project basis) to help you solve a specific problem in your firm. When the project is done, the consulting is done.

- *Books* will get you the highest ROI on your personal development, by far. And you are reading one right now! You can get millions of dollars in value from a book, but the learning, accountability, and action are all on you to execute.

SMB Team's coaching program is designed around all of the above, hence why it has produced so much success for our clients. However, you can design your own personal development plan by mixing and matching the opportunities above.

The bottom line: once you scale up your marketing and your team, you need to learn how to become a leader who *deserves* to have a bigger team working under you. That means you need to learn to dial in your communication habits so that your team's heads don't spin off every time they talk to you. You need to learn how to build a world-class intake system for your firm as you scale up your marketing. You need to learn to be savvy enough about marketing so that you can go to the root cause of what's not currently working, rather than using the excuse that average attorneys do, which is "marketing doesn't work."

Rather, the educated lawyer who has been properly coached will look at marketing and say, "Huh—it seems like the geographic radius we set up for Campaign Two is in the wrong geographic radius. Maybe we need to edit that. I'll go tell my marketing team." How would you know anything about geographic radiuses and marketing? Cause you've spent money *getting answers*.

The 10% you spend on your own development allows you to *contextualize* your marketing and intake system. It helps you learn how to better manage and grow your team. It helps you get people excited to work for your law firm. In short, it's this budget line item that will help you become the leader that you're destined to be. You're not just learning it all through trial and error, all by yourself. You're learning it through investments in yourself.

It's important to also remember the rule of 40, which says the combination of your annual growth rate and profits should be 40% or greater. So, if a firm is growing 20% year over year, it should be profiting at least 20%. And, if a firm is growing 40% year over year or more, it's okay to profit 0% because of how much you're reinvesting in hiring and marketing.

Once you reach $10M in annual revenues, we advise transitioning from this reinvestment heavy model to traditional P&L budget management. At $10M in revenue, your law firm can profit $2M per year and run itself with a leadership team.

The 20/40/10 Rule will be the most worthwhile math you ever do. These are the numbers that put you on your way to your dream life.

> **Quick-Hitting Hack:** Growth requires reinvestment. In other words, you need to reinvest some of the money you earn back into the growth of the law firm. Some law firms—especially those that get windfalls from big case settlements—plow that windfall money back into marketing, and that's how they grow. Reinvestment requires more discipline if you're dealing with small, predictable, average case values, like a DUI firm. In that case, you can't wait for a home run case to bring in a huge amount of cash. You have to build that reinvestment discipline into your budget. That's what the 20/40/10 rule guides you in doing.

BILL HAUSER NARRATES

Five Numbers to Rule Them All

Earlier in this chapter, I described my parents walking into their accountant's office and asking the question, "So—did we have a good year, or a bad year?" They didn't understand how to interpret the numbers of their business. As a result, they had no idea where they stood. Were they charging enough? Spending too much? Did they need to hire more employees? Let some employees go? No one knew.

If you're generating a Vivid Vision, building an annual plan, coming up with revenue targets, and then budgeting accordingly—you seriously need to know how to interpret your numbers. Otherwise, you're going to find yourself in the same spot my parents were in, wondering what the heck is happening between your business and the bank.

We've talked about how to forecast revenue targets, and then figure out your ideal case buckets. We've also talked about how much to spend on marketing, payroll, and personal development. Now, we're going to teach you about the five numbers that must be hit in order for you to *reach* the revenue goals that you've set.

1. Lead volume
2. Conversion rate on those leads
3. Average case value
4. Profit metrics
5. Net promoter score

In our next chapter, we're going to talk about how to understand those five numbers. Then, we're going to explain how you can use them to help you build your short term quarterly goals.

And if that sounds boring to you, revisit the dream life you sketched out in Chapter 1. More freedom. More time with your favorite people. More time to do the things you really enjoy. More money to ease your stress and provide you with a greater quality of life. More confidence in your staff. More assurance that you're giving your clients a world-class experience.

Picture yourself sipping a fruity drink on a beach in Mexico with your favorite people close by. You left your cell phone in the hotel room because *you don't need it*. You have full confidence in your people to keep the firm running while you're off the grid, eating tacos, sipping a tequila sunrise, and doing sunset yoga on the beach while Enya plays in the background.

That dream life—or whatever version you prefer—is possible. KPIs and Quarterly Boulders may not sound particularly exciting, but they're crucial for *making* the exciting stuff happen.

Chapter 3 | Takeaways

1. Take some time to craft your Vivid Vision, a three- to six-page PDF document which breaks down every big picture three-year reality that you see in your head. It answers the question: *If you had no limitations, a windstorm of cash, and could retain every key hire, how*

would your law firm look and feel in three years from today?
The Vivid Vision addresses the following points:

- ○ Your firm's statement of purpose.

- ○ A description of your firm's values and culture.

- ○ An encapsulation of your growth goals along with specific financial targets you plan to hit in the next three years.

- ○ The core business activities which will help you achieve your target growth.

- ○ The impact you intend to have on clients.

- ○ Specifics about marketing and client experience.

2. Your annual plan should map out revenue targets for each month of the next year. These revenue targets should help put you on track for your three-year Vivid Vision.

3. After determining your monthly revenue targets, figure out your ideal case buckets: the percentage of different types of cases that will ensure you hit your revenue goals.

Align your budget with the 20/40/10 rule. 20% goes to marketing, 40% is dedicated to payroll, and 10% goes to getting answers via personal development. We recommend you base your percentages on your *target* revenue projections.

CHAPTER 4

GOLDEN NUMBERS AND GREAT BIG ROCKS

THE NITTY GRITTIES OF EXPLOSIVE GROWTH

"Without data, you're just an idiot with an opinion."

—paraphrase of a quote by W. Edwards Deming

We were teaching the concepts in the previous chapter recently at our Relentless Lawyer event, with 980 lawyers in attendance from all over the U.S. We asked them a question at this point. "Okay," we said. "You've got your Vivid Vision, you've got your Annual Plan, and now you've got your budget figured out with the 20/40/10 rule. Now, how are you going to *start* that revenue engine?"

Hands went up. Plenty of ambitious lawyers were ready to give the "right" answer. "More leads!" one of them called out.

Andy nodded. "Makes sense. We do marketing for lawyers, after all. Who here has ever felt like, if you could just get more leads, everything would be fine?"

Across the room, 980 lawyers all started nodding their heads. More hands popped up and waved. Some called out, "Yes!"

It's *obvious*, right? More leads equals more business, equals more money.

Except it *doesn't*. (Trick question.)

Lead abundance is important. So important, in fact, that's going to be the focus of our next chapter. However, before you can determine a good marketing strategy, you need to solidify your *business strategy*. You need to know what *kind* of leads to go after, so that you can get the kind of cases you're looking for. And in order to clarify your business strategy, you need to wade into some numbers.

Building a successful law firm is essentially a very simple math equation, but it does involve multiple factors. To put it as plainly as possible, you need five elements.

1. You need to get a certain number of leads.
2. You need to *convert* a certain percentage of those leads into paying clients.
3. You must make a certain amount of *money* per case.
4. Then you have to *remain* profitable.
5. And, finally, you have to make sure your clients are *happy*.

Together, these elements will determine whether your firm grows toward the goals you've set, or limps along at the same tired old pace. It's not rocket science, by any means, but it is systematic and doable.

In fact, we codified those five steps into **five key performance indicators (KPIs)**. Getting more leads is *one* of those indicators—but the other four have equal power in making or breaking your law firm's growth.

The 5 Key Performance Indicators

The 5 KPIs That Mean EVERYTHING

1. Lead volume
2. Conversion rate (the percentage of new cases you get out of your leads)
3. Average case value
4. Profit metrics
5. Net promoter score

These are the metrics *you must master* as a law firm owner to reach your dream.

THE 5 KPIS THAT MEAN EVERYTHING

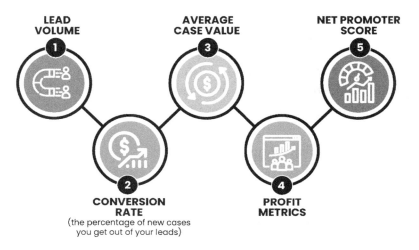

**These are the metrics you must master
as a law firm owner to reach your dream.**

Let's talk through each one.

1. Lead Volume

Lead volume is simply the number of new leads you get from marketing campaigns. All those new potential clients indicating their interest in your firm. Remember how you're spending 20% of your budget on marketing? Ideally, that investment will give you a healthy number of new leads for potential cases.

The goal with lead volume is to hit that magical status of lead *abundance,* where you have more leads than you need. In Part 2 of this book, we'll talk about how to get yourself there.

But wait—how many leads *do* you need to get to lead abundance? We'll explain how to determine your lead abundance number after explaining the next two KPIs.

2. Conversion Rate

Let's say you get 100 new leads and sit on them. You either don't pick up the phone or just wait for them to call you back. How is that likely to work out? Not very well. So, we get to metric 2, your *conversion rate*. You need to actually turn those leads into signed clients. That's why the conversion rate is a big deal. If you can't convert leads into cases, your marketing investment is a waste of time, effort, and money. Don't worry, we're going to talk about how to boost your conversion rate in Part 2. (Psst: the fortune is in the follow-up!)

Here's how you can determine your conversion rate:

Conversion rate % = number of signed cases/ number of new leads.

Eg., attorney Brian signed 10 new cases out of 100 new leads.

Since 10/100 = 0.1, attorney Brian's firm has a 10% conversion rate

Once you know your average conversion rate, you can predict how many new *cases* you'll get from your lead volume. You'll also understand how many leads you need to get in order to sign one new case. That information can help you predict your progress toward your revenue goal, provided you know your firm's …

3. Average Case Value (ACV)

The average case value (ACV) is also known as your average fee per case. It's just what it sounds like—the amount of money you get paid for a typical case. To determine your ACV, you simply divide your firm's revenue by your number of cases.

ACV = Revenue/Number of Cases

Let's say Attorneys Alyssa and Bernard both run a DUI practice. Last month, they both brought in ten DUI clients, but whereas Attorney Alyssa's law firm brought in $30K, Bernard's brought in $50K. Simple math tells us that Alyssa's ACV is $3K and Bernard's is $5K. So, how will their ACVs impact their firm's revenue goals?

Short answer is Bernard's firm is on track to earn exponentially more revenue than Alyssa's. And not just for the obvious reason that he made $20K more than her firm did. They got the same number of cases, but Bernard has an extra $20K to *invest* in marketing, hiring better employees, and increasing his profit. Because he spends more money on marketing, he then gets more cases. Because he spends more money on his employees, he then gets stronger employees, who then get better outcomes for his clients. That produces more five-star reviews than what Alyssa gets, causing even more clients to find him, while simultaneously lowering his cost to acquire. He's building a reputation in the community as the go-to lawyer for DUIs, and all those five-star reviews make it easy for him to charge $5K per case. It's a snowball effect—all made possible because he generates *more per case,* which he then invests in his firm.

On the other hand, Alyssa is doing everything she can just to get clients through her door—but because of her low case value, her revenues are also staying low which holds back her firm's ability to grow. Even if Alyssa is intentionally keeping her rates low for philanthropic reasons or because she thinks cheap prices will attract more clients, she's *holding herself back.* She has less to invest in attorneys, which means she has to resort to hiring low-performing employees. That leads to poor results for her clients and simultaneous burnout on her part because she has to pick up their slack. She thinks she's serving her clients with low prices, but actually, she's doing them—and her firm—a disservice.

> **If you're the cheapest, no one expects you to be the best. And if you're the best, no one expects you to be the cheapest.**

For contingency fee practice areas, the way you increase your average fee per case usually comes down to targeting better cases and/or working your current cases better.

For flat fee practice areas, is the answer to simply raise your rates? Usually, yes.

Your average case value should be five times higher than your cost to acquire a client, and ideally high enough to help you reach your firm's revenue goals. However, you also need to keep it low enough that clients are willing to pay it. Striking the right balance is what we call *average case value optimization.*

Quick-Hitting Hack: What are some ways you can increase your ACV? Here's a quick and dirty list of levers you can push to increase your ACV. Don't worry—we're going to get into all of these in greater depth in Parts 2 and 3.

- *Work your current cases better.* If you're a contingency fee-based firm, get the most out of every case you already have. This is one of the fastest ways to increase ACV.

- *Increase your fees.* If you're not a contingency fee-based firm, the fastest and easiest way to make more money is to charge more. Start by raising your prices by 10% today. You'll be shocked when new clients agree to the higher fees without a fight.

- *Change your targeting.* If you're attracting small value cases, your marketing approach might be off. What are the clients and cases that get you the highest ACV? For example, motorcycle accident cases tend to be worth more than car accident cases, so targeting bikers in your marketing might help you raise your ACV. Ensure your marketing speaks directly to the demographic of higher-value case types. More on this in Chapter 8.

- *Get as many reviews as humanly possible.* Social proof and testimonials give your potential clients high confidence that you will get them the outcome they're looking for, enabling you to get higher-value cases and charge more. We'll focus on this in Chapter 7.

- **Build your celebrity.** If you're producing video content and become a recognizable face, they will pay more money to hire you specifically because you are the one that they trust. In PI, the bigger cases usually go to the most known firm because of the law of large numbers. Chapter 8 goes into this concept in greater depth.

- **Sell the result.** In all your messaging, focus on your clients' dream outcome, not your legal services. People hire you for one reason. To get them a result. Focus your messaging on what they want, how they get it, and most importantly, what their life will be like after it's obtained. If you do this, you will get bigger cases and can command a higher fee. We hit this point in Chapters 6, 7, *and* 8. (That's how important it is!)

- **Explain what they stand to lose.** Do the math for them. Yes, it will cost them $4K to pay you for their DUI case, but if they lose their commercial driver's license, they could forfeit their career, salary, benefits, and pension. Make sure your clients know you'll fight tooth and nail for them to protect their career prospects, income, dignity, and reputation. That's the true *value* of having you as their attorney.

- **Contact your clients early and often.** If you're a personal injury attorney, for instance, ensure your clients get seen by a doctor immediately, attend all appointments, and complete their treatment so that insurance companies will struggle to dispute the gravity of their injuries. This early and frequent client contact will lead to a higher settlement.

The ACV is a huge factor in determining how much revenue your firm pulls in. And, good news! There are a lot of ways you can influence these numbers and make the metrics work in your favor. ACV is also impacted by how much you need to *spend* to get each new case. We're going to talk about that more in a moment when we get into profit metrics.

Revenue Equation for New Cases

These first three KPIs—lead volume, conversion rate, and average case value—will determine your **revenue equation for new cases**. In other words, it's those three numbers that will determine how much money your firm makes. We'll give you an example.

Let's say that you run a new ad campaign that brings you 100 new leads in the month of September. Your conversion rate on these leads is 20%, and your average case value is $10K. With these numbers, here's how much money you stand to make from new cases in September:

100 leads × 0.2 conversion rate = 20 new cases

20 new cases × $10K ACV = $200K revenue from new cases in September

But … are these numbers *good*? As any lawyer worth their salt would say, "It depends." If your revenue goal for the year was $500K, then congratulations, you crushed it. If your goal was $5M, then you're way off.

So let's look at how you can use these three numbers to hit your revenue goal. This is where things start to get exciting, all with the help of a few equations.

Let's say your goal revenue is $1M. Awesome! Now, you need to consider, "How many cases do I *need* to make that?" Let's bust out the calculator.

Step 1: Divide your target revenue by your ACV.

$1M/ACV

Eg., your ACV is $10K

$1M/$10K = 100 new cases

There it is! You need 100 new cases to be on the way to your dream life. Okay, now you have to figure out how many leads you need if you want to get 100 new cases.

Step 2: Divide the number of new cases you need by your conversion rate percentage.

100/conversion rate

Eg., your conversion rate is 25%

100/0.25 = 400 leads

Boom! Now you know how many leads you need to get through your marketing! Are you seeing how all the concepts in this chapter tie together? Your Vivid Vision helps you determine your Annual Plan, and your Annual Plan helps you set monthly goals. Now, these first three KPI numbers will help you understand *exactly* what numbers you need to pull to hit that monthly target. Are you excited about this? You *should* be excited by this! These are the building blocks that are going to make your dream life happen!

And bonus, once you can predict your future revenues accurately, you have the confidence to scale up more aggressively. You also have more clarity on what levers to push to make these numbers work better for you—for example, training your intake people so that you get a higher conversion rate. That means more dream life, more quickly!

Revenue Equation for New Cases

Lead volume × Conversion Rate = number of new cases

Number of new cases × Average Case Value = total revenue from new cases

You might be thinking, *Hang on ... What about the cost it takes to acquire a case? Where does that factor into the ACV number?* That's a *great* question. Profitability factors like marketing costs, a.k.a. Cost to Acquire, are a major factor in the revenue you get to take home. That's why we have two more KPIs to discuss.

4. Profit Metrics

A new case comes in—it looks to be a high-value divorce case, but there are signs it could get drawn out and messy. You can choose to assign it to two different attorneys. Kim is known for her effective mediation and ability to settle quickly. Darrel tends to take a little longer. He likes to pore over details and can easily get drawn into family drama.

Your divorce retainer fee is $5K. You're guessing Kim could get this case done within three months—maybe four. Then, she's ready for another new client. Darrel would probably need six months, or even more if he starts exploring rabbit trails. Their different levels of *efficiency* will result in a different level of *profitability* on that case. That's what we're talking about with this fourth KPI.

Profit metrics are a measure of the cost of doing business. Specifically, the marketing cost of acquiring a new case and the cost of paying your employees to do the work. It tells you what *profit* you are making on your cases with those costs factored in.

You can get all the cases you want, but if you aren't making a profit on them, you aren't going to be in business very long. You should always be optimizing the most profitable pieces of your practice. Don't let *low-profit* areas dilute *great-profit* areas.

Profit metrics have two main components, which we'll be looking at on a per-unit basis.

1. **Cost to Acquire.** How much are you spending to acquire a case? This is your total marketing expenses in a time period divided by the number of cases signed up during that time period.
2. **Cost of Goods Sold.** How much are you spending to process a case? This is the number of hours it takes to handle a case from start to finish multiplied by the hourly rate of the employees involved in that case.

Let's unpack each one and we'll explain how to calculate both.

Cost to Acquire

"Cost to Acquire" is what you spend to get a new client. For instance, if your average case value is $10K, but you paid $11K in marketing costs to acquire that client, then you're upside down. Let's geek out a second and do some math.

Let's say you spent $1K on running an ad and you get 10 calls from it. That means each call costs you $100. Your conversion rate with those new client phone calls is around 20%. So, of those 10 calls, you signed two clients. That means it costs you $500 to acquire a new client. That's your cost to acquire.

For most law firms with an ACV over $1K, that's no big deal. But if you run a low-ticket law firm, and your ACV is only $300, that number should be cause for concern. Ideally, you want your ACV to be five times higher than your cost to acquire. So, if it costs you $1K to acquire a client, your ACV should be at least $5K.

How can you *decrease* your cost to acquire? You get a better track record signing on clients by employing some of the marketing strategies we're going to teach you in Part 2. For instance, you put in a follow-up sequence of daily texts and two more people sign up two weeks later. Now you've just reduced your cost to acquire a customer from $500 to $250! And then let's say you can get one of those new clients to refer you to one of their friends. Now, you have five new clients! Your close rate has gone from 20% to 50%, and you've decreased your cost to acquire from $500 per client to a wonderfully low $200.

A few final tips about how you can leverage the cost-to-acquire number to increase your overall profitability:

- Make sure you factor in your ACV per case type when setting your cost-to-acquire goals. For instance, if Case A has an ACV of $10K and Case B has an ACV of only $5K, you should be willing to pay *twice* as much to acquire Case A vs Case B.

- The best way to track cost to acquire is on a zoomed out basis. For example, take your *total* amount spent on marketing for a month and divide it by the *total* number of new cases you signed up that month—that's your cost to acquire. This would include any money you spent on ad spend, vendors, freelancers, and full-time in-house marketing staff. If you have separate, dedicated intake staff, you could throw that in too. This is important because of the multi-channel environment we now live in. There are times when it is necessary to drill into individual marketing campaigns to identify what's working and what's not so you can reduce your cost to acquire.

All right, that takes care of the first element of Profit Metrics. The other major factor impacting your firm's profitability is the efficiency—or lack thereof—of your employees. We call this measurement "Cost of Goods Sold."

Cost of Goods Sold

To calculate cost of goods sold on a per-case basis, you need a few numbers. The amount of time it takes to work a case from start to finish and the hourly rate of that time. Here's one way you could figure that out with a salaried employee:

> Step 1: Find total hours worked per year.
> 52 weeks × (average hours worked per week) = work hours per year. Eg., attorney Jane works on average 38 hrs per week, including vacations. 52 × 38 = 1,976 hours in a year.

> Step 2: Determine hourly rate of employee.
> Salary/total work hours per year = hourly rate of employee. Eg., attorney Jane makes a salary of $75K. $75K/1,976 = $37.96/hr.

> Step 3: Determine cost of goods sold.
> Hours worked on case × hourly rate of employee = cost of goods sold. Eg. Jane takes 25 hours to resolve the case and has an hourly rate of $37.96 per hour. 25 hours × 37.96 = $949 cost of goods sold.

Both cost to acquire and cost of goods sold are crucial to your firm's overall profitability. If either or both numbers are too high, they will adversely affect your profit. For instance, let's say your average case value is $5K. It costs you $3K to get a case (cost to acquire) and then it costs you $2K to resolve the case (cost of goods sold). In total, that case costs you $5K. But—oh no! That means you're only breaking even. You may have *thought* you were making $2K off that case, but that's because you weren't accounting for cost of goods sold.

With this clarity, you might want to make some changes to become more profitable. For instance, you might assign certain cases to attorneys with a track record of efficiency, or increase your average case value. You'll get lots of ideas about how to tighten up your profitability in Parts 2 and 3 of this book.

Average Case Value – (Cost per Case + Cost of Goods Sold) = Case Profit

In a perfect world, for a case with an ACV of $10K, a law firm owner would spend no greater than $2K to acquire that case and $3K in cost of goods sold. As your firm gets bigger, this equation gets more complicated since there will be many people involved in your case acquisition and case management process. Understanding how to problem solve around these numbers can be transformational in creating a profitable law firm business model.

There's one final KPI that will impact your overall bottom line: customer satisfaction.

Here's why customer satisfaction matters. If you blow your clients away and they shower you with five-star reviews, you can *increase* your average case value and *decrease* your cost to acquire at the same time. On the other hand, if you get *bad* customer reviews, you could have great numbers in all other KPI categories, but your firm would still lose money. For instance, if Attorney Adam is "efficient" but sloppy, that could create bad word-of-mouth and scare people away from your firm. In that case, efficiency is not going to help your profit metrics in the long run.

None of what we are saying in this book is any kind of excuse for bad lawyering. Far from it! You don't build a five-star firm by doing crappy work. You create success by doing *first-class work* and focusing on hiring people who do excellent work *efficiently*. We'll discuss more about how to measure for efficiency using employee scorecards in Chapters 10 and 11.

Quick-Hitting Hack: We've devoted our entire Chapter 10 to the subject of how to hire all-stars, but here's a tidbit to hold you over until then. These concepts will be elaborated on in Chapters 10 and 11. To hire for efficiency, do the following three things consistently:

- Focus on how much revenue each employee should generate. If an employee isn't performing well enough to meet this standard, let them go and hire someone who can.

- Create an incentive pool with some of your payroll revenue and give your employees incentives to hit key targets in the form of bonuses.

- Publish your list of incentives so your employees know what they need to do to get those incentives.

And speaking of first-class work, we've now arrived at our fifth and final KPI.

5. NPS: Net Promoter Score

Nearly 20 years ago, my aunt hosted a birthday party at a well-known, expensive steak house. Afterward, nearly *everyone* at the party got food poisoning. This event became a family legend. We call it the massive gastric catastrophe. I wasn't at the party, but my aunt told me about it afterward. Even though the party happened nearly two decades ago, I've *never* forgotten the name of the business, and I've also *never* eaten there. When my friends suggest eating there, I tell them the story of the massive gastric catastrophe and we decide to go somewhere else.

Here's the kicker: *my aunt never told the restaurant.* She didn't think they were likely to do anything. Instead, she told me and who knows how many other people. Then, we all told however many other people. Just her experience alone probably cost the restaurant multiple thousands of dollars in revenue. Multiply that by all the people who were there and you can only imagine what a revenue catastrophe this incident was for the restaurant. Yet they never even knew it happened.

Most people don't complain to you when they've had a bad customer experience. What they do is complain to their friends and family and anyone else who will listen about their bad experience. The average person tells twelve people about a negative experience they've had—but they don't tell the business.[8] In fact, for every one complaint that makes it to you, there are probably 20 other people who feel the same way.

Here's the moral of the story: If you're not asking your clients about what they think about you, the vast majority of them won't tell you.

That's why you need to ask! The best way to determine the satisfaction of your clients is by collecting results from net promoter scores (NPS). Net promoter score is a measure of how happy your clients are. Growth will get you nowhere if your clients aren't satisfied with your firm's work. Did you treat them well? Did you advocate on their behalf with zeal and competence? Did you maintain regular communication with them?

Net promoter score will tell you and you'll get these numbers through customer experience surveys.

We've talked to enough attorneys to know that some stop right here and think, *GROAN, not surveys! Surveys are annoying. I ignore them. Why do so many companies DO these surveys?*

They do them because they work. They give businesses crucial information about how satisfied their customers are.

---

[8] Thomas, Andrew. 2018. "The Secret Ratio That Proves Why Customer Reviews Are So Important." Inc.Com. February 26, 2018. Accessed October 13, 2023. https://www.google.com/url?q=https://www.inc.com/andrew-thomas/the-hidden-ratio-that-could-make-or-break-your-company.html

You should do the same! Generate your net promoter score by surveying your current clients every three to four months. What should you ask them? Drum roll, please ...

On a scale of one to ten, how likely are you to recommend our law firm to a friend or colleague?

That's it! That's the question. People don't recommend businesses to their friends unless they are truly happy with their experience. By phrasing the survey this way, you will get the truest measure possible of how happy your clients are.

What average score would you guess most law firms get? Go ahead and guess. 7? 8?

Way off. Clearlyrated.com, which tracks these numbers for law firms, says the average for all firms is *3.2* out of 10—a 32 NPS score.

That's pathetic! No firm is going to scale up to impressive profit with that kind of satisfaction rating.

World-class firms—the 1% of firms who build a world-class client experience—score up to 7.0—a 70 NPS. That means most of their clients are giving them a nine or 10 out of 10. That's the absolute *minimum* you should be aiming for in client surveys.

But hang on—your average score from the surveys doesn't tell you everything you need to know. Think of my aunt. She was only *one* detractor, but she single-handedly blew a huge hole in that steakhouse's profit by spreading the news of the massive gastric catastrophe. On the flip side, an avid promoter can get you multiple new clients.

Clearly, not all survey scores are created equal. The promoters and the detractors pack more of a punch on your firm's success than the people who score you somewhere in the middle.

That's why NPS is calculated using percentages of your survey scores:

- Your clients count as a **Promoter** if they rate you a 9 or a 10, meaning they are likely to actively promote you. They get a +1.

- They count as **Passive** if they rate you a 7 or 8, meaning they are unlikely to talk about your firm either in a positive or negative way. Since they're not likely to talk about you at all, the percentage of *Passive* responses is not factored in the NPS equation. They get a 0.

- They count as a **Detractor** if they give you a 6 or below, meaning they are likely to actively discourage people from using your firm. They get a -1.

Use those percentages to determine your NPS.

> **% Promoters – % Detractors = NPS.** *Eg., out of 100 survey responses, you had 50 promoters, 30 passives, and 20 detractors. 50% – 20% = NPS score of 30.*

What's a good NPS score? Well, you definitely don't want to score in the negative, where your percentage of Detractors is higher than your Promoters. The Creators of NPS, Bain & Company say, "Above 0 is good. Above 20 is favorable. Above 50 is excellent. Above 80 is world class."[9]

At SMB Team, we have worked our butts off to reach a 75 net promoter score for the past three years in a row. But it hasn't been easy. We're working even harder now to get to 80!

If that math all sounds too complicated, we get it. We use a service to gather and calculate our NPS number. (Our preferred service is "Ask Nicely" but there are many others.) Bottom line: send out the surveys and track this number. If it's low, create strategies for your law firm to improve the client experience. (We'll teach you how in Chapter 12.)

If you aren't tracking your NPS, then you're driving blind. It's no different from a motorist trying to see ahead in a thick fog.

Success Metrics

Your Profit Metrics tell you how much money you're making. Your NPS score tells you how happy your clients are. Together, these two numbers tell the story of your firm's success and sustainability.

---

[9] Carpenter, Aaron. 2023. "What Is a Good Net Promoter Score (NPS)? - Qualtrics." Qualtrics. August 16, 2023. https://www.qualtrics.com/experience-management/customer/good-net-promoter-score/#:~:text=Above%200%20is%20good,Above%2080%20is%20world%20class.

Profit Metrics tells the story of the benefit to *your law firm*. Here is that equation:

Average Case Value − (Cost to Acquire + Cost of Goods Sold) = Profit Per Case

NPS tells the story of the benefit *to your clients.*

% Promoters − % Detractors = NPS

A bad NPS score is negative, i.e. you have *more* detractors than promoters. An excellent NPS score is above 50. A world-class score is 80 and above.[10]

If you have a low profit per case and a high NPS, that's a sign that you might be doing too much for your clients and you should charge more. If you have a high profit per case, but low NPS, that's a sign your clients are unhappy and word might start to spread. Taken together, your Profit Metrics and NPS tell the story of your firm's Success Metrics.

Every one of your five KPI numbers needs to be ruthlessly tracked and monitored. And what are they again? You want to memorize these like your kid's birthday. Let's rattle them off together!

1. **Lead volume**
2. **Conversion rate**

---

[10] Ibid

3. **Average case value (ACV)**
4. **Profit metrics,** *and*
5. **Net promoter score (NPS)**

When you live according to these five KPIs *and build goals around them*, your law firm will be unstoppable.

Now that you understand the numbers, you need to move the numbers in the right direction. As your firm's CEO, it is your job to create *goals* around these five KPIs. You and every member of your team need to be crystal clear about expectations around all the KPIs, so that you can push the growth you need to make your dream life happen.

The way to do that is by coming up with Great Big Rocks, what we call quarterly boulders.

BILL HAUSER NARRATES

Quarterly Boulders

Overwhelmed. That's how I felt. Completely overwhelmed.

We were two years into running SMB Team and things were cooking. The business was growing fast—but it felt like things were starting to spin out of control. I'd formed the company with a clear long-term plan, but when it came to goal setting in the short term, I had just been winging it. I set goals that had subjective timelines. Some goals were measurable; some weren't. Other goals were put out in the open, but no one ever took ownership of them. I didn't have a clear 90-day picture of how I was going to get SMB Team's long-term plan accomplished, or *who* was going to get *what* done, by *when*.

As a result, I felt buried by competing priorities.

Hoping to get some clarity on next steps, I spent $35K on a coaching program with some high-level entrepreneurs. At the first meeting, I walked into the room feeling anxious and scared. I knew I was the smallest person in the room, in terms of revenue. I tried to pretend like I was super confident about all the progress my team had made in two years, but deep down, I knew how overwhelmed I was with the "here and now" of my business. Everything felt so rapid fire.

How was I supposed to introduce myself? "Hi, I'm Bill. I'm a dog chasing my tail, running around in circles. I have unfocused and scattered priorities." I didn't want to admit weakness. But then it occurred to me—hadn't I paid $35K to get *advice* from these people for my company's pain points?

During the quarterly workshop, I opened up publicly about the challenges I was dealing with for the first time. All the high-level entrepreneurs around me started chiming in with the same advice. "Oh, you need to set quarterly rocks. That's what you need to do, just set your quarterly rocks."

I felt hope and skepticism at the same time. Was it really going to be that easy? Set some quarterly goals, and then all my problems would go away? They told me to read the book

Traction, by Gino Wickman. I read it from start to finish. The book talked conceptually about the importance of setting quarterly goals that are measurable, clearly assigned to people, with clear 90-day deadlines attached.

I got hyped up. I was pumped about setting quarterly goals. This was going to solve all my problems!

For the next three quarters, I set quarterly goals. But each time, something was off.

1. The first quarter, I held a meeting with my team and I informed them of all the amazing goals I had set for the next 90 days. Everyone looked shocked, like a deer in headlights. My announcement was a completely different style of leadership from the way we had run our business up to that point, because *I didn't get their buy-in.* They felt like the goals had been forced on them, instead of formed cooperatively. Huge mistake.

2. The next quarter, I held an offsite meeting with key members of my team so that we could all plan the quarterly goals together. My team had a ton of amazing ideas. Instead of stepping all over them, I gave them almost complete free rein to set the goals for the company over the next quarter, providing minimal input. As a result, they were super bought in. Except ... 90 days later, it became very clear that we'd set the wrong goals for the company. We'd been focusing on all the wrong priorities. I hadn't set clear enough parameters as a leader to clarify what was most important to our business. Another mistake.

3. The third quarter, I started wondering, "Do these things even work?" But I finally found the magic. We did another offsite, quarterly meeting with key leaders from every team. *This* time, I started by giving the team clear parameters around what was most important to our business for the next 90 days. During our brainstorming meeting, everyone's thinking was guided by those parameters. By the end of the meeting, everyone had bought into the goals, and everyone had set *the right* goals. Huge win!

However ... even though we'd gotten the formation of the goals right this time, the day-to-day problems of the company still sometimes got louder than the quarterly goals we'd committed to. My team came to me midway through the quarter and said, "Hey—X, Y, and Z problems happened. We should maybe slow down on the quarterly rocks we set. Right?" I felt like pulling my hair out when they asked me that, but the only person I had to blame was myself. Somehow, I hadn't communicated sufficiently just how important these quarterly goals were. Yet another mistake.

That realization helped us put the final piece in place. I started thinking to myself, "We're calling them quarterly rocks. But here's the problem with a rock: anyone can pick up a rock and throw it away." I didn't *want* my teams throwing away these quarterly rocks.

One day, I called my company together. "We're not going to call our quarterly goals 'quarterly rocks' anymore," I announced. "We're calling them Quarterly *Boulders*. And here's why. A boulder is an immovable object. It can be detonated—but it can't be moved. When we set these quarterly goals, we *will not* deviate from them, no matter what. They're either going to be fully detonated, meaning we are completely abandoning the goal that we set—or we ain't moving 'em. We're going to finish the quarter and we *will* accomplish these goals."

All of a sudden, the team's attention to the quarterly goals that we'd set increased. It was a noticeable cultural shift—everyone worked with greater urgency toward those goals. After two quarters of failure, we started making more progress than we'd ever made before. I had succeeded in helping my team become self-managing—one of the key elements in the Law Firm Growth Acceleration Model.

I didn't feel overwhelmed anymore. I lost my cognitive dissonance. I had delegated our goals and no longer felt solely responsible for them! That was the beauty of orienting my team around the *right* actions. All of us had perfect clarity about our priorities. Another huge win.

In that third quarter, the Covid-19 pandemic hit. But despite all that adversity and the potential distractions, we quadrupled our revenues throughout 2020 and 2021. We were so dialed into our quarterly goals, we actually *exceeded* all of our goals that quarter. What a win! *That's* the power of setting goals the right way.

And now, we're going to teach you exactly how to do it.

Defining Quarterly Boulders

Quarterly Boulders (QBs), as explained in the previous section, are not rocks. They are strong, sturdy, immovable objects. Embracing quarterly boulders is the most important operational behavior your firm will undertake.

Let's describe a Quarterly Boulder.

- A QB is a goal set at the beginning of a quarter.

- It positively and directly impacts one of the five KPIs.

- It has a number attached to it, which makes it measurable.

- It is assigned to *one* owner.

- It takes an entire quarter to get done.

- It has a firm deadline, typically the end of the quarter.

- It is a goal which *must* be met. No exceptions.

QBs cure complexity. Instead of people in your firm looking to the future with unease or bewilderment, they are given the clarity to focus on specific and attainable goals, along with the tasks necessary to complete those goals. This clears away any confusion for people about where to focus the best part of their effort and energy.

Do you have any idea what a game changer that is? Imagine your revenue quadrupling in a year. *That's* what kind of a game changer it is.

There are three types of QBs.

1. Company-wide QBs
2. Departmental QBs
3. Personal QBs

Where do you begin? Start with number one. At least 90% of law firms should focus first on setting company-wide QBs. You want to get everyone onboard the big ship and get it steering straight before working on smaller sections.

After three successful quarters, you could start expanding Quarterly Boulders to the department level. By that time, your managers will have seen how they work on a company-wide basis and will be ready to apply the concepts to their departments.

Then, after two full years of operating with Quarterly Boulders, everyone on your team should each have three of their own personal QBs.

There are three steps to identifying and then implementing these great big rocks in your firm. First, you **define** your goals and **assign** point people to each one. Second, you **roll them out**, with passion. Third, you **track their progress.**

Let's talk more about each step.

Define and Assign

If you select the wrong goals, it's like putting the wrong address into your GPS. Sure, you'll get *somewhere* but if it's the wrong place, you're not going to be happy about getting there. That's why defining your boulders is the most important of all these steps.

So, how do you know how to set the right goals? (Psst: take a glance at the first half of this chapter.)

Ding ding ding! Start with the five KPIs. Set goals for each one. This would look like setting five quarterly boulders—one for company-wide lead generation, intake conversion rate, average case value, net promoter score, and profit. And, all the goals for each of these five should come from your annual plan.

Don't leave any out. If you only set goals for lead genera-tion, what will happen to client happiness or your intake rate? Remember, these five golden numbers determine your rev-enues and profits! You want your team to understand why every KPI is important.

I can already hear you thinking, *I don't want my team to know my profits! Isn't that too transparent?* You *do* want your team to know everything about your business. This could be uncom-fortable for your earlier team members who aren't used to this transparency. It's your job to show them how a healthier business will result in them having more growth opportuni-ties in the business. If they can't get on board with this, they have to go.

In addition to considering the five KPIs, you want to avoid these common *Don'ts:*

- *Don't* come up with selfish QBs that mainly serve you. "Increasing my take-home pay" is *not* a company-wide QB and won't inspire your team. They should be com-pany-wide initiatives.

- *Don't* set more than six company-wide QBs.

- *Don't* make them short-term tasks. For instance, "increase Google budget to $20K per year" should not be a Quarterly Boulder. That's a five-minute task. Quarterly Boulders should take a full 90 days to accomplish.

- *Don't* make them monthly goals, such as "generate 100 leads per month." Instead, measure the goal on a quarterly basis. So 300 leads in this quarter. Let's say you get 99 leads in one month of the quarter. This allows you to catch up in the final two months of the quarter.

- *Don't* make the same mistakes we did (setting goals with zero input from your team and setting goals with zero input from you). You should set the parameters for the QBs and your team should provide input. As your team gets used to this, they should be the ones creating the action plans on *how* these goals will be reached.

Now, let's talk about your *DOs* for Quarterly Boulders.

- *Do* select important boulders that will have a positive impact on the KPI you want to improve. For example, let's say your boulder is to increase your intake conversion rate from 15% to 25% in one quarter. You decide the actions required to make that happen are rolling out a sales training system, hiring VAs to follow up with your leads, and designing a lead follow-up system. These are *projects* that, if accomplished, will help you reach your overall goal. If you assign a one month deadline to each of these three projects, then you can get all three of them done in one quarter, as milestones of your bigger goal. The key is that your quarterly boulders are outcome oriented and tie into your annual plan.

- *Do* assign these boulders to the right people. A detail-oriented boulder should be assigned to a detail-oriented person. Simple. This means you can assign a boulder to someone whose normal job doesn't relate to that boulder. For instance, assigning the development of a follow-up system to someone on the marketing team. That marketing person might be passionate about improving follow-up, so that the ad campaigns can get a better ROI! When assigning boulders, you want to match the project to a person's abilities, interest, and availability, not simply to their role.

- *Do* consider pre existing workload when assigning QBs. Before anyone accepts the responsibility of owning a QB, they need to have a discussion with their manager to agree that they can complete the boulder with their current workload.

As you're developing some of your QBs, you might have difficulty seeing how to attach numbers to them. This is understandable. Saying, "I want us to roll out a new intake system" does not give your team a quantifiable, measurable boulder.

The way to handle this is to define what "done" means. You say you want to "increase conversion rate to 25%." That's a goal with a number. In the milestone plan for the goal, clearly map out your three key milestones with deadlines. Milestone 1: Roll out sales training system. Milestone 2: Interview and hire three VAs to follow up with leads. Milestone 3: Design lead follow-up system. Each of these equals 33% of the milestone plan being completed.

Everything and anything can be quantified. You just have to look at it the right way and communicate to your team how they can achieve those numbers.

Quick-Hitting Hack: If you want to see the exact type of software SMB Team uses to manage and track our own boulders, scan the QR code to be taken to our book bonuses where you'll find a walk-through video about this.

Scan this QR Code to Unlock This Bonus

We'll give you an example of what this looks like for SMB. During the third quarter of 2024, here are the Company Quarterly Boulders assigned to the Executive Leadership team:

COMPANY BOULDERS

Status	Title	Due By	Owner
👍	Agency ROI & Strategy	Jun 30, 2024	
👍	Coaching Operations & Resource Overhaul	Jun 30, 2024	
👍	Launch New Client Sourcing Initiatives	Jun 30, 2024	
👍	Driver Model Profit	Jun 30, 2024	
👍	Sales Team Expansion to Close Sales Gap of $2.952M ARR	Jun 30, 2024	

Andy Stickel—that's the "AS" you see—is responsible for generating $8.52M in new revenue from marketing and sales. If you were to then navigate to the marketing department, you'd see department-level boulders designed to make the $8.52M revenue goal happen, such as revamping our content marketing and event sales strategies, along with redesigning SMB Team's homepage.

Each boulder describes a major quarterly initiative. The boulders require an entire team to pull off, but each one is assigned to a single owner.

Additionally, each department has their own set of boulders, called departmental boulders. These boulders are centered around projects specific to the department.

Status	Title	Due By	Owner
DEPARTMENTAL BOULDERS			
👍	$4M Relentless Lawyer Event Execution	Jun 30, 2023	
⚠	Company Process Workflows & Tech Stack Mapping	Jun 30, 2023	
👍	75 NPS	Jun 30, 2023	
👍	$1M Upgrade ARR	Jun 30, 2023	
⚠	$4M from Sales Team	Jun 30, 2023	

What might this look like at a law firm? Your Quarterly Boulders might entail increasing your lead volume by 100 leads per month by launching a new advertising initiative, getting 100 reviews, and/or designing a new website. Maybe you're looking to increase your ACV by $5K by adding a new practice area, increasing your prices, or changing your messaging to attract better cases. Consider the major initiatives that would help you take your KPIs to the levels you need, in order to achieve your annual plan. Then, write up your boulders!

And yes, you do need to actually *write* them up. SMB Team's Quarterly Boulders are named and then linked to a document that spells out milestones, deadlines, responsibilities, and so on. If you hope to lead a self-managing team, it's critical to write up clear plans for your Quarterly Boulders—more importantly to have your TEAM write up these clear plans since you're no longer doing all the work yourself ... right?

Quick-Hitting Hack: Want an easy way to remember criteria for a well-written Quarterly Boulder? Just remember to keep them CLEAR:

Concise. Clearly convey what "done" looks like in as few words as possible.

Linked. Link it to the overall company vision and objectives—the 5 KPIs.

Engaged. Ensure one responsible person is fully engaged, committed, and wants to own the boulder.

Action-oriented. It should come with specific actions, projects, or milestones.

Reviewed. Regularly review the progress throughout the quarter.

If you'd like to read a full write-up of one of SMB Team's Quarterly Boulders, you can go here and check it out.

(You'll find all the other bonuses from the book here or you can go to **yourdreamlawfirm.com**.)

Offsite Retreats

An excellent way to develop and assign quarterly boulders is with an offsite retreat. Take your team outside of the office on a quarterly basis so you can all focus on the QBs. Put on your board shorts and sandals, throw some burgers on the grill, and get excited to talk about Great Big Rocks.

In preparation for this, don't just pack your sunscreen. Look at the numbers. Audit your last quarter's KPIs and examine them for strengths, weaknesses, opportunities, and threats.

Once you're at the retreat, set the context for your team. Tell them where the company is and where you want the company to get to. This sets them up to think about appropriate and productive QBs.

Then, bring the entire team into a brainstorming session to dream up the next quarter's boulders. During this time, you want to inspire as much creativity as possible. Use a whiteboard to write down suggestions from everyone, so that everyone can see. Celebrate each idea. Get goofy if you want! The goal is to encourage participation. The entire team should feel welcome to contribute to the QBs. At this stage, no idea should be considered out of line or ridiculous.

The final step is to go through all those ideas and narrow them down. Pick the very best. Select the *right* three to six boulders for the next quarter and assign each one to a single person who will become that boulder's owner. This process gives your team focus, ownership, accountability, and makes them a part of the process.

Now you're ready for the next step. Rolling them out!

Roll Them Out!

Here's when you get to channel your inner Steve Jobs. It's time to get your team excited about the QBs you've assigned and defined. You're going to announce them with a whole lot of passion and then incentivize people to go after the QBs with incentives of cold, hard cash. Time for your team to roll up their sleeves and get to work!

Hold a meeting with the entire firm about two weeks before the end of the quarter. It should be a raucous event. Bump the stereo! Flash that strobe! You want to create energy! Talk about all the wins you had in the previous 90 days. Then talk about continuing the momentum so that you can build the firm to new heights. If the Steve Jobs comparison doesn't inspire you, pretend you're a world renowned coach, giving a pep talk to your team before a big game. Get everyone excited about the future.

Announce where you are going! Spell out the Quarterly Boulders you identified for the next 90 days. Introduce the owner of each boulder to the entire team and emphasize the seriousness of each goal.

Then, sweeten the deal. Tell everyone specifically what bonuses will come and who will get them upon the completion of each QB. That's right, you're going to use cash incentives to encourage people to throw their effort into achieving the QB they're assigned to. Give bonuses to the individual responsible for the QB when the QB is met. Better yet, give the entire team a bonus when the QB is met! You want everyone on your team to associate QBs with their own success, not just the firm's success. "When the company wins, I win" is a winning formula for everyone.

Keep it short. No more than 30 minutes. Beyond that, people's minds start to wander.

Quick-Hitting Hack: Scan the QR code below for a template that will help you launch your own Quarterly Boulders.

(You'll find all the other bonuses from the book here or you can go to **yourdreamlawfirm.com**.)

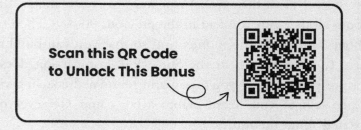

**Scan this QR Code
to Unlock This Bonus**

As part of the rollout, you should have documented the QBs and communicated details about them publicly. Here's how you do that:

- **Each QB should have *three or four* measurable milestones.** The owner of the boulder (with your help) will create a milestone plan, which breaks a big QB into three or four projects with deadlines. Milestone plans help you ensure your team has a bulletproof plan to accomplish the boulder. Each of the milestones can be further broken down into a project plan (which is a mini-milestone plan for each project).

- **Each QB owner should create a milestone plan within two weeks** of it being assigned to them. The milestone plan states exactly what each of the milestones will look like. Make sure you get the milestone plan from each QB owner before the start of the next quarter. Read it carefully. Give feedback. Have the owner revise it if necessary until you get it where it needs to be.

- **The final step for you is to sign off on it.** Once you're satisfied that the plan will lead to the completion of the boulder, put your actual signature at the bottom of the milestone plan.

Open communication reinforces the importance of the boulders. They become part of everyone's day-to-day working life, regularly reinforcing their high-priority status, and they get everyone in the right frame of mind to achieve them.

DELEGATE ALERT!

Once you've signed off on the plan, step away from it. You have delegated this task. Don't stick your nose or fingers into it anymore! Trust your teams. Trust your managers. You can't get trapped in the day-to-day. That's the job of the QB owner. You have higher-level stuff to focus on. And, if you don't have anyone on your team, this should serve as motivation for you to HIRE help!

And now … go ahead and breathe a sigh of relief!

Tracking Progress

After the meeting, don't stop communicating about the QBs. Publish weekly progress reports letting everyone know how things are going. Make them easily accessible to everyone in the firm so that people stay pumped!

This involves *tracking the progress.* You accomplish this with weekly leadership meetings with your leadership team—usually the owners of the QBs. In these meetings, discuss only the QBs. Do *not* talk about specific cases in your office. Do *not* discuss client fires that happened last week. That kind of stuff will only serve to detract from the importance of keeping the QB projects moving forward.

This is what you *do* discuss:

- **The progress of the QBs.** Are the milestones being met? If not, why not?

- **The status of the KPIs.** Are these metrics on track? If any are slipping, you need to find out why and work to correct them.

Even though QBs don't change until the end of the quarter, sometimes strategies for achieving those QBs *will* change. That's why you need these weekly meetings. To discuss strategy and identify new tactics as needed. Your team should not come to you in real time with every QB-related issue that comes up. That would require you to be constantly "on call." Instead, they should get in the habit of thinking, *That would be a great topic to bring up at the weekly leadership meeting.*

Quick-Hitting Hack: We'll discuss other sorts of meetings in future chapters. For now, just understand that QBs need a dedicated weekly meeting of their own. Here is a link to our weekly meeting template. (You'll also find all the other bonuses from the book here or you can go to **yourdreamlawfirm.com**.)

Scan this QR Code to Unlock This Bonus

Harness the Aggregation of Marginal Gains

We've talked about the 5 KPIs and why they matter. The most successful law firms devote time and energy to all five. Any firm that concentrates on just one or two will be at a distinct disadvantage in the marketplace.

We've also talked about Quarterly Boulders and why *they* matter. They are the best way to achieve goals that will propel your firm to greater success. They harness the talents and energy of your team in the most efficient and focused way possible.

Here's the crucial element of all these processes: *You don't have to make dramatic gains in any of them.*

Seriously. No big gains needed to get the job done. Even a 1% gain in all the KPIs will work wonders for your firm. Marginal gains, compounded over time, will be more than sufficient.

James Clear illustrates this perfectly with a story that shows the powerful impact of small marginal gains in his bestselling book *Atomic Habits.* The star of the story is the British cycling team in the early 2000s—although at the start, they look more like losers than stars. The British cycling team in 2003 was *terrible.* It had been terrible for 100 years. They never won any races. Never even came close! They were so bad that *bicycle companies wouldn't even sell them bicycles.* The team was such a dumpster fire, brands were embarrassed to have their name associated in any way with the team.

Coaches cycled through, always focusing on one main strategy. Get the team to pedal faster. Sounded reasonable. But it didn't work. It was their mantra for a century, and it just plain did not work. They were still terrible—even after trying their darndest to pedal faster.

Finally, they hired a new coach, Dave Brailsford, who introduced a radically new approach. Rather than focusing on simply pedaling harder, Dave guided the team in *marginally* improving every aspect of their cycling. That started with the athletes themselves. They hired new strength and conditioning coaches. But the pursuit of marginal gains went much further—and got much geekier—than just strength and conditioning. The team tested the fabrics they were using in wind tunnels to find the most aerodynamic ones. They rubbed alcohol on their tires to make them grip the road better. They tested bicycle seats to find the one that was the most comfortable. They even tested mattresses and pillows to find the ones that gave team members the best night's sleep.

The seemingly minor tweaks went on. They painted the inside of their repair vans white so any dust or other impurities in their bikes could be better seen and removed. They tested different gels to see which ones led to faster muscle recovery. They looked for *micro improvements* in all aspects of their bikes, their bodies, and their team. They were relentless, looking for tiny incremental changes, over and over again.

None of these changes made a big difference. But added up, they made a *huge* difference.

The team got better. Much better. Soon they began winning races, taking home trophies, and performing like stars. Within ten years of implementing their incremental improvements, they won the Tour de France. *That's* the power of marginal gains.

This sort of thinking applies to your law firm. Your firm will not hit the revenue you want it to if you're solely thinking about getting more leads for your firm, just like the

British cycling team could not improve by merely focusing on pedaling faster.

It's about making small changes in *all* aspects of your business. All five KPIs, backed up by Quarterly Boulders to give them heft and focus. Marginal gains lead to an aggregation of improvements. *That's* how you race across the finish line in first place!

Chapter 4 | Takeaways

1. There are five Key Performance Indicators that will help you bring your Vivid Vision into reality:

   a. Lead volume: how many new leads your firm gets per month.

   b. Conversion rate: the percentage of new leads converted to clients.

   c. Average Case Value (ACV): the average fee that you receive per-case.

   d. Profit metrics: the impact of your *cost to acquire* and *cost of goods sold* on your profit per case.

   e. Net Promoter Score (NPS): the measure of how happy your clients are, on a scale of 1 to 10.

2. You can predict the revenue you'll make from new cases by using the following two equations:

   a. Lead volume × conversion rate = number of new cases.

   b. Number of new cases × average case value = total revenues from new cases.

3. You can evaluate your Success Metrics (i.e. your success re: profitability and customer satisfaction) by using the following two equations:

   a. Average Case Value − (Cost to Acquire + Cost of Goods Sold) = Profit per Case

   b. % Promoters − % Detractors = NPS

4. The five KPIs should inform three to six Quarterly Boulders (QBs) that identify your goals for the next 90 days. QBs start at a company-wide level, eventually move to the department level, and after two years of implementation, can be made at the personal level.

QBs should be defined with collaboration between the CEO and team leaders, assigned to just one owner, and rolled out via Steve Jobs-style quarterly presentation. And then you should meticulously track their progress over the next 90 days during weekly leadership meetings.

PART 2

GROWING YOUR FIRM

*How to Generate Lead Abundance, Form Your
Marketing Strategy, and Level Up Your Intake*

FREEDOM ENTREPRENEUR

PROFIT + FREEDOM

SELF-MANAGING
TEAM

THE ABYSS

INTAKE

REVENUE

LEAD GENERATION

THE NEW WAY OF MARKETING A LAW FIRM

HOW TO GENERATE LEAD ABUNDANCE

"Prove you can help people by actually helping them."

—Frank Kern

ANDY STICKEL NARRATES

As my six-year-old son's head went underwater, he thrashed his arms violently and gasped for air.

I had been trying to teach Mason to swim for the last year, and the old way wasn't working. He was terrified of putting his face underwater even though he desperately wanted to swim.

Up to that point, I had been attempting to teach him how to swim without putting his head underwater, but it wasn't working. I knew that something had to change.

After about an hour of coaxing (and yes, I bribed him with a video game ... sue me), I convinced him to try to put his face in the water. He squeezed his face so tight you'd have thought he ate a lemon whole. Finally, he put his face in the water. Just for a second at first, then for five, then ten.

Twenty minutes later, he swam for real for the first time.

Sometimes achieving our goals is as easy as making a simple adjustment, even if that adjustment terrifies us.

When I first started my business, I was the person you hate. I emailed thousands of lawyers per month with some B.S. story about their website not being optimized and not ranking on Google. You know the emails.

It worked ... kinda. I mean, we did get clients. But they weren't our dream clients and, even when we got them results, they would often leave us for the next cheapest company that came around.

One day I was on a sales call with a victim of my email spam when he said something that shook me: "I know you're no better than all the other marketing companies because you use the same shady marketing tactics as them. You're basically Spamerella."

That was the last time I ever sent a spam email. The crazy thing was, I knew my company *was* different. We got results for our clients. We cared about our clients! But how could I prove I was different if I didn't *act* differently from the other guys?

That's when I had a radical idea: what if I started creating as much content as possible through videos, with the goal of helping lawyers grow their law firms—even if they never decided to hire me? I'd just … give them all my secrets!

My thesis was simple: arm lawyers with enough content and information to make millions, and do it for free on YouTube. A handful of them would recognize that I did, in fact, know what I was talking about. They would appreciate the non-spam approach so much that *they* would reach out to me, to hire *me*! They'd be chasing ME down!

I didn't realize it at the time, but this epiphany launched me from the *old* way of marketing, into the *new* way of marketing … And by tapping into the new way of marketing, I took my marketing company to a new stratosphere of success.

The New Way of marketing—and the related tools, tricks, and tips we'll share in the chapters to come—is your ticket to lead abundance. Why should you care about lead abundance? Here's why:

1. **Freedom.** You get more cases and better clients. This means you don't have to take on any more crazy clients with bad cases or those you suspect won't pay their bills. Put simply, you get to pick and choose your cases—and it all doesn't depend on you.

2. **Money.** Lead abundance means you can control your top-line revenue growth, *increase* your average case value without taking on more cases, and/or *decrease* your cost to acquire. This will make you more profitable and a lot more money.

That's the promise we'll be unpacking in this chapter: more freedom and more money, growing out of the new way of marketing.

But first, let us convince you that it's time to put the old way out to pasture.

Old Way vs. New Way

What is the old way versus the new way of marketing a law firm?

- The old way depends on *hoping and praying*: you put up an untargeted ad and hope someone calls. Or, you do a good job for a client and hope they pass your name on.

- The new way not only relies on ads and referral business but also involves *providing valuable information* to potential clients and showing up when they're actually in need of your legal services.

There are mainly two old ways of law firm marketing. Let's look at each one.

Old Way #1: Shooting Spiders with a Shotgun

This strategy is so simple it hardly even counts as a strategy. You place an ad in the yellow pages, or put up a billboard, or buy a TV ad, or whatever. Maybe you do all these things. Each ad says some variation of the same thing: "Hey, I'm a lawyer. Hire me."

The "old way" *can* work, but to make it work and completely saturate the market, you have to spend a lot of money—way more money than what most firms have altogether, let alone what they've allocated for marketing.

Here's the basic problem with this version of the old way: there's no *reason* for anyone to call you. Your bus ad says you do personal injury cases. Great! But you're not the only one. There are *tons* of personal injury lawyers. What makes you different? What sets you apart from the rest? Just because you have an ad on a bus, does not mean you're building real trust in the marketplace.

We call this strategy "shooting spiders with shotguns" because it is so inefficient. Your ad is seen by thousands of people, *most of whom do not need what you're offering.* While this will provide you top of mind awareness, if you're not willing to do this for three years straight, and spend millions of dollars, you're not going to get a great ROI. You're spending a huge amount of money on each client you get. It's the same level of ridiculous as using a 12-gauge shotgun to shoot the itsy bitsy spider. Much better to use a more targeted method.

Old Way #2: The Referrals Rut

Forget about shooting that spider with the shotgun. Referrals seem like a good option to go all in on. After all, they're cheap. That's good, right?

Wrong.

Here's the problem with referrals: *you are 100% dependent on someone else.* What happens if your referral source decides they don't like you anymore? What if they retire, or they die, or they begin working for your competition?

That source of referrals is dead. The stream dries up. Your firm grinds to a halt.

This happened to a well-known attorney who had an eight-figure business based on referrals from a single law firm who sent him all the smaller cases they didn't want. One day, they decided to bring all those cases in house. His referrals evaporated overnight and he had to scramble just to survive.

Now, we're not saying to get rid of referrals entirely. And make sure you provide an amazing service to your clients so you get a lot of them. Accept good ones that come your way. Just don't make them your *only* way to get clients. A good marketing to referrals ratio is about 50/50. That means 50% of your clients should come from your marketing and 50% should come from referrals. But that's not *always* the case. We know firms that have scaled with a 90/10 ratio—90% from marketing. If you want to grow *fast*, you need multiple scalable lead generation systems—mostly outside of referrals.

If your firm is dependent on a reactive flow of referrals, you are not *designing* your firm. You're truly dependent on whatever clients happen to call you that week and you will alter your firm's makeup to accommodate the referrals coming in. This will lead to you accepting clients you don't want or like—but you'll have to, because that's all you're getting.

But with a robust marketing platform, you have enough leads to *pick and choose* your clients. That's how you get the kind of freedom and money you want.

Out with the old, in with the new. So, what is the new way? Here's a clue: free samples.

New Way: Provide Value *Through* Your Marketing

When you go to Costco, what do you see? (Besides cases of paper towels stacked to the ceiling?) You see people at every second aisle giving away samples of sausages, muffins, slices of pizza, and more.

Why on Earth would a store give away stuff? Anyone who's lunched their way through Costco's buffet of samples knows why: because it prompts customers to take out their credit cards and *buy* stuff.

People love to buy things that they sample.

This is the foundation of the new way. Provide value up front. Give people a sample of what you are offering. Then, they will *buy* what you are offering.

You have a product. It's called legal services, but what is it, really? It's expertise, advice, and knowledge. Give away some of that knowledge in the form of a free sample, and you'll have clients wanting to *pay for* your knowledge.

To see how this works, consider a 35-year-old woman with kids who's thinking about getting a divorce. Let's call her Sara. If Sara decides to end her marriage, she's going to need legal services. Late one night, headphones in, she types into YouTube, "I'm a mom with kids and I want a divorce. What do I need to know?"

This is where you step in. You made a YouTube video titled "Five legal considerations for women with children seeking a divorce." In the video, you laid out exactly what a married woman with kids needs to get right when shopping for legal representation in the dissolution of a marriage. It's full of real, concrete, actionable steps for someone in her situation.

In the dark, on her laptop, Sara feels reassured by your advice. Your face becomes associated with clarity and empowerment in her next step. Then, that first video leads her to *more* of your videos. What she typed into YouTube (the second highest traffic website in the world) then triggers your YouTube video ad. This ad goes through the pros and cons of hiring a divorce lawyer. She clicks this ad, which allows you to "retarget" her on Facebook. So, she logs onto Facebook and sees a third video from you on five ways an antagonistic spouse might hide money from her. She then finds you on Instagram and watches your video about the best way to ensure she retains primary custody of her children.

Each video arms Sara with more and more crucial information, cementing your face as the source of helpful, practical advice. You start feeling like her personal confidant—she likes you, she trusts you, she feels like she knows you. Now, when Sara's ready to contact a law firm, is she going to go to your competitor? Hell, no! She's been watching your videos. You're like a celebrity to her! She's going to go with the firm that has already shown her how to avoid traps and pitfalls. She's going to go with *your* firm. That's entirely because of all the value you already have provided to her through your marketing.

Listen: why do people hire a lawyer in the first place? It's because they have a problem. If you create content that helps people solve their biggest and most common problems, people will look at you as the authority. You'll be the expert. You'll develop a tremendous amount of goodwill *which will lead to new cases*.

When you have a content strategy in place, combined with targeted ads to promote those videos to the right audience, and you're showing up on Google with glowing 5-star reviews—*that's* where magic happens.

But how do you get potential clients like Sara to find your videos in the first place? And should your videos be about *anything* related to the focus of your law practice or should they be more specific? And do you personally have to make the videos?

We're going to get into all these details in the next few chapters. But before we talk brass tacks regarding strategy, we need to get a few big picture concepts ironed out: *when, who, where,* and *how.* There are any number of potential clients floating around out in the internet universe. So—who do you target? And where should you serve your marketing? And how should you market to get your right fit clients?

In our last chapter, we said you needed to iron out your business strategy before determining your marketing strategy. Now that you've got your ideal Case-Buckets, Quarterly Boulders set and have more clarity on your firm's KPIs, we're ready to dive into how you can apply all of that to the *when, who, where,* and *how* of marketing.

When: the Four Stages of Marketing

Potential clients tend to go through four stages on the way to hiring you:

1. **Unaware.** In this first stage, your potential client doesn't yet know they have a problem, or they *don't* have a problem. They are blissfully going through life, not worrying about any legal issue. They don't know they need an estate plan. Or they haven't yet figured out their spouse is cheating on them. Or they haven't yet gotten into that car accident, or arrested for DUI.

2. **Research.** Your potential client has figured out they *do* have a problem, and they start typing research keywords into search engines. The Research stage is where Sara was, in our earlier example about a mom looking for a divorce attorney. Potential clients in research mode are Googling things like: *what happens to a house in a divorce?* Or, *how much money can I get from the asshole who put me in the hospital with his reckless driving?* People in this stage are not *quite* ready to hire. They're simply gathering information.

3. **Vendor Selection.** In Stage 3, potential clients stop searching for information and begin shopping for an attorney. They're still using a search engine, but their search terms are more like "bankruptcy lawyer near me," or, "best criminal defense attorney in my city." They've gone as far as they can with their research. Now they're looking to hire a professional. Note that *only about 3%* of any given market is in the Vendor Selection stage, also known as the Demand stage.

4. **Hire.** The final stage. Your potential client has found the attorney they want to handle their case and they hire them directly. If you did everything right, that attorney is you!

Pop quiz: When in these four stages should you target potential clients with your marketing?

Most people pick Stage 3, because that's when clients are closest to hiring. Is that what you picked?

That's what *most* people pick. The vast majority of law firms advertise to potential clients in Stage 3. And, that's great! As we already broke down, Stage 3 is the fastest way to create a scalable lead generation system to climb the Lawyer Legacy Staircase. But, since everyone does it, it's also an expensive choice in a crowded field. You're fighting the laws of supply and demand: there's a very limited supply, given that only 3% of potential clients are in Stage 3, yet there's high demand for their attention from all the other law firms advertising in the same space. You might need to pay $50 or even $200 per click for some of those "Stage 3" keywords, like "personal injury attorney near me," or "divorce lawyer."

Now, does that mean you *shouldn't* advertise to potential clients in Stage 3 at all? No. Just because it's expensive doesn't mean that you shouldn't advertise there. When someone types in "car accident attorney near me" or "DUI attorney," you still want your name in front of them. But if that's your *only* source of advertising forever, it gets expensive. It also means you're missing a golden opportunity to capture the attention of the 97% of potential clients still in Stage 1 *and* 2. Ideally, you'll devote portions of your marketing budget to advertising in stages 1, 2 *and* 3, and dollar cost average.

Stage 2 is the "road less traveled" we want you to explore. In Stage 2, the supply of potential clients is quite high, and demand for their attention is low. In other words, hardly anyone is advertising there—which means it's cheap.

Targeting clients in research mode during Stage 2 also gives you an enormous advantage. In that less crowded market, you're able to introduce potential clients to your value-rich content, full of good advice for their research-based questions. You have the opportunity to cement yourself in those potential clients' minds as their go-to source for wisdom about solving their problems. That will translate to *leads.*

We've learned that 85% of people prefer to hire the company that helped them do their research. That means if they find *your* YouTube videos, Facebook Ads, or blog posts helpful while they are researching, they will likely hire *you*, completely bypassing your competitors. By far, the cheapest and most targeted way to advertise is catching people while they are in Stage 2. And if your marketing provides them with free information that helps them understand their situation, they will be chomping at the bit to hire you.

> **The cheapest *and* most targeted way to advertise is catching people while they are still in the research stage. If your marketing provides them with free information that helps them understand their situation, they will be chomping at the bit to hire you.**

Notice, in our example of Sara researching a divorce attorney, she found videos that were very specific. They likely targeted a specific gender, a specific age, and a specific parental status: that's why she found them. That's why she trusted them. And that was no accident.

The New Way is all about niche marketing. It works best when you define a very specific and narrow audience and tailor your marketing to that niche. Now: we're at "who."

ANDY STICKEL NARRATES

Who: "Niche Down"

Dad brag. My daughter, Malayla is an excellent softball player and takes private lessons. She wants to get a scholarship to a D1 college and we want to help her get there. So, when we were seeking out a private instructor, did we hire a PE teacher? No. We hired a softball coach who *only* coaches middle and high school girls, with the goal of getting them a scholarship. We hired *a niche coach.*

Your potential clients are looking for that same niche expertise, which is why you need to niche down. "Niche down" means to think about *who* will hire you. Who are your ideal clients? What kind of expertise are they looking for?

Perhaps you're a personal injury lawyer looking for more traumatic brain injury cases. If Donna is the mother of a child with a traumatic brain injury, do you think Donna wants to hire a general personal injury attorney, or would she rather hire the attorney she perceives to be the "go to expert" on traumatic brain injuries? Obviously, Donna would prefer to go with the second. If Clark gets arrested for a DUI, would he want any ol' criminal defense attorney, or does Clark want to work with a DUI Specialist? If James is a father going through a divorce, does James want any family attorney, or a Father's Rights attorney?

People want to hire specialized professionals because they feel confident in that person's niche area of expertise. That's why we sought out a niche softball coach for Malayla. In the same way, your potential clients want an expert in the area of law where they need legal help. You should become that expert. You should be a niche attorney.

What niche clients do you want to target with your marketing? You might be tempted to give an answer that aligns with whatever form of law you like geeking out about— but that actually *shouldn't* be your first consideration. Your first consideration should be the numbers you identified after reading through Chapter 4. Remember your ideal case buckets? What kind of cases did you decide you wanted to get more of? *That's* where you want to niche down in your marketing.

It might be personal injury cases from motorcycle accidents. It could be landlords trying to evict bad tenants. It might be startups looking to go public. It could be professional drivers hit with a DUI who are now in danger of losing their CDL. Whatever it is, whatever niche clients you're looking for, *go all in* on those niches for a bit. Craft your videos to target the niches represented in your ideal case buckets. This marketing approach will allow you to position your law firm as the go-to expert for those case types, making you less dependent on referrals. And that's freedom, because then you get to choose your clients.

To be clear, you don't need to niche down your entire firm. You can still take on a wide range of cases. But you do need to niche down your *marketing messages,* usually by developing multiple niched marketing campaigns. If you try to talk to everyone, you'll reach no one. If you tailor your messages to specific audiences, they'll hear you.

Here's an example. Let's say you're a PI firm interested in representing more car accident cases. Now, consider, what kind of people typically hire you for car accident cases? Let's say you brainstorm and come up with three types of clients: parents of teen drivers, people dealing with DUIs, and Uber/Lyft drivers who are on the road a ton. Ask yourself: what kind of information might those people be interested in *before* the accident ever happens, when they're still just in the research phase?

Consider the parents of teen drivers. Do parents of teens want to watch a video titled: "What to do after your teen gets into a car accident"? No. If it's before the accident, the video isn't relevant. If it's after the accident, they're too busy making sure their teenager is okay. But those same parents *would* be interested in these videos:

- "Top five most dangerous intersections in [your city.]"
- "How to keep teens from texting and driving."

- "Three ways to keep your teens safe while behind the wheel."

- "Best app you can use to make sure your kids aren't speeding."

- "Three most common causes of accidents in teenage drivers and what you can do to prevent it."

You're not creating content for the teenage drivers—they wouldn't be the ones hiring you. You're going to create content that their *parents* will be interested in. These videos help establish you as an expert in this niche, ensuring that potential clients know, like, and trust you. Now, imagine you turn this into a 10K-person Facebook group filled with parents of teen drivers in your market, putting out helpful content daily. When a teenager gets into an accident—or their parent/friend of the parent/friend of the teen/relative gets into an accident—you've already established yourself as a personal injury attorney that this community trusts. They've been watching all of your content on social media. Why wouldn't they hire you?

Who are your ideal clients? You don't have to pick just one, although it might make sense to start with one type of client as a focus of your marketing spending. Eventually, you can market to many niches at the same time, so long as each segment is specific and narrow. Each niche should comprise one piece of your marketing. And with each niche you target, remember that *people* hire you. Cases don't. Think about *who* you are trying to attract. What are their emotions? What are their fears? What do they need to know?

Quick-Hitting Hack: Here's a four-question test to determine if your marketing has successfully addressed a good niche:

1. **Can your target audience self-identify?** ("I'm a parent of a teen driver.")

2. **Do they have a specific set of unique problems?** ("I'm worried about my teen's road safety. I'm stressed about the increase to our car insurance. I think my teen uses her phone while driving.")

3. **Do they have specific demographics?** (Demographics refers to statistical data such as age, gender, income, etc. collected for a particular population. For instance: middle-aged parents of teens driving in [this city.])

4. **Do they have specific psychographics?** (Psychographics refers to information about a particular population's attitudes, aspirations, and other psychological criteria. For instance: anxious moms looking to reconnect with their adolescent children.)

We worked with a personal injury attorney who niched down on motorcyclists. He created a Facebook group, YouTube channel and separate website where he posted all kinds of content about motorcycles, especially motorcycle safety. How to avoid a motorcycle accident. Dangerous intersections for bikers. Best safety gear. Three common ways motorcyclists are killed. And so on. The group developed a large number of followers. One day a friend of someone in the group—who was not in the group himself—got killed in a motorcycle accident. The guy who *was* in the group went to the family of the deceased biker. "You need to hire this attorney to handle the wrongful death case," he told them. "He knows absolutely everything about motorcycles and motorcycle accidents."

That lawyer had established his authority and got an important case because of it. He went all in on his target niche, and brought his audience valuable information they cared to know.

Appeal to people where it counts: in their emotions. Give them information that comforts them and helps them find peace. *That's* how you establish your authority as an expert.

We have a tool to help you get to know your particular group of target clients, so that you can niche down effectively and ensure your marketing successfully nails the New Way. We call it the DDP.

ANDY STICKEL NARRATES

DDP: Know Your Audience with the Defined Demographic Profile

One year ago, my wife and I decided to go to Cancun for our anniversary. We hired a travel agent to help us out.

This travel agent was *amazing.* When she got the trip all planned out, she invited us to a PowerPoint presentation to show us pictures of the stunning resort she'd found. Each suite had its own private pool. Grown-ups only—no children allowed. We'd have our own private butler the entire time. We'd step out of our room right onto the beach where waiters would bring us drinks. Seven great restaurants. Breathtaking weather. Stunning ocean. "This is your place," she said. "You will love this vacation. Once you are there you will not want to leave. That's how truly amazing it is."

We were blown away. *Completely* sold. We handed over our credit card without a second's thought.

Guess what the travel agent didn't mention?

The airplane ride.

There was no PowerPoint slide showing us arriving at the airport three hours early for an international flight. Nothing about the TSA gauntlet: standing in line, removing our shoes and belts, getting scanned, waiting to board. No mention of the hours we'd spend squished in an uncomfortable seat on a plane, surrounded by strangers. Skipped over the part where we'd have to wait in line at Cancun to go through customs, collect our bags, find the Uber pickup spot, and so on.

And those omissions were very effective marketing.

The truth is, no one wants the plane ride. They want the *destination* that the plane will take them to. How does this relate to marketing your law firm? Simple. Ask yourself: am I selling the resort? Or the plane ride?

No one wants bankruptcy. What they *want* is to get out of debt. That means you, as a bankruptcy lawyer, shouldn't sell bankruptcies, even though bankruptcies are the path out of debt. Advertising your help with the bankruptcy process is like doing a PowerPoint of a miserable plane ride.

What you sell is *freedom*. Freedom from debt! *That's* the resort.

Nobody *wants* a divorce. Divorce is the plane ride. What they *want* is to move on with their lives and experience greater peace and be happy. That's the resort.

When you're marketing your law practice, take that travel agent's lead and sell the *desire*, what people really want. You do this with what we call a DDP, or Detailed Demographic Profile. It's a quick way to ensure your marketing speaks directly and powerfully to your target clients. It looks like this:

I help <**audience**> get <**desire**> without <**fear**>.

Let's see how this works for different kinds of lawyers. Consider estate planners. They make wills and trusts. Should they sell wills and trusts to their clients? Absolutely not! People don't care about wills and trusts. No one wakes up in the middle of the night yearning to get a will or a trust. Who wants to think about being dead?

What they *want* is peace of mind. They want to know the government is not going to take their money. They want to know their kids, spouse, and pets are going to be taken care of when they die. So, the DDP for them would look like this:

I help **wealthy people** get **peace of mind** without **taxes robbing their assets**.

Get it? If you're an estate planner, your website's landing page should not wax poetic about wills and trusts. Instead, it should feature images of people looking happy and reassured after forming a strong estate plan that cares for their family members. Your website should emphasize the *benefits* of having that peace of mind.

How do we know this? Because we implemented a similar program at SMB Team. We revamped our messaging to emphasize the benefits of a higher income (that's the resort) rather than the ins and outs of SEO marketing or the best way to fire employees that don't perform (that's the plane ride.) That messaging shift led to a noticeable increase in sales and more overall engagement as people resonated with the new language.

We know a family law attorney who works with first responders on Long Island going through a divorce. That's a niche, for sure, which is great. But what was his DDP? At first, he was stymied because he didn't know what first responders wanted. After a little research, it became obvious. Every single first responder, when asked what their greatest fear was, told him they were afraid their exes would get their pensions.

The DDP then fell into place: I help **first responders** get **to move on and start a new life** without **losing their pensions.**

Say you're a divorce lawyer specializing in fathers. What's their fear? Not having any time with their kids. Boom! You've got your DDP: I help **fathers** get **freedom from a bad marriage** without **losing a relationship with their children.**

Another example, this time for a bankruptcy firm: We help **families** get **freedom from debt** without **destroying their credit.**

Lawyers often get stuck on selling what they do. After all, a lot of them are dealing with pretty stressful plane rides: divorces, estate planning, bankruptcies, and so on. What you need to understand is no one wants the thing you sell. Not really. What they want is the *result* of the thing you do. That's the resort and that's what you need to sell in your marketing!

> **Quick-Hitting Hack:** Here's a test to determine if you're selling the airplane ride or the vacation:
>
> 1. Is your marketing focused on *them* rather than *you*?
> 2. Is the main focus on *how the client will benefit?*
> 3. Is the benefit *important* to the client?

That takes care of *when* and *who*. How about *where?*

Where: Fishing for Marlins

The "where" used to be pretty straightforward because law firms had basically one way of marketing. They took out a yellow pages ad. That was it.

Then, the internet came along. Some lawyers jumped on it for marketing—and a lot didn't. A lot still don't. Many of our clients say they don't use social media. When we mention "SEO" (search engine optimization), their eyes glaze over. "It's not my thing," they say.

Our response to them is, "So what?"

There are two types of people on social media: *producers* of social media and *consumers* of social media. Just because you're not a consumer of social media doesn't mean you can't produce it. Last we checked, there are 3 billion monthly active users on Facebook, 2.7 billion on YouTube and 1.5 billion on Google. In fact, producing social media is productive in a way that consuming social media is not. Neither one of us is a big consumer of social media—but we're both huge *producers* of content in those spaces.

So, who cares if you spend time on those sites or not? *Your clients* spend time there. In fact, they spend a lot of time there. If you want to catch a marlin, do you hold off fishing in the ocean because you might get seasick? Of course not! If you want to catch a marlin, you go where the marlins are. It's the same with social media. You market where the clients are.

I'll illustrate this with a story about a client we work with, Patrick Slaughter.

Patrick is a high-end divorce attorney. For a long time, he relied on traditional ads and word-of-mouth marketing with some referral action thrown in. But it wasn't working for him. He wasn't getting the leads he needed to grow his practice.

One day, as he was browsing YouTube, he found some videos by this guy (*ahem*) named Andy Stickel. He liked what he saw. The videos offered real value for free. Patrick decided that was the right way to go, and he started producing videos of his own that were similar to mine, posting them on social media.

His videos explained the ins and outs of divorce, child custody issues, and child support issues. These videos helped people solve their problems. Within a short time, Patrick was getting leads in droves. A phenomenal number of leads, all based on his videos. He went where the marlins were.

Most of your target clients are spending a huge amount of time surfing the internet—that's where your big fish are swimming. As you think about the *where* of your marketing, go where you're most likely to get the attention of the clients you want to catch. That's just being smart.

However, it's not the whole story. Remember that your *business* strategy must come before your *marketing* strategy. Going to the ocean is the right place to fish for marlins, but if you use the wrong kind of bait, you're still not going to catch the fish you want. You need to think critically about how you're communicating, and this consideration should be guided by your business strategy.

Patrick Slaughter's story, once again, helps us see why. After Patrick got that first deluge of leads, he realized he still needed to do some fine tuning, regarding the *how*.

How: Business Strategy > Marketing Strategy

There was one major problem with all of Patrick's new leads: the majority of the people calling him weren't his right fit clients. Most new leads couldn't afford him and asked for pro bono services. (That's why they appreciated his free advice so much.)

Others seemed downright loco, like the client who tells you a secret cabal of government-controlled aliens is trying to take her house from her, and she needs a lawyer. "But don't worry," she says, "because I'll direct you with strategy and legal tactics the whole way." Thanks, but no thanks.

His team developed an internal hashtag to flag all the crazy or ill-fitting clients that were contacting his firm from those original videos: #nopenopenope.

Patrick had gone where the big fish swim, but the big fish weren't biting. Somehow, his videos were getting the attention of *wrong fit* clients.

Patrick called us up and explained his problem. "What am I doing wrong?" he asked. We looked at his videos together. They weren't the best things ever, but they were adequate. They got the job done. So why was he getting low end clients only? In the videos he was telling people how to deal with family law issues. What he *wasn't* doing was telling *rich people* how to deal with family law issues that were unique to people of means.

"Who are you trying to target, Patrick?" we asked.

"Affluent people."

"What are affluent people worried about when they're getting a divorce?"

He rattled off a list of examples. "What to do with the second home … who gets the boat … how to rewrite the will … traveling with the kids …"

"So, rich people problems," we summed up. "You need to make content about rich people problems."

He went back and revamped his videos, offering quality content about problems that *only* wealthy people tend to have. For instance, how to protect a vacation home during a divorce, what to do about brokerage accounts, step-by-step instructions about how to handle their kids' passports so they could travel with a divorced parent outside of the country, and so on. He explained how to divide investment accounts and rental properties. His new videos niched down even further than his first set, targeting the unique questions which only wealthy people pursuing a divorce would have.

Patrick's ideal case buckets informed his strategy. He wanted to bring in more high net worth clients. Once those videos went up, Pat started getting the clients he wanted—the high income folks who could afford his fees. There were still some wrong fit clients contacting him, but it didn't matter because he got so many *good* leads that he began charging for consults. He was in such high demand that people paid *just to talk to him about a case.*

The lesson here is that your business strategy must come before your marketing strategy. Define exactly *who* you want your clients to be, based on your ideal case buckets, then create value content specifically for that niche. Be as specific as you possibly can. Then, give that audience value-rich content.

Once you get clear on this, these become your demographic targeting settings on Google, YouTube and Facebook advertising. And, it will guide the content you create.

The Magic Math of Marketing

At the start of this chapter, we told you that implementing the new way of marketing could help you *increase* your average case value, and *decrease* your cost to acquire. That might have seemed outlandish. After all—isn't marketing going to be a huge expense? How could spending all that money help accomplish profitability in those other areas?

Let's consider two law firms. Firm Boohoo gets ten leads a month. They have to take them. They have no choice if they want to stay in business. The average value of those cases might be $3K.

Firm Rockstar, on the other hand, gets *300* leads a month. How do they get all those leads? They've implemented the new way of marketing, being strategic about when, who, where, and how. And as a result of that lead abundance, they get to pick the ten cases from those 300 that they actually want. With that freedom, they choose the ones that give them, say, $6K per case. They've *doubled* their revenue over Firm Boohoo even though they've ultimately accepted the same number of cases.

Are you catching this? A substantial marketing investment and subsequent lead abundance results in your ability to *increase* your average case value.

We're not done yet. All that extra money gives Firm Rockstar confidence to grow their business. They attract quality candidates, hire A-players, and invest in more marketing. With better people, they're getting their clients better results. That means satisfied clients who give more good reviews. Better reviews puts Firm Rockstar higher on Google searches and generates organic search traffic for the firm. This leads to a snowball effect. More satisfied clients, more good reviews, more good clients.

That's how we accomplish principle number two. The increase of satisfied clients accomplished by your lead abundance results in more clients *for free*, meaning you have now *decreased* your cost to acquire (CTA).

Let's illustrate this. Imagine you spend $1K on a marketing campaign that gets you 10 calls. Out of that, two new clients sign up:

- Your CTA is $500
- $1K/2 new cases = $500

But what if you put in a robust follow-up sequence that contacts those other eight calls who initially turned you down? Perhaps two more clients sign up. You've just *reduced* your CTA to $250.

- $1K/4 new cases = $250

Then, what if one of those clients refers you to someone else and you snag them? Now your CTA is $200! And on it goes. All this is possible with a refined marketing system that pursues all these possible ways to acquire clients.

Behold the magic math of marketing. By increasing your marketing budget, you can *increase* your average case value and *decrease* the cost of acquiring a client.

There's more to it than that, obviously—we wouldn't have three more chapters about marketing if there wasn't—but we want you to understand this fundamental principle:

Effective marketing is crucial for your firm's growth, its increased revenue, and for your personal freedom.

There's a reason the fastest growing law firms spend 20% of their gross revenues on marketing, year after year. You should do the same.

In fact, that's where we're going to wrap up this chapter. Talking about what you *should* do as your firm's leader. And, more importantly, what you *shouldn't* do.

Embrace the Exponential

Imagine that a colonel gathers three of his captains together. He's trying to decide which one he'll promote to major, so he gives them a test. "The battle we'll be facing in the weeks to come will be intense," he says. "I need you to help your units level up. What's going to be your first priority?"

One captain says, "We're going to double down on our equipment and preparation. Make sure everything's in top condition and packed efficiently."

One captain says, "We're going to work on our hand-to-hand combat."

The third captain says, "My first priority will be to get my troops to the high ground."

This last response gets the Colonel's attention. "*Yes,*" he says. "Get to high ground. How?"

The third captain shrugs. "I would leave that up to the platoon leaders to make the call during battle. But the strategy would remain our first priority. Get to high ground."

The colonel promotes the third captain. Why? Because that third captain was focusing on a strategy that would lead to *exponential* advances. Whoever can take the high ground will have an enormous advantage over the enemy. The first two captains were focused on technical improvements, but neither suggestion could move the needle like getting to the high ground.

The same concept applies to you as your firm's leader. We started this book with the Lawyer Legacy Staircase, urging you to take action in order to rise higher to greater impact, profit, and freedom. Here's one key thing you can do to help yourself climb that staircase: Embrace the exponential.

When it comes to marketing, it's easy to get bogged down in technical details. Learning how to run Facebook Ads yourself. Researching keywords. Building your own website. Turning the knobs, as it were. These are necessary prerequisites to launching any sort of marketing campaign, but focusing on technical stuff like this will only lead to small, incremental changes—and it's all stuff you could easily delegate or outsource.

What will lead to big changes in your marketing ROI? Strategy, vision, branding shifts—the kind of work that *only* you can do. This would include decisions that relate to the *when, who, where,* and *how*—decisions that answer questions like, "Which ideal case buckets should we target with our marketing?" When Patrick Slaughter initiated a strategic shift in his videos, making content that attracted the affluent clients he was looking for instead of pro bono clients, that shift led to *exponential* gains.

We repeat this phrase a lot at SMB Team:

"Outsource the incremental. Embrace the exponential."

On Steps 3 and 4 of the Lawyer Legacy Staircase, you'll often see the Solo Practitioner and the Small Business Manager getting tangled up in the weeds of marketing. They're distracted by the incremental.

The people who have climbed to Steps 5 and above, however—the Law Firm CEO and Law Firm Owner—those leaders have learned to outsource the incremental and embrace the exponential. The sooner you can do likewise, the faster you can climb your own staircase. If you run your Facebook Ads yourself, that might add an incremental increase to your law firm. But if you decide, "We're going to change our messaging to attract better clients," that will provide an exponential return. *That's* the stuff you should be focusing on.

As much as possible, don't mess around with the low-level technical stuff yourself. Things like PPC ads, social media ads, website design, SEO, and so on. Even if you're still functioning as a rainmaker at Step 3, working as a Solo Practitioner, you're still better off contracting that stuff out to technicians. Save your time, energy, and expertise for where it's most needed.

If you're at Step 4, Small Business Manager, you've likely moved into Demand Marketing. Try not to get too distracted by the nitty-gritty details of Google Ads. Instead, focus on guiding your firm's Google Ads strategy.

Once you've climbed to Steps 5 or 6, and ideally even before that, focus *exclusively* on the leadership only you can provide, like being the face of your brand. Empower your directors to make marketing strategy decisions aligned with the Vivid Vision and Quarterly Boulders you helped lead. Concentrate your time and energy on building marketing omnipresence and *exponential growth* strategies.

This is good news for you because you don't *have* to learn all the intricacies and little details of technical tools. You don't *have* to figure out how to size an image on Facebook and make sure it has the correct DPI. That's low-level stuff! Turning the knobs and working the camera for the YouTube videos is at the bottom of the chart. It is literally beneath you.

While the technical stuff is necessary, improvement in those areas will lead only to modest increases in revenue. Improving a strategy will lead to bigger gains—like streamlining your intake procedure. That will help take you from functioning as the manager of your firm's growth, Step 4, to functioning as a Law Firm CEO, Step 5. And the biggest gains come when you invest your time and energy into the top level of omnipresence. That's what leads to huge, exponential growth, taking you to Step 6 and beyond.

By the way, this concept is true for every aspect of running your firm. You should spend your time exclusively on higher-level work. Do you answer the phone and get the personal information of the person calling your firm? No way! Talking with unqualified clients is a $10 per hour task. That's why you delegate it. Creating a new Unique Selling Proposition for your firm, on the other hand, is a ten thousand dollar an hour task. That's why *you* do it.

Remember in a previous chapter when we told you that lawyers who do the most end up making the least? Don't be the lawyer who tries to do everything yourself. It will kill your growth faster than anything. Instead, delegate the lower-level "survival" tasks and take on the top-level tasks, which lead to high impact.

Quick-Hitting Hack: Scan this QR code for free access to our Lead Abundance Framework, the methodology we teach hundreds of lawyers from across the nation. It builds on what we've outlined here and will equip you with the knowledge to really ramp up your marketing strategies.

**Scan this QR Code
to Unlock This Bonus**

ANDY STICKEL NARRATES

Pick Your Hard

I regularly go to a gym to work out.

I hate it. Absolutely *loathe* every minute I spend there. But I do it anyway.

I have friends who can't wait to get in there and lift those weights or run an hour on the treadmill. They'll go crazy if they don't put in time on the bench-press or the pull-up bar. I am not one of those people. Working out is *hard*. So hard that I have a trainer to keep me on track with my program.

But you know what else is hard? Having health problems due to a lack of exercise. *That's* hard. Not having freedom of movement because you lack muscle mass is hard. Being out of shape is hard. Having to change your diet because of cholesterol issues is hard. If you acquire enough negative issues from lack of exercise, your life will be pretty damn difficult.

That's why I go to the gym. I picked my hard. I chose the discomfort of working out over the discomfort of reduced health.

We're telling you to do hard things. Pivoting your strategy is hard. Creating videos when you are camera-shy is hard. Forming a business strategy and quarterly boulders is hard.

But here's the thing. It is *harder* to have a low-performing law firm. Not knowing where your next client is coming from, going around begging for business, doing all the work your-self … Burning out and becoming a workaholic and watch-ing your marriage start to crumble—that's *hard*. That's a more debilitating "hard" than doing what it takes to ramp up your business and make it work for you.

You have a choice. Pick your hard.

We've given you the tools and knowledge to get started. We've tried to make your "hard" as easy as possible. You know how important it is to do the New Way of marketing and pro-vide value through your marketing materials. You have tools to evaluate the *when*, *who*, *where*, and *how*. You understand how to focus your attention when it comes to marketing your law firm. You're ready to do some hard things.

Now, we're going to turn you into a strategic marketing genius. In the next chapter, we'll look at the fundamental principles of marketing. These "11 commandments" will guide you in taking your marketing to the next level, giving you that much more momentum toward your dream life.

Chapter 5 | Takeaways

1. The New Way of marketing involves *providing value* to your target clients with a video content strategy, com-bined with targeted ads to promote those videos to the right audience, and showing up on Google with glowing 5-star reviews. This strategy will beat a reac-tive referral strategy, or traditional marketing, every day of the week.

2. Set your marketing coordinates by identifying the *when, who, where,* and *how* of your marketing.

a. When: Prepare your marketing materials for potential clients in the research phase.

b. Who: "Niche down" by identifying a very specific target demographic of clients. Use the DDP (Defined Demographic Profile) to identify their biggest desires and fears.

c. Where: The most efficient and effective place to do your marketing is online, via content marketing combined with SEO, PPC and social media campaigns.

d. How: Your marketing content should be informed by your business strategy. Ensure your messaging appeals mainly to the target clients you identified after doing the work from Chapter 4, looking at your ideal case buckets, considering your QBs, and so on.

3. A robust, effective marketing campaign can enable you to *increase* your average case value (ACV) and *decrease* your cost to acquire (CTA).

As your firm's leader, you should only engage in marketing decisions that relate to strategy and omnipresence. You do not need to learn the technical details of SEO marketing, Facebook Ads, or website design. Those are areas to delegate.

CHAPTER 6

THE 11 COMMANDMENTS OF MARKETING

CHOOSING YOUR OVERALL MARKETING STRATEGY

"Watch what everyone else does—do the opposite. The majority is always wrong."

—Earl Nightingale

ANDY STICKEL NARRATES

During my college years, I worked as a cook at a pizza place called Carrabba's Italian Grill. While I was there, they hired a new kitchen manager. He was dedicated and energetic—really wanted to do a good job. But the weird thing was, he didn't start managing the kitchen right away. Instead, he spent two weeks under me as a pizza cook. I showed him everything I knew about how to bake pizzas, and he soaked it up.

Next, he switched over to the appetizer station and put in two full weeks there, learning from the appetizer guy. After that, it was two weeks at the salad station, then two weeks on the grill.

He did this because he knew the best way to lead the kitchen effectively was to know the ins and outs of every station in the kitchen. That's how he would know when things were being done right and where there was room for improvement.

He never intended to make all the pizzas himself, but by working all those stations for all those weeks, he learned how to recognize if the people who were preparing the food were doing it right.

This chapter is intended to equip you like that savvy Carrabba's kitchen manager. If you want effective marketing for your firm, you need to know enough about marketing to assess whether your approach makes sense and can be expected to bring results. That doesn't mean doing the technical work of marketing yourself. It simply means it's on you to understand enough about marketing to ensure the right people are cooking at the marketing station and know what they're doing.

You can't count on marketing companies to keep you informed and in the loop—and we say that even though one of our core services is marketing! Most marketing companies out there will B.S. you until the cows come home. They're trying to hide their "insider knowledge" from you. This is nonsense—remember, the highest value use of your time in marketing involves staying up to date on trends and directing high-level strategy. Still, lawyers fall for this line of crap from marketing companies all the time.

> **Quick-Hitting Hack:** Want to know the easiest litmus test to see if your marketing team will be effective? Here's the surest way to evaluate them: *Does your marketing put the client first?*
>
> If it does, great. You've probably got a winner with your marketing crew. But if their proposed ad copy is all about you (your fancy degrees, your swanky office space, your impressive connections), they don't know what they're doing. Marketing should be focused on the benefit to the *client.*

Let's look at an example of how a lot of marketing companies approach law firm marketing with a completely counterproductive strategy. Imagine you buy a clickable ad on a popular website. Your ad says, "Father's Rights Lawyer: Helping Dads Through Divorce." But when people click on the ad and arrive at the homepage of your website with no mention of Father's Rights, they click around in frustration, looking for what was promised to them, until finally, fed-up, they leave. You lost a client because your landing page did not match the message of the ad.

We know of a guy whose sole job was honing Adobe.com's landing page. He tried all kinds of things to bring in more traffic—different fonts, various button designs, all manner of graphics and videos, a multitude of background colors, and so on. None of it made a difference. The *only* thing that got the company a significant increase in conversions was he ensured Adobe's pay-per-click ads on other websites matched Adobe's landing page message.

Most lawyers get 3% to 5% conversion on their pay-per-click ads. That's the industry average. In our marketing agency, our ads for law firms convert at a rate of 16% because we know to not send traffic to a homepage and what needs to be on a landing page in order to convert.

You need to know what you're looking for. You need to understand what the marketing company is supposed to be doing so that you can determine whether or not they're doing a good job. Unless you know that the message on the landing page and the message on the ad need to be congruent, it wouldn't even occur to you to check for that.

It isn't always that these firms are trying to cheat you, either. A lot of marketing firms simply do not know what they are doing. We have many stories of lawyers hiring five, six, or seven marketing firms that don't get meaningful results for them. They waste a firm's time and lose them money.

That's not what we want for you. Building a broad understanding of marketing strategy is the best way to make sure you don't get screwed by crappy marketing firms. It also keeps you from falling into Agency Jumping Syndrome, when you keep hiring agencies that promise big results yet don't deliver, then hire another agency and get the same outcome. By educating yourself about marketing principles, you can create your *own* marketing strategy and then hire the right team by ensuring their marketing plan makes sense and aligns with your business strategy.

THE 11 COMMANDMENTS OF MARKETING

We're going to educate you on how to recognize good marketing principles—not only so that you can fine-tune your own approach, but so that you can recognize a good marketing agency from the bad ones. This chapter will take you from station to station in the marketing universe, to teaching you all you need to know about marketing a law firm.

The 11 Commandments of Marketing to Grow Your Firm

Welcome to the marketing kitchen! Here's a tour of what you're going to be learning …

- Station 1. You're going to learn what **groundwork** needs to be laid, understand your clients' fears and desires, build strategic partnerships, and gather social proof.

- Station 2. Then, we're going to teach you **the pitch**, how to do offer creation, establish a unique selling proposition utilizing the first mover advantage, and embracing an *all-in* strategy.

- Station 3. Now, let's talk about **the afterglow.** What needs to happen *after* your clients encounter your pitch? We'll look at the importance of follow-up and using a "didn't hire" survey to gather key data.

- Station 4. We'll cover **global principles.** Our tour ends with discussing how to become brand dominant and tracking your ROI as a whole.

Ready? Let's toss some dough.

Station 1: Groundwork

Where do you begin? You always begin with your ideal clients. Figure out the message that will most resonate with them, build up strategic partnerships with businesses who can send you referrals, and gather social proof.

ANDY STICKEL NARRATES

1. Understand Your Client's Fears and Desires

When I was a college student, way back in the Jurassic, I didn't go to the dentist. For one thing, I didn't have any insurance. But also, I just didn't care. I was young and figured my teeth would last forever.

After I graduated, I still didn't go to the dentist. It wasn't that I was afraid of dentists. The drill and the needles didn't bother me. What *did* bother me was the judgment I expected. What would the dentist say when they found out I had avoided all dental work for—by that time—*nine* full years?? Thinking of the dental hygienists' disapproving looks or shocked incredulity made me shudder. Better to just stay away.

I'd see ads for dentists that said things like "Pain free dentistry." They didn't move me. I saw ads that said, "All Insurance Accepted." Didn't care. I even saw ads that said the first appointment would be free. Again, I did not bite.

You know what did inspire me to walk through a dentist's doors? I saw an ad with the tagline: "Judgment-Free Dentistry." I made an appointment that day.

Remember the DDPs we discussed in the last chapter, the "Defined Demographic Profile"? All those dentists who weren't luring me into their chairs had the wrong DDP. They didn't know my true fear—judgment—and as a result, they were selling the wrong thing. They thought people were afraid of the *cost* of dentistry or the *pain* of dentistry. Certainly, for some people, this was the case. But for me, I was afraid of being scolded by a dentist who would tsk-tsk me for waiting so long in between fluoride trays. I was afraid of being shamed.

As it turned out, I'd done a perfectly fine job taking care of my teeth, and when I finally sat down in a dentist's chair, there were no problems to address. But what *got* me into that dentist's chair? Reassurance that I wouldn't be judged either way. One dentist figured out a lot of people were afraid of getting shamed about their teeth and came up with a DDP that addressed my personal fear. It was *that* dentist who snagged my business.

So, the first principle for successfully marketing your law firm is knowing the fear of your potential clients.

Lance Fryrear, a criminal defense attorney in Washington state, went through a similar experience. His early marketing emphasized his experience, knowledge, and his success rate in handling cases. He assumed his clients feared being in the hands of an amateur.

Sounds reasonable. But it was wrong. His marketing had flat-lined because of it.

Once he realized this, Lance revamped his intake procedure to include a survey of his clients. He used a tool in our online law firm marketing university to survey them about their fears, frustrations, and desires. He zeroed in what they *actually* wanted and what they *actually* feared—not what he guessed they needed.

The information he learned from those surveys was pure gold for his marketing. He discovered that people weren't solely afraid of getting an incompetent lawyer to represent them. That was definitely a fear. But others were still considering the pros and cons of hiring a public defender and whether they should even pay for an attorney in the first place. They didn't even know the differences.

Once Lance figured this out, he completely changed his marketing and his intake interview. Instead of convincing people that his years of experience would be an asset to them, he started explaining how much more likely they were to get a favorable outcome if they hired a criminal defense lawyer instead of accepting the PD the state was offering.

He addressed the real fear they had, not the fear he *thought* they had. He then applied this to dozens of other fears he identified by interviewing his clients, which improved his marketing messaging and his intake process greatly.

Quick-Hitting Hack: We have a worksheet to help you better understand your clients' fears and desires. It's called the Fears, Frustrations, Wants, and Aspirations worksheet, or FFWA. We recommend using it during intake to turn that process into powerful data collection to fuel your marketing. You can find it here.

You can also check out Andy's video, *How We DOUBLE Google Conversion Rates for Law Firms*, which unpacks this concept further and is also available at this link.

(You'll find all the other bonuses from the book here or you can go to **yourdreamlawfirm.com**.)

Scan this QR Code
to Unlock This Bonus

If you haven't taken the time to thoroughly research your target clients' true fears and desires, your marketing is likely not resonating with your clients. You need to listen to your clients more!

We quoted our friend and mentor, Myron Golden, in an earlier chapter. Here's another wise quote we like from

Myron: "Whoever can articulate the problem the best is automatically thought to have the best solution." This means if you can demonstrate that you clearly understand what your clients fear, they will trust you enough to hire you.

So, do what it takes to find out exactly what they fear. Ask them questions. Do a survey. Gather *facts*. Then, tweak your marketing accordingly.

2. Build Strategic Partnerships & Referrals

A strategic partnership can be a lawyer's best friend, yet most lawyers pay very little attention to them. Harvey Mackay wrote a book about networking called *Dig Your Well Before You're Thirsty*. We *love* that title! It implies the point that you want to lay a foundation of network connections that can send you a steady stream of potential clients *before* you're in dire need of them.

What kind of strategic partnerships would make sense for your law firm? Ideally, these partnerships would be with other people or organizations that your target clients are likely to need. Ask yourself this question: "What products and services do my target clients potentially need *before* the case and during the case?" Make a list.

Here's an example list for a family law attorney:

- A therapist to deal with the stress and trauma.
- A child therapist for the same reason.
- Real estate agent to sell their house.

- Mortgage broker to deal with paying for a new house to live in.

- Apartment, if they don't want to buy a house.

- A new bank because their joint account will be dissolved.

- A temp agency because the client might have to go back to work.

- Tax attorney, because now their tax situation will change.

- Self-defense class for a woman now living alone.

- Criminal defense attorney if there's domestic violence issues.

- A gym because people often like to get into shape following a divorce.

We could go on. The point is, every person, organization, or service on this list presents an opportunity for a family law attorney to form a strategic partnership and generate referrals. For instance, you could say to the child therapist, "I'm a family law attorney. In my practice, I meet clients with kids who need therapy. I want to start sending you leads for free. I would love to meet you and find synergies between our practices." Maybe this leads to them sending you some clients. Give *them* value in exchange for them giving *you* value. This is networking at its finest. It helps both of you.

Do this sort of thing with every strategic partner you can think of. Make strategic partnerships with a real estate company, a local bank, a gym, a criminal defense attorney. Find a creative way to provide value to each other.

Think big on these partnerships. Most lawyers don't have a large enough network. A personal injury attorney might think, "All I've got is chiropractors and auto body shops," and stop there. Those are good, but there could be a lot more. What about restaurants, physical therapists, dog sitters, home chefs, and so on? The key is to find businesses that your clients will need.

Dig your well before you're thirsty!

Then, once you have your partners, don't neglect them. Send them gifts as a way of saying thank you. A box of chocolates, a dozen donuts, a mug with their logo on it. (Not your logo—that's not a gift, it's a promotion.) Or go bigger. SMB Team worked with a partner who gave us a lot of work. We knew he was a Dallas Cowboys fan, so we sent him two tickets to a Cowboys game so he and his son could go. He will remember that game forever and think of us each time he does.

You can't have too many partners. The more you cultivate, the better off you will be.

Don't try to collect them all at once. A lawyer we know, John Fisher, has several hundred strategic partners. He built this empire by sending out one email a day, requesting a partnership with a business or service. Just one a day! He kept up that streak for years. Most of the people he approached turned him down, but it didn't matter. Slowly, as he kept his streak going day after day, over years, he accumulated a solid and substantial group of partners. He calls this method "streaking" because it's all about keeping the streak alive. Incidentally, this also worked for John in getting reviews. Once a day, he asked for reviews from former clients. As a result, his firm has over 500 reviews.

Creating a strategic partnership is not a one-and-done thing. These relationships need to be cultivated and pursued, with ongoing effort. Stick with it over the long haul. Streaking makes it easy. No, don't run around naked. Just approach one new business a day.

> **Make multiple outside businesses your strategic partners. Exchange referrals with those partners and include those businesses and their services as part of your offer to potential clients.**

3. Gather Social Proof & Reviews

How do you choose a restaurant for date night? You probably look at reviews on Yelp or Google. When you go to Amazon to buy a toaster, how do you select the one you want? Most people look at the reviews from people who bought that toaster. When you order an Uber, how do you know you can trust the driver? You make sure the driver has mostly five-star reviews.

Reviews function as powerful social proof. It's people talking to other people, saying "buy this" or "whatever you do, don't buy *this*," and the stories of their experience are compelling.

Now think about someone buying the services of a lawyer. Hiring an attorney is potentially one of the most important decisions anyone can make in their lives.

Are they going to want to see reviews of the law firms they are considering? Of *course,* they will! They'd be foolish not to. But what if your law firm doesn't have any reviews anywhere? You may as well not even exist.

You *need* reviews. Lots of them. In fact, they're so important, Andy wrote an entire book about how to get more good reviews for your firm, called *5-Star Attorney: A Proven System Any Law Firm Can Use to Earn More Reviews, Attract More Qualified Leads, and Increase Profits.*

We're not going to repeat the content in Andy's book. Instead, we'll give you the highlights and invite you to learn more by picking it up yourself.

- Google ranks are based on reviews. If you want your law firm to be at the top of search inquiries, you need to have good reviews.

- Bazaarvoice Visual Syndication Network analyzed 50 million online reviews for all kinds of businesses to calculate the dollar worth of a review. They found that when *any* business hits 200 reviews, their revenue increases by an average of *44%.* Let's say your firm is doing $1M per year in revenue. Multiply that by .44, then divide by 200. You get $2,200. That's how much each review is worth to your business. That's *huge.*

- How do you get great reviews? You can't always count on satisfied clients remembering to leave you a review, so you have to *incentivize* them. We don't mean bribing them with gift certificates or bottles of whiskey to write good reviews. We mean incentivizing your *staff* to make sure reviews get posted. You could, for example, give a $100 bonus to any staff person responsible for securing a client's five-star review. That's an incentive for your employees to gently reach out and keep prompting until the satisfied client remembers to sit down and rave about you. And it's cost-effective. Remember how each review is worth somewhere around $2,200 for a firm bringing in one million in revenue? Even if you were to pay your staff *half* that amount per review, you would still come out ahead because you've paid them once and that review stays online forever, helping generate new revenue every year.

- Another hack we've seen some firms do is to offer a donation on behalf of your client for a 5-star review. The script is like this, "Attorney so-and-so loved serving you during your case. He/she would love to make a $50 donation to X charity on your behalf if you left us some feedback on your experience. Would you be open to us donating to X charity on your behalf?" Then if they say yes, send them your Google review link. Since you're not directly incentivizing the client, many firms do this.

Quick-Hitting Hack: Clients sometimes hesitate to write reviews because they don't know what to say. We recommend sending them an email along these lines, with the five questions below: "Hello, [Client!] Thank you for your willingness to write a review of your experience with our firm! We've found that many of our clients sometimes struggle knowing what to write. If that sounds like you, feel free to use the following prompts to guide your answers:

1. What was the problem you had before coming to our law firm?

2. Why did you pick us?

3. What did we do for you?

4. What were the results?

5. How did those results impact your life?

This script, properly executed, will prompt most people to post a review. And not just any review, but a good one. A believable one. A good review tells a story that other potential clients can relate to which will make them want to hire you!

- Even bad reviews are good. In fact, you *need* some bad reviews. Most people don't believe five-star reviews if there are *no* one-star reviews. They will think all that praise is either fake or bought. And, as a bonus, you can earn further goodwill with potential clients by responding to those bad reviews using the TEARS method.
  - **T**hank them for their feedback.
  - **E**mpathize with their situation.

- ○ **A**pologize for their frustration.
- ○ Show a willingness to **R**esolve.
- ○ Invite them to **S**witch channels and discuss the issue in a private forum (either email or phone call).

A well-written response in the TEARS method is not actually for the sake of the negative reviewer, but for the hundreds of potential clients who will read it and conclude you seem like a pretty stand up law firm owner. That's great marketing!

Embrace reviews and incentivize your staff to make sure you get them. Lots of them. The more, the better for you and your business.

Station 2: The Pitch

You've laid critical groundwork. Now, it's time to actually reach out to your target clients with a pitch! Let's talk about four strategies that will help elevate your pitch above the competition's.

4. Make a Stellar Offer

Imagine you need a babysitter. There are two in the neighborhood that you could hire.

Babysitter A—we'll call her Abby—says, "I'll watch your kids."

Babysitter B, Bobbi, says, "I'll watch your kids, and as soon as you leave, I'm going to cook them a healthy dinner, do all the dishes, and play games with them all night. Then, I'll read them a bedtime story and have them in bed and asleep by the time you get home. I'll also straighten up the house. And by the way, I'm trained in CPR, first aid, and child development."

Abby charges $10 per hour. Bobbi charges $20. But most people would still choose to hire Bobbi, despite the fact that she's *twice* as expensive.

Why? *Bobbi has the better offer.* She is giving much more value per dollar, even though she charges twice as much. When you get an offer that good, you don't turn it down, even if there's a cheaper option! What if Bobbi charged $22 per hour? We're guessing you would still choose her as the better person to babysit your kids.

Contrary to popular opinion, most people would not cite price as *the* most important factor when buying a product or service. It's an important factor, sure—but what's even more important to people is the *value* per dollar. Remember, if you're the best, no one expects you to be the cheapest. And if you're the cheapest, no one expects you to be the best.

Imagine you run a family law practice. Remember Sara from Chapter 4, the mom looking to get a divorce but maintain primary custody of her kids? We discussed some of Sara's questions in the previous chapter, but let's say that by the time she contacts your firm, new questions are looming. The divorce is feeling more real, and she's worried about how it will affect her kids. They're ten and twelve, and she's concerned they could be traumatized by their parents splitting up.

Your law firm *could* just provide Sara with a divorce. But what if you went the extra mile? Suppose you teamed up with a family therapist. And suppose you made this offer to Sara: "When you hire us as your attorney, we're going to give you two free sessions with this child therapist to help your kids deal with their new situation."

Just like Bobbi, the $20 per hour babysitter, that offer from your law firm provides more value. Most potential clients would want to go with you and would feel like you care.

Remember that the solution you're presenting to your potential client's problem creates new problems. In Sara's case, you're providing a solution to her unhappy marriage—the divorce—but the divorce creates new problems for her, like concerns for her kids' mental health. She's also going to be dealing with navigating life as a single mom, moving out of her current residence, untangling her various assets, possibly seeking a new job, and so on. When you form your offer with those new potential problems in mind, you can provide value that goes above and beyond legal expertise to help the potential client.

Presentation is also important here. Think of how infomercials typically work. A company selling a knife set doesn't just come out and say, "Here's this awesome knife set." Instead, they first talk about *one* knife and how great it is. Then they say, "If you buy this knife, we'll *also* give you a set of paring knives." Then, "If you buy this knife in the next hour, you'll *not only* get the knife and the paring knife set, but we'll throw in a cutting board and a knife sharpener." And so on. They break down the product into its component parts to make it seem like the customer is getting a truly awesome deal.

If you look at any criminal defense attorney's website, you'll see something like, "Come in for a free case evaluation!" But if a potential client looking for a defense attorney is looking through several websites, they're not going to be impressed by this. A "free case evaluation," when offered by every attorney, is a ho-hum offer.

But what if you take a different approach and spell out everything you're going to do during that case evaluation?

Come in for a free case evaluation and talk with an expert attorney about all of the following:

- Comprehensive review of your arrest record
- Full explanation of all your charges
- Discussion of potential weaknesses in your case
- Clear explanation of potential penalties and fines
- Review of potential defenses for your case

You probably do all of those things at every consultation anyway, but your potential clients don't know that. Breaking down those consultations into every component part helps clarify the tremendous value you provide during those sessions. Now, which firm is the potential client going to contact for a free consultation?

Yours. You've given the impression of exceptional value to the client and they're impressed. Even before they step foot into your office for that consultation, they're moving closer to sign with you.

And yes, crafting an offer is important, even for your free services. Don't be fooled, thinking that you don't have to sell something just because it's free. If you want to get potential clients through your doors, you've got to sell your services like Babysitter Bobbi.

You can do this for any type of law practice. Do a brain dump of what you do during a consult. Write it all out. Then, frame your offer so that each item on the list is presented in turn to your potential clients. Do that and you're sure to increase the number of leads that convert to paying cases.

Here are a final few ideas to juice up your offer to clients, so they can't possibly turn you down.

- What other services can you provide? Consider including those as "add ons." If you're a family law attorney, you could tell your potential clients that not only will you handle their divorce, but you'll also throw in a free estate plan, since the divorce is going to upend whatever financial plan they had in place. Or if you specialize in personal injury, offer to do a free defense of any traffic ticket the client might get in the next ten years. Think about the skills that you already have and how they could be employed to add additional value to your offer.

- You can create more perceived value *without* discounting your prices by offering "free value." For example, you may have seen ads for cruises where they say, "If you sign up for a cruise, we'll give you $400 to spend on board!" They don't *discount* their price, but they do give extra value. We know one lawyer who applied this strategy to his practice. When someone hired him for $5K, he put $1,500 into their trust account. Just like that. Free and clear. The client got more value, and the lawyer did not devalue his brand by discounting his rates.

- Consider what you could offer your clients if you increased your fee by ten times. Think outside the box. Maybe you pick up your client for court in a limo. You buy them a $1,000 suit for court appearances. You supply a case of champagne when you win. You take them and a dozen of their best friends to an NBA game to celebrate. Go crazy. Make the offer so enticing that the client would be insane to not hire you. Then, when you've got this insane offer mapped out, dial it back a little to something more reasonable. You might offer them an Uber ride to court, or give them a discount coupon at a clothing store where they could buy a suit. Take your insane imaginary offer and translate it into something saner. By doing this exercise, you'll come up with ideas that will sweeten your offer.

All these examples of adding value are not meant to be the final word. Use your imagination and think of ways *you* can add value to the services you provide. Don't be like Abby, whose offer was simply, "I'll watch your kids." Be Bobbi who dazzled you with her unbelievable offer.

5. Get a Unique Selling Proposition (USP)

To illustrate the Unique Selling Proposition, a timeless marketing principle, let's take a drive down Route 66, which runs from Chicago to Santa Monica. Back in the day, it was called

"The Main Street of America" because that's how a lot of people got to the West.

Every long-distance highway has gas stations and motels, and Route 66 has hundreds of them. At some point, one of the motel owners along Route 66 decided to get creative about a way to ensure drivers stopped at *his* motel, over all others. His solution inspired many other similar efforts. So, what did they do?

The motel owners turned themselves into tourist attractions. One of them built their motel in the style of Native American wigwams and called itself "The Wigwam Motel." Another one made itself look like Main Street in an old western movie. Roy's Motel and Cafe distinguished itself by its giant neon sign, which you could see from miles away.

Each gimmicky location was *differentiating* themselves from the competition. They gave themselves a *Unique Selling Proposition* (USP) and in doing that, they created interest and amped up their business.

As the owner of a law firm, you should consider doing the same. We're not implying you should erect a giant neon sign in front of your firm. But you *do* need to find your USP.

Here's a perfect example. One of our clients was a family law and criminal defense attorney who hired us to help her scrub her Google profile. When people Googled her name, an old DUI case against her from her years in college came up, which she felt deeply embarrassed about. She thought that DUI would hurt her business. Who would want to hire someone so reckless as their lawyer?

We could have helped her bury the result, but we had a better idea. We said, "Wait a second. You don't *want* to bury that. You need to *lean into it.*"

She was baffled.

We explained, "That's your differentiator! You need to tell your clients, 'Look, I understand that good people can make stupid decisions. And I understand that just because you get arrested for a DUI, it doesn't define you. I know exactly what it's like to be sitting in that defendant's chair, and that's why I'm going to defend you wholeheartedly.'"

She was also divorced, so we continued, "Tell your divorce clients, 'I know exactly what it's like to not know if you're going to get alimony. I know what it's like to be dependent on a settlement to pay your bills. I know what it's like to worry about what this will do to your kids. I've had to navigate those questions personally, and that's why I'm going to make sure this process is as smooth as it can possibly be for you.'" She thought her experiences detracted from her reputation as an attorney. Actually, they served as amazing USPs.

Ask yourself what makes your law firm unique. Is it your personal story? To see how to use your personal story to create your USP, here are some examples from practicing attorneys:

- Dan Newlin, who we've mentioned before, is a personal injury attorney who became a lawyer after working for years as a deputy for the Sheriff's Department. After seeing hundreds of people get injured in car accidents and then screwed over by their insurance companies in court, he decided he wanted to come to their defense as an attorney.

- An immigration attorney is herself an immigrant and had to navigate the immigration process firsthand.

- Michael Barszcz is a medical malpractice attorney in Orlando who used to be a medical doctor and can speak with an unusual level of accuracy, understanding, and insight on behalf of his clients.

All these lawyers use their USPs in their ads and social media posts. They lean into what makes them unique. They attract clients in the same way the giant dinosaurs on Route 66 used to attract motorists by the thousands.

So, what makes up your Unique Selling Proposition? Is it your unique way of handling cases? Your "promise" to all clients? Your niche specialty? Your personal story? Or the big checks you get for clients? Can you break this down for each case type you handle? All of these will differentiate your law firm in the marketplace.

> **Quick-Hitting Hack:** We've created a tool to help you create your own Unique Selling Proposition as a law firm owner, so you can truly convey why they should choose you over all other firms. You can access that tool here.
>
> (You'll find all the other bonuses from the book here or you can go to **yourdreamlawfirm.com**.)
>
>
> **Scan this QR Code to Unlock This Bonus**

6. Jump on the First Mover Advantage

McDonald's does not make the best hamburgers, yet McDonald's sells more hamburgers than anyone else in the world. Why should a seller of decidedly mediocre hamburgers rise to the top of the hamburger chain wars?

For one simple reason. They were the first restaurant chain to figure out a system selling hamburgers at scale. Hamburgers used to be made one at a time, by hand. McDonald's mechanized the process so they could produce hamburgers by the hundreds every hour. And because they were the first to figure that out, they still dominate the market.

McDonald's reaped the benefits of *first mover advantage*, which describes the momentum you get as a business from being the first to break into any given market. The golden arches captured the market early and have held onto it ever since.

There are many examples of first mover advantage. Coke was first in the cola war. Pepsi was second, and it's *still* working to catch up. Uber and Lyft provide almost identical services, but Uber was first, which means Lyft will always be second. And so on.

If you want to capture a market, be the first on the scene.

For a long time, lawyers weren't allowed to advertise. When they were finally given the green light to advertise, the smart ones jumped on the yellow pages, TV, radio, and billboards. The *smartest* ones advertised heavily on those platforms right off the bat. Everyone saw their ads (and criticized them) constantly. Some of those lawyers crushed their competition and maintained their dominance for years.

Later, when the internet started cranking up, lawyers who grabbed domain names early on rode the wave of first mover advantage. To this day domains like personalinjurylawyer.com, duilawyer.com, and caraccidentlawyer.com are phenomenally popular. The owners of those domains make fortunes every year.

The same thing happened with Google Ads and Facebook Ads. As soon as those came along, the lawyers who jumped on them and were the *first* to use them made a ton of money.

As we write these words in 2024, social media is the new thing. Lawyers who arrived early on the scene and crushed social media are bringing in lots of new cases and tons of revenue.

We can't predict what the next marketing opportunity will look like or where it will come from. But you can be sure *something* new is going to come along in the next year, month, or week.

Look for it. Maybe have someone on staff whose job it is to sniff out the next big thing in marketing. When you find it, test it, and if it works … pounce. Grab on and don't let go. Firms that move first always make the most money. Make sure you're that firm! But, don't abandon your more predictable marketing streams as you test new ones.

7. Choose Your All-In Strategy

What happens if you don't get there first? In that case (in any case), you can still dominate the marketing space by choosing an *all-in* strategy.

The most successful people in marketing are typically not dabblers. They don't try a little bit of TikTok, a small Google Ads effort, a few billboards, sprinkle in some radio pitches, and try 50 other things. Instead, they find one to three things that they go absolutely *all in* on. Typically, this works best when they choose a medium that aligns with their strengths so they can sustain their enthusiasm and consistency.

Going *all in* like this can generate massive results for your business, creating a blue ocean opportunity for your firm where nobody can compete with you in your chosen space. What are some examples of an *all-in* strategy? It varies. Some firms go *all in* on Google Ads, using that as their dominant channel. Other firms go *all in* on TV, doing mass advertising with the majority of their budget. Some firms go *all in* with SEO, and others generate eight figures of cases a year from going *all in* on social media.

What's the one marketing strategy you want to go *all in* on? There's a huge opportunity available to you when you identify that, figure it out, then become excellent at marketing yourself in that focused approach.

From there, build up other marketing channels as secondary channels, rather than trying to be a jack of all trades and doing a "little bit" of hundreds of other marketing approaches. Keep in mind that your *all-in* strategy can change as your firm's priorities evolve. On Step 3 of the Lawyer Legacy Staircase, when you function as a Solo Practitioner, your *all-in* strategy might be to lean heavily into your network and generate word of mouth as your main marketing effort. Your *all-in* strategy may shift to Google Ads once you're navigating Step 4 (Small Business Owner), then evolve to social media ads when you reach Step 5 (Law Firm CEO).

There's no one right or wrong way to do this, and there are pros and cons to every strategy. If you decide you want to go *all in* on "top of mind awareness" approaches, like TV or social media, it's likely that you're not going to be as strong on Google. And that's okay—you're choosing to devote your time, effort, focus, and marketing budget to go *all in* on those "top of mind" forums. Similarly, if you've gone all in with Demand Marketing, you're going to be there when people search for you—but not necessarily pop up in their view when they *aren't* searching for you.

Ultimately, you want to arrive at omnipresence in the marketing spheres, where you're utilizing a mix of multiple approaches. But until you have the massive budget and team that omnipresence requires, lean in on one to three *all in* strategies. Go big, stay consistent, learn how to market in that space with *excellence*, and watch the amazing impact on your lead generation.

Station 3: The Afterglow

You've made your pitch—now what? Don't let those potential clients get away! Continue to woo them with your follow-up and by gathering data.

ANDY STICKEL NARRATES

8. Follow Up Religiously!

I've been revisiting my college years with my examples and stories, so what the heck. Let's stick with that vibe.

When I was a broke college kid, as many are, I got the bright idea of starting a business where I converted VHS tapes to DVDs. This was when the world was making the transition phase from mostly VHS to mostly DVD.

I put out signs on the side of the road at various places around town where people would see them during rush hour. The signs were simple: "I can convert your VHS to DVD," and my phone number. Those signs worked like a charm. The first week I put them out, I got 40 calls in one afternoon. "I've got like 50 home movies on VHS," one person told me. "I'd love to get them onto DVDs. Once I get home, I can collect them and bring them over."

I was charging $10 per tape. I figured my fortune was made! … But it wasn't.

The first two weeks, I did not get a single person to actually bring me their VHS tapes. Not one. I was still getting calls from people interested—dozens a day—but no one actually brought me their tapes!

Luckily, I had saved everyone's name and phone number in an Excel spreadsheet. After two weeks with no one bringing me their tapes, I called every single one of them back. I'd say,

"Hey, a couple of weeks ago we talked about your VHS tapes. Are you still interested in transferring them?"

"Oh yeah!" they'd say. "I'm so glad you called!" They told me they had forgotten about the tapes, or they'd lost my number, or they got too busy. There were lots of reasons they didn't call back, but none of those reasons involved them not wanting me to do the transfers.

The first week I called people back, I made $5K. I felt like I'd won the lottery! Really, all I did was apply a marketing principle called *follow-up.*

I continued my follow-up call-back system and kept getting customers. Sometimes I would have to call people back as many as five times, but if I kept at it, eventually almost everyone brought me their tapes.

This taught me an important lesson: *the fortune is in the follow-up.* Following up on initial calls has been a core principle of any business model I've been involved with ever since then. It's crucial.

The fortune is in the follow-up.

We want you to try a little experiment right now. Put down this book and go find five law firms in your area that compete with you. Click around their website. Give them a call inquiring about their practice. Just a simple call for information.

Now, pay attention to how many of the firms call you back. See how many of those firms follow you around with ads on your social media accounts.

We're willing to bet not even one of them will do that. This means you have a golden opportunity if you commit to a robust system of following up on initial contacts, because there's a good chance you'll be the only one doing it in your market.

The research group Forrester found that most people will hire a business after a *minimum* of five "touches" with that business.[11] That applies to law firms as well. Five touches could include seeing your Facebook ad, a blog on your website, spotting your billboard ad, stumbling across a YouTube video, or any number of other visible points of contact.

Five times.

Why not help them get to five quicker? When someone calls you, have a system in place that calls them back in under 30 minutes if nobody answers their call or if they submit a form.

Follow-up can happen in one of two ways.

1. **Traditional Outreach.** Follow up with potential clients through a text, phone call, or email.
2. **Social Media Retargeting.** Use social media remarketing to follow people around on the internet with ads after they've visited your website at least once.

---

[11] Clark, Benedict. 2023. The B2B Customer Journey: Back to The Basics. Acquire: Customer Journey. 23. June. https://acquire.io/blog/b2b-customer-journey#:~:text=More%20than%20half%20of%20all,to%20purchase%2C%20according%20to%20Forrester (accessed: 15. November 2023).

Both are effective, although the second method scales more easily. Its disadvantage is that it can feel kind of creepy, so you need to be careful when using it. We'll come back to that issue later.

Use either method or both, but *don't* neglect follow-up. Follow-up gets you clients. It's true in any business, including lawyering.

9. Find Out Why They Didn't Hire You

Follow-up is crucial both before *and* after you work with clients. Do it with clients who hire you and clients who don't. For instance, what if the potential new client doesn't hire you and you follow up with them afterwards with no response? That's when you ask them to complete a **didn't hire survey.** Send it about two weeks after the unsuccessful consultation.

Here are the questions your "didn't hire survey" should ask:

- Were you considering hiring our law firm?

- Are you still looking for an attorney?

- What ultimately led to your decision to not hire our firm? Please be as specific as possible.

- Is there anything you think would prevent you from being successful in your case?

- Anything else that you'd like to tell us?

- Would you like us to follow up with you? If so, please leave your phone number below.

There are many reasons people won't hire you. Once you know those reasons, you've got what you need to do a better job educating potential clients of the value of hiring you. You won't necessarily get the one that got away, but that lost opportunity at least gave you information you can use to land the next client. Revise your intake and consultation script accordingly.

You can gather similarly important data from **exit surveys.** If a client communicates that they were dissatisfied—find out why. Even the clients who are satisfied might have helpful information to communicate: "Hey, just so you know, [this and this] happened." You'll learn so much from those surveys that you couldn't discover any other way, and once you know about points of breakdown, you can start making changes to improve them.

We've visited Stations 1, 2, and 3. Marketing commandments to follow before the pitch, during the pitch, and after the pitch. Our final two commandments have to do with principles you want to keep in mind *all* the time.

Station 4: Global Principles

In the Carrabba's kitchen, the global principles were things like, "Cleanliness at all times" and "Only use fresh food." In your marketing kitchen, it's "Become brand dominant" and "Track ROI as a whole."

10. Become Brand Dominant

One of the best outcomes of consistently investing in your marketing is that you strengthen your brand recognition.

And your brand is like a moat. Once it gets big enough, it becomes hard for others to compete with you and can act as a buffer against negative reviews or bad press. When there's *so much content* out there connected to your brand, the good content overwhelms any potentially negative stuff. That's the gift of becoming brand dominant. It's also a strategy to lean into if you didn't manage to seize the "first mover advantage" momentum.

Make no mistake—brand dominance is *absolutely* a possibility for you. A lot of lawyers get intimidated by more successful lawyers. They see someone pulling tens of millions of dollars in revenue every year and think, *I can't compete with that*. Or they see them spending millions on advertising, and they look at their marketing budget and think, *I'm doomed to being second fiddle*.

Wrong. Anyone can be competitive!

The thing to remember about that super successful firm is that they started out where you are. No one (unless they inherited an already successful business) *starts out* successful. They build that success through smart marketing and persistence.

Don't compare their *after* to your *before.*

Instead, build brand dominance with three basic principles:

1. **Quantity.** Put out a lot of stuff. And, when you find something that works, double down on it. When it comes to content, Andy has 1,600+ videos on You-Tube and has filmed hundreds of Facebook Ads. Before Andy made any videos, he kept his video

camera on his desk for six months and sweated over making his first video. That's where he started! He doesn't have 1,600 videos because he's some kind of superman. He just finally got started and then kept at it. Brand dominance comes from putting out a *lot* of stuff.

2. **Consistency.** Don't just try a lot of marketing initiatives for one month and then give up. This is a lifelong commitment. Regardless of what you go all in on (PPC, SEO, content marketing, offline, etc.), stay consistent with it. If you want to make content, then make it on a regular basis. Do one video a week for three to five years. Or put up ten Facebook Ads every month for one year. Create confidence by keeping to a schedule. (We'll talk more about this in the next two chapters.)

3. **Omnipresence.** Your ultimate goal with your marketing is to appear *everywhere* to your target clients. Dominate one to three platforms and then build up your secondary marketing on all other channels. Don't stop until your potential clients see you everywhere they go. You want to be "inescapable."

Do these three things over the long term and you will eventually achieve brand dominance. That's been our strategy. We create videos that help lawyers solve problems. This book is an extension of the same effort. We've been helping lawyers day in and day out for years. As a result, we're one of the top brands that lawyers think of when they need help growing their law firm via coaching, marketing, fractional CFOs, or virtual assistants.

Again, we're not telling you this to brag. We're telling you this to show you that brand domination is not some magical thing. It happened because we made it happen. You can do the same for your piece of the market.

11. Track ROI as a WHOLE

The final commandment of marketing is to track your marketing ROI *as a whole*—don't get mired in the details of which ad is more successful or which marketing expense doesn't seem to be paying off. Everything is connected, and your visibility through your marketing works together as a whole to bring you new clients.

Here's an example to illustrate what we mean. We had a client who was doing very well with her marketing. Staci's firm had a robust organic SEO system in place, and it was bringing the firm good leads. She was so happy with her online marketing that she figured the firm's offline marketing could be cut.

She came to us and said, "I'm going to get rid of my billboards."

"We don't think you should do that," we cautioned.

"Why not? Those billboards don't do anything for my SEO."

"You don't know that. There's a good chance people are Googling you *because* of your billboards."

Staci eyed us suspiciously. She went ahead with her decision and got rid of several billboard ads that had been displayed prominently in town for years.

That was a mistake. Practically overnight, her firm's SEO leads plummeted. It was like someone had turned off the tap. All because she scrapped the billboards.

There's an old saying in marketing: "I know half the money I spend on advertising is wasted, I just don't know which half." The flip side of that is that you also don't know which half is *not* wasted.

The whole advertising world is like an interdependent eco-system where one small disturbance can lead to a larger effect, like the butterfly effect. In the billboard example, someone may have been driving to work and registered the name of the law firm, but they couldn't follow up with a phone call right away. They were driving!

Later, when they got home, they might have taken out their phone, looked up the lawyer they saw on the billboard, and then clicked on Staci's firm's website. Or, they search using a generic term and recognize her law firm from the billboards, causing them to click. Staci thought all the interest in her firm was coming from online sources, but she was wrong. Offline sources contribute to online sources.

Whenever we launch an ad campaign on Facebook, our organic search numbers always go up. Why? Because people who see the ad go to Google and search for us. Google sees we have a higher click-through-rate and lower bounce rate (people quickly leaving the website and returning to Google) and responds by increasing our search rankings. The whole system feeds on itself in a positive feedback loop.

Don't get us wrong, we believe trying to pinpoint where signed cases come from is vitally important. But, in most instances, you aren't going to know the whole story of how *this* ad led to *this* case. A saner approach is to look at the overall expense of your marketing. Check your total marketing budget against the number of signed cases you're getting. That tells you your overall ROI, which is a better measure of your marketing's overall effectiveness.

Say you spent $15K on marketing last month and you got 30 cases. That means you spent $500 per case. That's your CTA (Cost to Acquire). That's the number you should be looking at and evaluating. Is it a good CTA? Not so good? Do you need to increase your marketing budget to improve that number? Do you change strategy, like implement a better follow-up system or generate a better offer? Use your overall CTA to evaluate your marketing, not one small segment of it—because it all ties together.

The key takeaway from this section is that one piece of advertising can lead to another piece of advertising and they work together collectively to produce your leads. Having a wide range of advertising across multiple media forms is the proven road to success.

Market Like a Circus Genius

Marketing is nothing new. The strategies we've outlined in this chapter are all time-tested ways to get customers. They work in any industry, and they will work for your law firm.

There's a great book by Joe Vitale and Jeffrey Gitomer called *There's a Customer Born Every Minute: P. T. Barnum's Amazing 10 "Rings of Power" for Creating Fame, Fortune, and a Business Empire Today—Guaranteed!* It outlines all the strategies P. T. Barnum, the circus magnate, used to get rich. He had 10 key

LAW FIRM GROWTH ACCELERATOR

strategies, and guess what, they're pretty much the same as the ones we've talked about here.

P.T. Barnum died in 1891. That's more than 130 years ago.

What can he teach you about marketing your law firm in the 21st century?

Plenty.

Most people think of P.T. Barnum as the circus guy, but before he did circuses, Barnum got rich with a museum similar to a Ripley's Believe It or Not. He used every strategy that we've presented in this chapter to get people into that museum. He understood what people wanted, their fears and desires. He gave them extra value. He advertised everywhere—newspapers, pamphlets, billboards, playbills, sandwich boards, kids in the streets shouting invitations to the museum, whatever was available in his day.

Later, when running his circuses, P.T. Barnum leaned into these marketing strategies with even more gusto. He had a memorable USP. This was the Greatest Show on Earth! He made sure he was brand dominant. When people thought CIRCUS, they thought BARNUM.

Marketing doesn't change. What changes is *tactics*. These days, marketing your law firm will probably include things like SEO and social media. Those forms of advertising weren't even a thought in P.T. Barnum's day. The *tactics* and *tools* have changed—but the strategies have remained constant.

At the end of the day, marketing is a simple process. It's *communicating a message* to people where they are *spending their attention.* Right now, the two biggest marketing opportunities are search engines and social media. That's where people's attention is *today.* With that in mind, there are two ways you can get in front of potential clients:

1. **Demand Marketing.** This is a reactive strategy. You get leads when potential clients search for you. They are in demand of your services.

2. **Awareness Marketing.** This is a proactive strategy. You build awareness in potential clients *before* they're looking for you.

Your job is to align the right message, using the right vehicle, to the right people. So, in the next two chapters, we're going to break down how both opportunities work and how you can best take advantage of them.

Chapter 6 | Takeaways

1. Marketing tactics will change, but solid marketing principles are timeless.

2. Some of the most important marketing principles include:

    a. It's vital to understand the desires and fears of your target clients and speak to those with your copy.

    b. Social proof—like reviews—are crucial for getting clients in your door.

    c. You can distinguish yourself from the competition with a stellar offer and a Unique Selling Proposition.

    d. Implementing a strong follow-up system is crucial.

3. Marketing effectiveness is best evaluated when looking at your Marketing ROI as a whole rather than in component parts, since the advertising world functions as an interconnected ecosystem.

4. The most important criteria to look for when hiring a marketing team: Are they putting the client's needs first and foremost in their advertising recommendations?

CHAPTER 7

DEMAND MARKETING

HOW TO CREATE A PAGE-ONE GOOGLE STRATEGY THAT WORKS

"Don't push people to where you want to be;
meet them where they are."

—Meghan Keaney Anderson

Imagine a guy named Mike gets into his car one evening to head home from work. In the crush of rush hour traffic, Mike ends up getting rear-ended. He pulls off to the side of the road, gets out of the car, and checks himself out. Thankfully, he feels fine. He decides he's not really injured. Then he looks over his car—the bumper's crunched and both tail lights are out.

Mike decides he'd better document the damage to his car. He pulls out his phone and Googles, "What do you take pictures of after a car accident?" The first listing is a blog post. It's run as a sponsored ad from a personal injury lawyer, but the article looks good. Mike clicks on the link, registers a few key points, and then gets distracted when the police pull up. Mike turns his phone off, shoves it in his pocket, and goes to talk to them.

Later that night, Mike is back at home and unwinding. He scrolls through Facebook and notices an ad—it's a video from the same personal injury law firm whose blog post he'd clicked before. The video's title is: "Three Tricks Car Insurance Companies Use to Screw Accident Victims Out of Paying Their Medical Bills." Mike watches about 45 seconds of the video, then scrolls down to something else.

A few minutes later, it occurs to Mike that he should check the weather since he's playing golf the next morning. He opens his Weather Channel app, and the Google display ad is *another* one from that same personal injury law firm. This one is just an image with the law firm's logo and name. He barely notices it because he's looking at tomorrow's high temperature, but subconsciously, it registers. Mike shuts his phone off, plugs in the charger, then goes to sleep.

In the middle of the night, Mike wakes up. The pain from the accident is finally starting to kick in. He gets up to take some ibuprofen and pulls up YouTube, typing in "back pain relief." He clicks on the first video and waits while the ad plays. It's another one from that same law firm. He watches for 35 seconds, clicks "skip" as soon as he can, and watches the video about back pain relief stretches. As he does, though, he's still thinking about that law firm. *Maybe I need a personal injury lawyer,* he thinks, rubbing his neck.

He's now seen the name of that personal injury law firm about four different times. The next morning, he goes to Google and actually searches for the name of the firm to check them out.

The firm pops up and he notices that they have *tons* of five-star reviews. He thinks, *Okay. That's pretty interesting.* He Googles "personal injury attorney" to research a few more options. That same personal injury law firm is at the top of the list. Number one, with more reviews than anybody else. Mike hits the phone icon button next to the law firm and calls them.

And *that's* how people book appointments. It's also why it's so hard to track cost to acquire.

This beautiful happily-ever-after comes about as a result of two types of marketing working harmoniously together. We're going to spend the next two chapters discussing how to use both of them to make more dreams come true.

- Several different PPC and SEO strategies ensured that the personal injury firm showed up high on page one of Google. That's *Demand Marketing* which you use to ensure that your firm's name is in front of people who are actively *in demand* of your services. This chapter is going to teach you more about PPC, SEO, and getting on page one of Google (the right way).

- The "follow-up" approach, where the ads for the personal injury firm started following Mike all over the internet. That effect is accomplished by putting a pixel on your landing page or website. A pixel is a little piece of code that tracks internet behavior and tells websites like Google, Facebook, and Instagram to show them more ads after they visit one of your pages. We're going to do a deep dive into more Awareness Marketing tools like these in our next chapter.

LAW FIRM GROWTH ACCELERATOR

Remember, the internet and advertising world is like an interrelated ecosystem, where everything works together. By learning more about how you can use both Demand and Awareness Marketing tools, you can optimize your firm's ability to both get potential clients' attention *and* secure them as signed clients.

Demand vs. Awareness Marketing

We first talked about Demand and Awareness Marketing when we discussed the different steps of evolving your identity on the Lawyer Legacy Staircase in Chapter 2. Demand Marketing tends to help lawyers get to Step 4, when they're operating as a Small Business Manager. Demand Marketing will usually bring in the highest quality leads, but since only 3% of the market is here at any given time, you can usually handle them with a small team. Despite that modest introduction, Demand Marketing can cause tremendous growth for your firm.

Only while you have a demand strategy in place, Awareness Marketing is usually the best way to help you get to Step 5, where you function more as a Law Firm CEO. It will generate far more leads for you, but with more leads comes the necessity of a system and team to sort through them all, since they will be less qualified. Only with that enhanced infrastructure will your firm be able to identify the right-fit cases and ensure that no golden leads fall through the cracks. You need a larger, more competent team to handle the influx of leads that come with Awareness Marketing.

Now, we have seen many firms go "all in" on Demand Marketing and use that marketing channel to become Law Firm CEO. But, most times, if you want to reduce your cost to acquire and increase your lead volume greatly, expanding into Awareness is the answer.

We'll jog your memory, because that was many pages ago. The difference between the two marketing approaches is simple.

- **Demand Marketing.** This mainly refers to Google Ads, Local Services Ads, and SEO marketing. Your potential lead does a Google search for your law specialty ("personal injury lawyer," for example). You react by showing them an ad or your organic listing pops up. The person is in *demand* of your services, which is where the name comes from. This method is also called "reactive" marketing since they are reacting to a Google search.

- **Awareness Marketing.** This mainly covers social media marketing and other forms of traditional marketing that involve building *awareness* among your potential clients, even when they're not actively looking for you. This is also called "proactive" marketing since they are taking the initiative rather than waiting for a Google search.

Demand Marketing is when someone is searching for you and finds you. Awareness Marketing is when someone is *not* searching for you and sees you.

Now let's talk about how to get your firm a starring role on the number one most-used website in the world. Google.

Your Page-One Google Strategy

Your page-one Google strategy is your *top* Demand Marketing strategy. That means you need to learn how to embrace Google Ads, Google SEO, and your website.

Google Ads is, in essence, paying to play by showing a sponsored ad at the top of Google when a prospective client in your market types in a relevant keyword to your practice area.

SEO stands for search engine optimization. It means you're optimizing your website to show up high on Google (for free) when a prospective client in your market types in a keyword relevant to your practice area. That optimizing process includes writing content a certain way, building your website a certain way, and having other websites linking to you intentionally, all so that more organic search traffic leads to your website and/or calling you. Building up your SEO takes considerable time, which is why we also recommend a Google Ads strategy which can feature you on page one of Google almost immediately.

Now, why is page *one* of Google such a big deal? For one, people go to Google when they have a need (i.e. they are more likely to be "in market" to buy something). And few, if any, people go to page two when they review Google results. If they don't find what they want on page one, they generally just type in new search terms to get a fresh page of results.

It's not just getting on page one that's crucial. It's getting *as close to the top* of page one as possible, for the right search terms.

Here's why. Most people focus their attention on whatever is near the top of that first page. That means the top firm is going to get their pick of leads and they're going to take the quality ones. The remaining leads—the less desirable ones (cough-crazy-clients-cough-cough)—will fall to firms further down the list. If your firm is near the bottom of page one, you're most likely getting calls from clients who have been turned down by or couldn't afford several attorneys before they called you.

You don't want to be one of those firms, trying to find good leads where there aren't any. You want your firm to be front and center at the top of Google's page one.

But let's say, as things currently stand, your firm doesn't yet have good Google rankings. You've set a goal to grow your law firm this year and you know that means you need to get more leads from Google, which is how the majority of "ready-to-hire" clients will find you. So how do you get to page one?

There are two ways to get your firm on page one. You can *buy* your way in, or you can *build* your way in.

- **Buying your way in** is your short-term strategy to get yourself on page one of Google. You simply buy ads. In doing so, you can get yourself on page one, on *day* one. But don't confuse short term with temporary. You're never going to want to stop running your Google Ads.

- **Building your way in** is a great long-term strategy. You do this by generating organic SEO (search engine optimization) through creating a *ton* of content, getting your website linked on other high-authority websites, and gathering loads of reviews. The reason this is a long-term strategy is because you need *time* to build those organic results. In fact, one element that contributes to your SEO is simply the age of your website domain. The longer it's existed, the more Google trusts that you're a reliable web page to serve in their search results. Building your way in is done through accumulating content, authority, and trust. It's a good strategy and well worth the time! Having all that content on the internet can pay dividends long into the future. However, depending on your market and practice area, it typically takes six to 24 months before you see results from a robust SEO strategy.

The smartest lawyers have a combined strategy for their page one Google plan. They allocate a large piece of their budget to showing ads on page one so they can get leads immediately (buy your way in), and they *also* allow time for building up their website's rankings through posting blog content with targeted keywords to generate more organic SEO traffic (build your way in). Over time (if done right), that second strategy will move your firm to the top of the Map listings and make you an overall page one Google baller.

There are four methods to dominate page one Google search results and they can be nicely divided between those two categories.

Buy Your Way In (Ads):

1. Local Services Ads (LSAs)
2. Search Ads

Build Your Way In (SEO):

3. Local SEO, including the Map Pack
4. Organic SEO

We've listed these in the general order you'll want to engage them. Let's look at each one.

BUY Your Way In: Google Ads

Buying your way in is done primarily through the use of ads. Google Ads fall into the category of PPC (pay per click, or sometimes pay per call). And using Google Ads is one of the most powerful ways you can grow your law firm. At the time of this writing, Google is the number one highest-traffic website in the world. It gets more eyeballs every day than any other website! Google Ads is the only way to get your law firm to show up on page one of Google practically overnight.

However, there are a lot of false beliefs that attorneys have around Google advertising. Many lawyers assume that Google Ads are too expensive and their small firm won't be able to compete. But most assumptions about Google advertising aren't true. We're going to help you identify cost-effective ways to use these marketing tools and strategies to ensure you're maximizing your potential profit with every click.

More than 77% of Google's $307B in revenue comes from advertisements shown through Google Ads (that's $238B). People don't spend $238B on something that doesn't work.[12]

What percentage of your marketing budget should you devote to Google advertising? After interviewing and coaching hundreds of law firm owners and their firms, we've seen that firms who do $5M or less in revenue per year (and are growing fast) spend about 50% of their entire marketing budget on Google Ads. Yes, really—50%. While this can vary based on practice area, this should show you the power of Google Ads.

Google Ads will consistently be one of your most powerful ways to get clients. The two main forms they come in are Local Services Ads (LSAs) and Search Ads.

LSAs (Local Services Ads)

Activity time! Pull out your phone and type "personal injury attorney" into the search bar. The pictures that come up at the top are Local Services Ads (or LSAs) which feature businesses in your local area. How does Google know where you live? Easy. It uses your IP address or GPS to track your location and recommends businesses near you. You'll see the word

---

[12] Bianchi, T. (2024, February 7). *Google: Distribution of revenue by segment 2023*. Statista. https://www.statista.com/statistics/1093781/distribution-of-googles-revenues-by-segment/

"Sponsored" next to the listing, confirming that someone paid for that placement.

Google allows both LSAs and search ads to appear on page one search results. We're going to discuss LSAs first because they usually appear at the top of the page.

Google introduced LSAs to lawyers in 2020, which makes them newer than some of the other page-one results. The really cool thing about LSAs is they're not exactly Pay Per Click, they are Pay Per *Lead,* which means you don't pay for them unless someone *calls* you. The price per call can vary anywhere from $10 to $1,000—depending on your practice area or market. Best of all, you can dispute and get refunds for leads that are not relevant to your practice area.

Quick-Hitting Hack: For a full explanation of how to set up your LSAs, scan this QR code.

(You'll find all the other bonuses from the book here or you can go to **yourdreamlawfirm.com**.)

Scan this QR Code to Unlock This Bonus

LSAs can be the most profitable advertising method in some markets and produce next to nothing in other markets—it all depends on your budget and setup.

We have learned many methods on how to optimize your firm's Local Services Ads based on the three major ranking factors. They are Radius, Reviews, and Response Time.

- **Radius**. This has to do with the proximity of the searcher in relation to your Google Business Profile location. If you have one Google location, and someone searches for you from 20 miles away, you are less likely to get that lead than your competitor, whose office is one mile from the searcher. This is separate from the geographic radius you select when setting up your ads. One way many attorneys are crushing it on LSAs is by setting up multiple Google Maps locations for their business if they target a large market.

- **Reviews**. If your firm has no reviews, you are not able to run LSAs. If your firm has bad reviews or a low overall rating, then nobody is going to call your firm. If one firm has 500 five-star reviews and is competing with a firm with 10 reviews and a 3.4 rating, it's not hard to know who's going to get the call. Reviews are make-or-break for your LSAs.

- **Response Time**. This is an actual ranking factor—and important. If you get 10 leads from LSAs and don't respond to all 10 of them fast enough, Google will stop showing your LSAs to prevent Google users from having a bad experience when contacting your firm. The cheapest and easiest way to get your LSA ads working is by rapidly attending to every single lead.

If used correctly, these ads can grow your firm by over $1M in revenue per year. We've seen firms add over $5M in annual revenue just from this one strategy.

Google Search Ads

Now, scroll slightly further down. Just underneath the LSAs, you'll see another type of ad. These listings look more like a typical Google result, but will once again have a word like "Ad" or "Sponsored" at the top:

Other than signing up a lot of clients, why should you invest in these types of Google Ads? These ads are not just marketing tools. They are also ways for you to gather information about your clients. When you start a Google search ads strategy, you're able to generate leads and—using a tool like CallRail®—you can simultaneously do market research on which keywords produce the highest volume and quality of signed cases. That information is golden! Knowing what keywords produce your best cases will help you know what keywords to double down on for all of your marketing. The key is to study what gets you the best cases, not necessarily the most or cheapest leads.

The number one rule when it comes to Google advertising is to avoid wasting money by showing ads to people who will not hire you. We accomplish this by asking three questions:

1. What keywords produce the majority of signed clients?
2. What devices do the majority of signed clients use when searching for a lawyer?

3. What are the demographics of the majority of signed clients?

For example, our data shows that the keyword "injury attorney" will pull in leads at typically the same cost of the keyword "accident attorney." But, the keyword "accident attorney" is three times more likely to turn into a qualified car accident case. Why? Because the word *injury* is more vague than *accident*. Somebody could've stubbed their toe and think they're entitled to money. When someone types in the word *accident*, it's more likely they were in a car accident.

We also know that 80% of car accident and criminal defense signed clients come from mobile devices. Compare that to business law and estate planning, where most signed clients come from desktop.

It's also important to pay attention to the demographics of the majority of your signed clients. For example, the majority of signed clients at a car accident firm may come from lower 50% income brackets within a 20–mile radius from the office location. Whereas, a high net worth divorce client will come from the top 10% income bracket and is willing to drive further for the right attorney.

So, by focusing on the correct keywords, targeting the proper devices and adjusting to the ideal demographics and search radius, you can vastly increase your ROI simply because you're not showing ads to the wrong people.

Quick-Hitting Hack: Is "Buying Your Way In" using 3rd party lead generators worth it? Most lawyers have gotten a cold call from someone offering to *sell you leads*. Is this too good to be true? Yes and no. At the end of the day, you should do things that produce a low cost to acquire signed cases. Experiment with some of them and see if you can make a return on it. But, be wary. Most of these 3rd party lead generation companies are getting their leads from page one of Google and just re-selling them to many law firms (not exclusive to you), and producing low-quality leads. You have to be fast and lucky to be the first attorney to contact any of those leads. Most times, you're better off investing your marketing time and money elsewhere—especially into things that build your brand and give you data, which is an asset for the future of your firm.

And, we haven't even talked about the *other* types of ads you can run in the Google advertising suite, like YouTube Ads and display ads (we'll get to these soon).

And speaking of *building* your way, it's time to discuss your long-term SEO strategies to get those page one Google results. Remember, the following two SEO methods take considerable time to generate, but they'll pay dividends long into the future.

BUILD Your Way In: SEO

Keep scrolling now and you'll finally get to the unsponsored search results. That's what we refer to as SEO.

It's valuable to be one of the top search results in the SEO category, but as we've explained, it takes quite a bit of time to get there. This is no reason, however, to neglect SEO as a page-one method. It's listed last on our list only because it tends to be the last piece you get in place—but not because it's the least useful. It's actually one of the most powerful strategies you have.

SEO comes in two varieties. Local and organic.

Local SEO

Local SEO refers to Google Maps. As the name suggests, it helps prospective new clients find businesses in their local area. These results are informed by a few things.

1. **Proximity to the Searcher.** Based on a searcher's IP address, which can be used to track their location, local SEO results favor businesses that are closer to the searcher's location than businesses that are far away. For example, typing a search term into Google while you are physically in Dallas will have different results from someone typing those same search terms while in Houston. Your firm is therefore more likely to show up on local SEO results for searchers who are close to you.

2. **Relevance.** How relevant is your firm to the thing that's being searched? That's what informs this criterion. Relevance is determined by your website content, from the sites that link to you, and from your reviews. When your content and reviews include keywords, phrases, and synonyms that match

your potential clients' searches, you're more likely to have a high relevance factor. This is yet another reason why reviews are so critical to your business and to your SEO. You can also improve your relevance by posting content on your website that incorporates keywords and topics that your best-signed clients are typing into Google. (Remember, you can learn what those are using CallRail® or a similar tool!)

3. **Prominence.** This is a measure of your authority in the internet community. How many other websites list your firm? How many link to your site? How many directories are you listed in? Google checks every website in existence, looking for mentions of your website. When they find an authoritative site that mentions you—like, for example, *The New York Times*—Google interprets that as other credible sources "vouching" for you, which improves your SEO. One way to enhance your prominence factor is by asking your strategic partners to link you on their websites. You can also enhance your prominence ratings by properly filling out all the business profile forms with the same Name, Address, and Phone Number (NAP) on sites like Find Law, Avvo, Justialawyers.com, Yelp, Apple Maps, Bing, Yellow Pages, and so on.

The most visible local SEO results—and the most clicked on—come in the Map Pack.

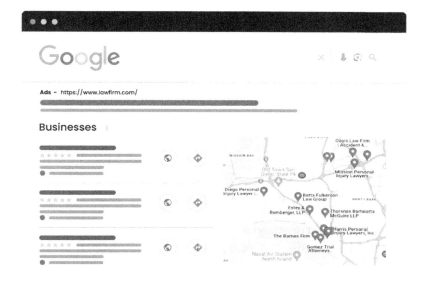

The Maps results are like the prom queen of page one. That's where the majority of "ready to buy" leads come from with your SEO—the non tire-kickers. People click on your maps profile when they are ready to hire a lawyer. Everything they need is right there. Your address, how long you've been in business, directions, and even reviews. Even if someone became aware of you on Facebook, YouTube, or Google Ads, chances are they are going to visit your Google Maps profile at some point to look up your reviews and call your main business phone number. Even better, there's an aura of authenticity about the Maps results because they're not titled "Ads" or "Sponsored."

How do we know most clicks come from the maps section? We once worked with a DUI attorney in Orange County, CA, who was number one in both the maps and organic listings. He was getting 50 calls a week, every week, from his SEO. A jealous competitor reported his listing as fake and, even though the claim was false, Google suspended his Maps listing. He remained number one for all the same terms in the *organic* listings—but no longer appeared in the maps listing at all. As a result, his phones dried up. His leads vanished almost overnight. We quickly worked with Google and were able to get his maps listing reinstated about a week later. As soon as his firm appeared on those map listings again, his calls started back up, at the same volume as before.

The moral of the story? It wasn't the *organic* listing that was making his phones ring with ready-to-buy leads. It was the *Maps* listing. That's the power of local SEO.

Getting your firm ranked on these maps can gain you lots of quality leads, *but*, as we explained, it can take months or years for this to happen and depends on many factors. Google is incentivized to give people the very best search results so that it maintains its reputation as the very best search engine. It will consider your firm a stronger and stronger search result to feature as you build your online presence through reviews (people have opinions about you), content (you produce material people are interested in), links from other websites (other businesses trust you), and the age of your domain (you've been around a while). All of those factors—plus a hundred others—impact Google's algorithms to feature your site as a trustworthy, high-ranking result.

All that to say, you should certainly work towards getting your firm ranked in the top three of the Map Pack. It may take a while, but it's such a great asset when you do.

Organic SEO

"Organic" typically brings to mind images of fresh fruits and vegetables on market stands. That's not exactly what this "organic" describes.

Organic SEO describes results that show up beneath Google Maps. For law firms, this is typically where a higher percentage of your *research-oriented,* rather than *purchase-oriented* leads and searchers will come from.

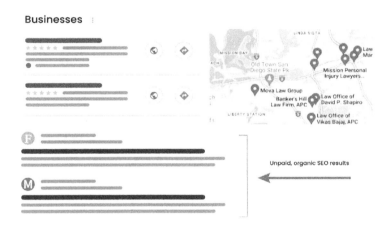

Here's an example. If you were to type into your search bar, "pizza near me," Google would determine your search was looking for a *local business* and *purchase-oriented.* You're indicating you intend to buy pizza. Google is going to help you out by prioritizing the kind of *local SEO* results we just covered in the previous section. It will point you toward businesses near you that sell the thing you're looking for. Google isn't going to give you pizza recipes or videos about how to toss pizza dough because your search terms indicated you didn't want to *make* pizza. You're just looking to buy it.

But what if you were to type in "low-calorie pizza crust"? Now you've entered a *research-oriented* search query. In this case, Google isn't going to provide you with Map Pack listings for Dominos or Pizza Hut, because that's not helpful for what you're looking for. It's going to provide you with highly-reviewed recipes for low-calorie pizza crust. That's a search that will prioritize *organic SEO listings*. The results in this example also aren't location-specific. They're provided to you based on their relevance to what you searched and their prominence.

In Chapter 5, we told you about the four stages of marketing, and that comes into play here. For service businesses, Organic SEO listings capture the highest percentage of searchers who are in an earlier stage of their buyer's journey. Since there are so many ads and map listings above the organic SEO section of Google, most of the "ready to buy" leads have already contacted other law firms by the time they get down there. And, if only organic SEO listings show up on Google, that usually means the searcher entered a *learner's search*. That's why we call them research-oriented. They may or may not need to buy something. Local SEO results, on the other hand, tend to be directed at people in Stage 3 who are entering a *buyer's search*. They're purchase-oriented and ready to pick a vendor.

Let's move away from pizza and consider how this might work with a law firm. Imagine that Leilah from L.A. types into Google, "How is child support calculated in California?" That's a research-oriented query and Leilah's results will most likely *not* feature the Local SEO Map Pack with law firms in L.A. Instead, she'll see government websites titled "Child Support Services," followed by drop-down suggestions under "People Also Ask," and then she might start seeing some articles or blog posts.

Imagine that Leilah clicks on one titled, "California Child Support in 10 Steps." Let's say the article was posted by Kramer and Kramer Associates, a family law firm in Sacramento. Most likely, the law firm wrote this article to capture the keywords "California Child Support" and strengthen their organic SEO. Leilah might click on that article and poke around on the site, exploring the child support calculator and spousal support calculator. It's a helpful site! However—if and when Leilah needs to hire a family law attorney—she's not likely to hire one in northern California. She would want to find one closer to where she's at in L.A.

That's the limitation of organic SEO results. They're excellent for research-oriented learners in Stage 2 of the marketing journey, but they won't always translate to Stage 3 or Stage 4 buyers. And, there's no way to target people only within a 20-mile radius of your office the way you can on paid ads. For this reason, Local SEO results—and especially the Map Pack—will result in more signed cases for your firm than organic SEO results.

Still, there's value in publishing research-oriented content. Having high-quality content on your site makes Google think that your site is more authoritative and also will typically attract backlinks from other sites who want to link to your content, thereby improving your relevancy and prominence. Thanks to that improved SEO, when people based in northern California type in "family law attorney," Google is more likely to feature Kramer and Kramer as one of the top picks in the Sacramento Map Pack.

There are financial benefits too, even if your organic SEO doesn't lead to many new clients for your own firm. If your site is set up for it, you have the opportunity to capture the lead and then refer that lead to another law firm. Kramer and Kramer, for instance, might capture Leilah as a lead and then refer her to a firm in southern California, subsequently benefiting from eventually receiving a referral fee or reciprocal referral. And don't forget, the body of content you produce to enhance your organic SEO will live on the internet forever, slowly building valuable traction for your firm and ultimately establishing itself as a valuable asset.

Now you know the four elements that, together, determine your Google ranking. When you buy *and* build your way in, through a combination of the methods we just described— LSAs, Search Ads, and local and organic SEO—you are starting to achieve the omnipresent effect. That means it's *you* showing up on LSAs, Google Ads, and Google Maps. Any person searching for you sees three of your ads with one search, *all* at the top! You can bet they are going to be *extremely* likely to click on one of those. And then—ta dah—you've got yourself another potential new client. Once we layer in the social media marketing, your omnipresence strategy will be taken up to a whole new level.

> **Quick-Hitting Hack:** Remember how important follow-up is in turning these leads into real clients. Most people who click on one of your ads or visit your website may not be ready to contact you right then. But you can invest in a follow-up strategy like placing a pixel on your website. This small piece of code tells other websites like Facebook to show ads for your website. It's a remarketing follow-up strategy. For a relatively low cost, your ads will "follow" your potential clients as they visit lots of other sites, keeping your firm top of mind. Remember, the fortune is in the follow-up. It's the glue that ties everything together.

But wait—how did all this search engine goodness begin? Even after you do all the work to tee up your page-one Google results, how does someone like Mike-who-got-rear-ended connect with you in the first place?

Words.

Mike typed *words* into a search bar. Words like "personal," "injury," and "attorney." Words open the door for you and your potential clients to meet. Words alert your potential clients to your firm's ability to meet their needs. And words boost your SEO listings—if you use them properly.

Everything that gets your firm to rank on Google starts with *words* that express a need. You, as a law firm trying to snag Mike's business, need to know the keywords people like him use in their Google searches. Then, you need to match those keywords in your marketing.

For the rest of this chapter, we're going to do a deep dive into how you can use *words* as a vital piece of your Google page-one strategy. Yes, it's as geeky as it sounds. It's also going to make you a hell of a lot of money. We think that's pretty exciting.

WAM It Up

WAM it up! No, that's not an M.C. Hammer throwback. That's our acronym for Word Alignment Marketing (WAM)—your key to success in search engine marketing. The WAM method lines up search words with your advertising. Put another way, it's how you ensure the words in your ads match the needs your potential clients will be typing into Google.

For example, if you are a personal injury attorney, you don't want the kind of keywords that someone who was at fault in an accident is using in their search, like "How much will my insurance go up if I was at fault in a car accident." You don't want at-fault car accident clients! That's bad word alignment.

How do you find the *right* words? How do you find the money-making words that will bring you quality leads?

By now it should not surprise you to know that Google comes to your rescue. They keep a record of every single thing that people type into Google. And we mean *everything*. Such as:

- How many times per month people are typing certain keywords into the search box.
- Where those people are.

- What sites their searches lead to.

- What words are the most popular in your practice area.

- What keywords, phrases, and synonyms are most often found on pages relevant for the kinds of cases you want to handle.

All this information is pure gold for you and your marketing efforts because it takes away the guesswork. You know exactly which keywords to bid on with your ads and write articles on for your SEO. You also know what topics to make videos on! Google is a search engine, sure, but it is also one of the most powerful research platforms *ever* for this reason alone.

> **Quick-Hitting Hack:** Find a video on YouTube that explains Google's "keyword planner." Watch it, study it, and learn how to use this tool. Then, use the knowledge you can gain from the keyword planner to fine-tune your ads. Keep in mind that the most *popular* keywords are not always the most *profitable* keywords. You may want to experiment with the words you use until you find the best formula for getting new leads.

Let's look at an example of how WAM works.

In our research, we found that in every market for civil rights attorneys, the phrase "civil rights lawyer" was typed in a lot more than the words "police brutality lawyer."

Does this tell you that "civil rights lawyer" will get you a lot more clicks if you use that in your ads for your civil rights law firm? Probably. However, there's also going to be a lot more *competition* for those keywords, which means any clicks attached to those words will be more expensive. It's also possible that the leads you get from those "civil rights lawyer" clicks won't be as qualified as leads you get from someone who's typed in "police brutality lawyer."

But let's say you decide to hitch your wagon to the latter key phrase "police brutality lawyer." You're now paying *less* for each click that comes your way through those keywords, and you're also getting *better-qualified* leads. These are potential clients who tend to have more compelling cases. That's an example where the *popularity* of a keyword needs to be considered in balance with the potential *profitability* of a different keyword.

Here's another example.

"Nursing home abuse lawyer" sounds like a good specific set of keywords for someone in that specialty—but once again, popular keywords may be expensive and put you in the arena with quite a lot of competition. What if you were to go after keywords that were more specific? For example, it's well known that bedsores are a common feature of nursing home abuse. So, maybe "bedsore lawyer" might bring you more business. It's this type of experimentation and exploration that Google's keyword planner can help you evaluate.

Put this book down for a minute and go try out some keywords based on your practice area. Type them into Google. See if your competitors pop up. If they do, that's a clue that they are good keywords. If they don't, that's an indication that the keywords you just typed in are up for grabs! This might be a place where you can stand out. For instance, if someone searches, "neck pain after a car accident," there's a very high likelihood that they were in a car accident and they're having neck pain—in other words, they could use a personal injury lawyer! But if you search for that phrase, you're probably not going to see a lot of ads popping up. That should tip you off that there's an opportunity there for research keywords which would target people in the research stage of their buying journey. Those terms would likely be cheap and would feature you in a space where your competitors aren't also crowding the field.

Now, take this experiment even further. Go into Google's keyword planner and see how those keywords perform. Are they getting results? Are they leading to law firms? How often are those particular words typed in? Look at all aspects of those keywords and use that data to help you make decisions about what keywords are going to be worth your time and money.

This is the WAM method. It's figuring out which keywords align with your law firm and your law firm's marketing, then leveraging that information to enhance your search results.

Let's take this a step further and get creative with what we call the Niche Demand Blueprint. Everything we're about to share with you is frickin' gold.

Niche Demand Blueprint

Most searches look like <problem> <lawyer>. We've already seen examples of this. It's <car accident><lawyer> or <divorce><lawyer> and so on.

But those aren't the only way to go. We've identified at least *eight* different categories of search keywords that you can use to ramp up your lead numbers. Together, they form your Niche Demand Blueprint, and they can be off-the-charts powerful. They are:

1. **Core Keywords.** This is what most people type in when they're looking for a specific kind of lawyer. "Car accident lawyer." "Divorce lawyer." Core keywords are usually typed in by people in the third stage of marketing—vendor selection. Because so many other firms are also bidding on these keywords, they're usually more expensive. But, they're the most "sure thing" in terms of generating cases.

2. **High-Value Keywords.** These are keywords that would produce a *higher-value* case. They are typed in less than core keywords, but they can snag lucrative cases. Examples are "truck accident lawyer" and "high profile divorce lawyer."

3. **High-Traffic Keywords.** These are words typed in frequently that relate to your law practice but don't specify a need for a lawyer. Good examples would be "car accident NY," or simply, "divorce." You could show an advertisement on Google every time someone types in "divorce" in your local market and offer them an ebook. We have a client who does this with incredible results. Cost per click is very cheap because the word "lawyer" is not included. However, you could run the risk of getting a higher percentage of

unqualified leads. You can also make a YouTube video like "most common car accidents in NY." The world is your oyster when you understand the usefulness of high-traffic keywords.

4. **Research Terms.** Remember how we coached you to target your advertising to people still in the second stage of their consumer journey, the research phase? Research terms capture those potential clients. These words are typed in by people looking for answers to their questions, such as "car accident settlement calculator," "state farm car crash insurance policy info," or "how to file for a divorce." They don't mention lawyers, but they *do* mention events that might lead to someone needing a lawyer. These terms are relatively cheap and they are a big opportunity for you. Most competitors are not aware of these terms and are certainly not tailoring their marketing to take them into account. Use research terms for your videos, blogs, and even your Google Ads keywords.

5. **Arbitrage Terms.** What is arbitrage? Let's say you find a rare pair of Air Jordans on sale for $20 at Goodwill in mint condition, and then you turn around and sell them on eBay for $250. That's arbitrage. Paying a little for something that most people ignore and then getting a lot back. Arbitrage terms don't refer *directly* to your practice area, but they are terms your ideal client might search for. For instance, someone researching "car wreck body shop" might

LAW FIRM GROWTH ACCELERATOR

need a personal injury attorney. Someone researching "divorce counseling" or "marriage therapy" might soon be in the market for a family law attorney. These keywords are very cheap and very few of your competitors are using them creatively in their content or ads.

6. **Negative Keywords.** Let's say you've bid on the term "divorce lawyer," so that anytime someone in your local area types that word combination into Google, they see your ad. That's all well and good—but what if they type in "*free* divorce lawyer," or "pro bono divorce lawyer"? You shouldn't pay money to market under the word "free." Take another example. You probably wouldn't want to use a search term like "*at fault* car accident lawyer" because you don't want "at fault" clients. That's where this sixth term is relevant. *Negative* keywords can be bad for your business and should therefore be avoided. Google enables you to specify what words you do *not* want to market under with "negative keywords." For instance, you're willing to pay for the term "divorce lawyer," but if someone types "*free* divorce lawyer" and "free" is one of your negative keywords, Google will not show your ad. Also, it may not make sense to make content on the topic of "how to handle your divorce for free." Negative keywords are a beast. There's so much more to them, like excluding geographic areas you don't serve and the names of your competitors, etc.

Quick-Hitting Hack: Here's another strategy you could employ with negative keywords. Use them as a marketing opportunity to build a subscriber base. For example, if someone types in "free divorce lawyer," you could serve up an ad that educates them on why they should be paying a premium for a good divorce lawyer, along with the dangers and pitfalls of choosing a free (or cheap) divorce lawyer. (As part of the Google advertising platform, you can specify which ads the negative keywords apply to.) In essence, you're treating negative keywords in the same way you treat research terms. Educating potential clients and raising awareness about your firm.

7. **Geo-Specific Keywords.** As its name implies, these search keywords mention a specific place. For instance, you might be surprised to learn that "Las Vegas lawyer" is typed in more often than "car accident lawyer" in the greater Las Vegas market. Counter-intuitive, right? But that also means there's an opportunity here. Geo-specific keywords tend to be *cheap*. In fact, we know many attorneys who have gotten millions of dollars in cases from just using their city and "lawyer" as keywords without specifying a practice area. A criminal defense attorney can do well by using the name of the town where the courthouse is located along with "lawyer." If you do this, the key is to use "negative keywords" for all of the practice areas and locations you don't serve.

8. **Competitor Keywords.** Now this one is not recommended for everyone. But, do you have a big fish competitor in your pond? One way to compete with them is to bid on the name of their firm. For example, you could use the name of that big fish law firm or even the lawyers who work there in *your* keywords. For example, in Florida "Morgan and Morgan" is typed in three times more than the words "car accident lawyer" because M&M has a huge brand, which means they have high name recognition. Some firms in Florida bid on the keyword "Morgan and Morgan," showing an ad for their firm when someone types that in. One caution here. Make sure your ads aren't deliberately confusing to clients, attempting to pass off your firm as your competitor. In other words, no one should click on your ad *thinking* that they're clicking on "Morgan and Morgan." That kind of deceptive advertising can and will get you sued. Instead, be upfront about the fact that you're a competitor with this other firm, and state why *your* firm is better than theirs. For instance, you might serve up an ad that says, "Go with a Smaller Firm than Morgan and Morgan." Look for firms in your area that have high search volume and consider beckoning some of those leads over to your firm. But be careful here if you do.

A successful Google page-one strategy is all about selecting the right keywords to dominate. The above eight categories are pure gold! Use them to come up with creative keyword ideas for your Google Ads, SEO content, and even video content. Once you know the words your clients are typing in (i.e.

what's really going through their minds), you will never run out of marketing ideas to grow your firm, and you'll always know what to test next.

> **Quick-Hitting Hack:** By the way, all the legwork you do to boost your status on Google will translate right into You-Tube. Google owns YouTube, so everything you're doing on YouTube ties into all these keyword concepts. That's a big opportunity if you're developing videos as a key element of your marketing strategy! (Which, Chapter 8 will tell you, is a *great* idea.)

Putting It All Together

Once you've brainstormed creative ideas on different keywords you want to target in your marketing, it's time to lift your head out of the nitty gritty data analytics and remember that your clients are *human.* They are emotional people.

Remember the first commandment of marketing: Understand your client's fears, frustrations, wants, and aspirations. Ultimately, your marketing can't be just a cluster of keywords—that might appeal to an algorithm, but not a real human. It's not enough to get your firm's name to appear as a link on page one of Google. You also need people to decide to *call you.* Real humans are looking for a message that appeals to them on an emotional level.

Take Mike, for instance, the guy who got rear-ended. Imagine that Mike types in "car accident lawyer." Those are the words. Those are his search terms. But now, consider his *emotions.*

Deep down in the back of Mike's mind, he's thinking, "I don't trust lawyers. How expensive is this going to be? I doubt this is going to be worth my time."

Mike doesn't know yet that he doesn't have to pay a car accident lawyer up front for their representation—he only needs to pay if his lawyers won him a settlement! So this is where your advertising messaging can get his attention with something like, "If We Don't Win Your Settlement, You Don't Pay!" That addresses his *fear* of legal representation costing more than it's worth as well as his *desire* to be compensated for his injuries.

Once you land on a message that incorporates the keywords you know will be effective, *plus* a message that targets your clients' fears, frustrations, wants and aspirations, you need to make sure this message transfers through all your internet ads, your website, and your online presence. Use your copy to make crystal clear why you're the firm to help your potential clients overcome their *fears and frustrations* about hiring a lawyer, and enable them to achieve their *wants and aspirations*.

Let's say you did it. You got your law firm on page one of Google. Your ad copy addressed your clients' fears, frustrations, wants, and aspirations with a great offer and a unique selling proposition. So they *click on your ad* (trumpet fanfare) and it sends them to your website.

Now what?

Forming Your Website & Landing Page Strategy

Yes, it's finally time to talk about your website. You might have thought this was the most important part of your marketing strategy, but there's a reason we've waited until now to bring it up. But before we do, here's a quick review.

What have you learned about so far about marketing in the last few chapters?

- You've discovered the *new way* of marketing, which offers real, practical value to your potential clients.

- You're now familiar with the *when, who, where* and *how* of forming a marketing strategy that is aligned with your business strategy.

- You're aware of the eleven commandments of marketing—timeless principles that will make your marketing effective.

- You now know about what goes into getting you on page one of Google and how to leverage keywords to your Google Ads and SEO advantage.

You're going to use *all* of that information to build your website. It should be built in such a way that uses all of those principles and tools to your advantage.

And, news flash, chances are high that you're doing it all wrong.

This is because most people who design websites build them to look good. They might throw a little bit of SEO optimization on it, but they mostly focus on the visual appeal. That means pleasing colors, an attractive design, pretty pictures, a nice logo, and so on.

But none of those things matter if your site doesn't generate traffic from Google searches! Your website is not an art piece. It's there to bring you leads. It must have the right technical infrastructure and compelling content that gets people to contact you.

Too many attorneys get a website based on their personal taste, which is the *least* compelling way to design a website. Think of it this way. Would you rather have a pretty website that wins awards for design, or a website that makes you money?

Let's focus on getting leads and making money. Then*, and only then*, we can worry about layering in an attractive design on top.

There are three elements that make a website successful in bringing you leads. It's what we call the Tripod Concept.

1. When people land on your website, they should be inspired to contact you with a phone call or an online form. This is what we call *conversion rate optimization.*

2. In addition, your website should be *optimized* to rank high in Google (for free).

3. Lastly, it should reflect your *personal brand.*

Note the order of this tripod. **Conversion rate** first, **optimization** second, and **personal brand** third. It's the exact reverse of how most lawyer websites are set up. They build for personal brand and taste first, which means optimization gets neglected and conversion rate never happens. *Gah!*

By following these principles (and many more), your website will be much more likely to rank high in local SEO and organic SEO, which will generate much more traffic to your site. Then, once people visit your site, they will convert into actual leads at a much higher rate.

Now, that's your law firm's website. But, what about all of those people who click your Google Ads? Where are we sending them? To your website—right?

No! This is one of the biggest paid advertising mistakes we see lawyers make—sending traffic to the SEO-optimized pages of their website.

Instead, when someone clicks your ads, they should be sent to a dedicated page that is solely designed to turn that click into an immediate phone call or form submission. That page is called a landing page.

Here's why this is so important. Let's say you have a car accident page on your main website. For SEO purposes, the headline on that page includes the words *car, accident, lawyer, San Francisco.* You decide to run a Google Ads campaign targeting Oakland, California (12 miles away from San Francisco). Assuming 100 people click that ad in Oakland, all 100 will be sent to your San Francisco page. Most of those 100 people don't want to drive 12 miles to meet their lawyer, so they bounce from the page and find someone closer.

Not to mention, that SEO-optimized page is not built like a landing page with a form submission box at the top of the page, compelling sales copy, and limited navigation. So, even more people bounce and end up *not* calling you. That's why you need a landing page that is specifically built to convert clicks from ads into phone calls.

Also, good landing pages do not follow SEO best practices, because they don't need to—you're paying for the traffic, not relying on Google to send it to you for free. Your landing pages should follow direct response marketing best practices—so they can turn a high percentage of your leads from ads into signed cases.

Let's look at what a law firm's landing page *should* have, in order to turn your advertising campaigns into ROI machines. Based on our data, it needs these seven elements:

1. **Benefits**. The most important part of your landing page is the headline and sub headline. These should be right at the top and answer a client's most pressing question. *"What's in it for me?"* Lead with how you will benefit them. It should be a statement like, "We help people injured by hospitals receive fair compensation" (for a medical malpractice attorney) or "We help fathers get through divorce without losing their relationship with their children or being taken advantage of financially" (for a divorce attorney). Remember in Chapter 5, we said you want to sell the resort, not the plane ride? This is where the resort goes. Don't bother touting your Harvard law degree. No one cares if you went to Harvard. They care about what you can do for *them*.

2. **Image**. When people go to a landing page, they want to see the product. For legal services, the lawyer is the product. Include a picture or video of yourself. A

huge bonus if this video is directly relevant and valuable based on what they searched.

3. **Features**. Usually, beneath the image or video is where you highlight your credentials, experience, and results. Most people lead with this, but it should come second. You can also mention your media appearances, but don't go overboard. Less is more here. You need just enough to reinforce your benefit-oriented statement.

4. **Proof**. Here's where you back up your claims of awesomeness through proof like client testimonials, or some review stars. Keep this brief. If you load up the page with too much of this, it can appear desperate or fake.

5. **Offer**. There must be a *reason* for visitors to your site to contact you. Provide a spot at the top of the page (no scrolling needed) where clients can input some of the basics of their case information under a heading marked, "No obligation case evaluation," or "FREE consultation." Get them in the door by emphasizing the low risk, high-value benefit you offer them. Ideally, you will create an offer better than a "FREE consultation"— something differentiated and specific to their case type.

6. **Form**. This is where people can contact you by typing in their contact information. Make it an extremely obvious component of your page. The button to send the form should be a different color from anything else on the page, and you don't want to label the button with "Submit" or some other weak wording. Instead, use a phrase that includes what they get like, "Free Consultation."

7. **Trust**. Build trust with your potential client by including things like "Free consultation; no obligation to hire." You can also incorporate symbols such as the Better Business Bureau logo, Verisign, local bar association emblems, chamber of commerce logos, and other markers of a secure, trustworthy, and reputable practice. Remember, most people seeking an attorney are doing it for the first time. They're in unfamiliar waters, afraid of the cost and obligation of hiring a lawyer. If you can throw them a life preserver and alleviate those fears, you'll help take their fear of commitment away.

All seven of these elements might seem like too much for one page, but it's not. They should all be there. They work together to get a potential client to contact you. That's the whole point of a landing page.

Quick-Hitting Hack: Check out Andy's video "The Perfect Law Firm Landing Page" where he shows you exactly what a good lawyer landing page looks like.

(You'll find all the other bonuses from the book here or you can go to **yourdreamlawfirm.com**.)

Scan this QR Code
to Unlock This Bonus

If you follow these practices for your website, you will be much more likely to get results from your SEO. And, if you segment your landing pages from your main website, you will be much more likely to get a high ROI from your Google Ads and Facebook Ads campaigns.

Once your SEO starts getting traction, your domain will turn into a valuable asset that ranks on the first page of Google. It'll work for you for years and won't cost you a dime.

It will make your phones ring for nothing. In fact, it may even be something you can actually *sell* if you ever want to and make over seven figures on.

Like any investment, the payoff takes time. But many valuable things in life take time. After all, you don't expect to pay your bills using your stock investments or your mutual funds. Those things generate value *as time goes on*. The same is true for SEO as it gradually elevates your website. It will pay off in the long run, not the short term.

And speaking of investing time in your advertising … it's high time we explained the other side of the marketing coin: Awareness Marketing.

A Mix of Demand and Awareness Marketing

In this chapter, we've taught you how to get yourself in front of clients who are actively *in demand* of your services. When a potential client like "rear-ended Mike" types terms related to your practice area into Google, these are the strategies that will ensure he finds *your* firm, clicks through to *your* website, and decides to input his case information to *your* intake people.

But remember what we taught you in Chapter 5 when we discussed the four stages of marketing. Only 3% of people fall into Mike's category. "Vendor Selection" is Stage 3, when a potential client is ready to hire. The other 97% of people browsing the internet are not there yet. They may be in Stage 2, research mode, or they may be in Stage 1, still entirely unaware of your firm. For those people, you're going to employ a different type of marketing strategy. *Awareness Marketing.*

As we explained in Chapter 2, when firms move from a marketing approach that mainly employs Demand Marketing to one that adds Awareness Marketing—*that's* when they see their firms scale up to the next level.

Nine times out of 10, Google will be your best choice to work on first. Focusing on your Google search results through PPC ads is a fast way to get started and will generate a higher percentage of quality leads than you could generate through social media. Those new quality leads will give you the revenue to enhance your SEO over time, especially as you improve your website. And as a bonus, all those new leads will force your firm to hone its intake system. (We're going to teach you how to create a dynamite intake system in Chapter 9.)

With all that infrastructure in place, it's time to pour gasoline on the fire. Building your social media presence through Awareness Marketing will cause the steady burn of Demand Marketing to erupt into a conflagration of leads.

Chapter 7 | Takeaways

1. The best first step you can take to increase your lead volume is to invest money into your page-one Google strategy. Start with *buying* your way in through PPC with LSAs and search ads. Then, work on *building* your search engine traffic to improve your placement in the Map Pack and local SEO listings.

2. Use your words! Use the information about keywords we taught you in the Word Alignment Method (WAM) and Niche Demand Blueprint to ensure your firm's name pops up for the right keywords when typed in on Google. Also, use these to drive your social media, video, and SEO strategy.

3. When building your website, look and aesthetics are less important than optimizing your conversion rate and technical SEO. Separate from that, your landing pages are designed strictly for conversion rate (from your paid ads) with no technical SEO! Make sure your landing pages include benefits for the client first and foremost.

Working on Demand Marketing first ensures you have time to get your intake system primed to handle an influx of new leads. The research you do regarding keywords also gives you invaluable insight into your clients' questions and concerns. That infrastructure and information will set you up for success as you turn your attention to Awareness Marketing.

CHAPTER 8

AWARENESS MARKETING

ESTABLISH YOUR SOCIAL MEDIA PRESENCE BY SOLVING REAL PROBLEMS

You can get everything in life that you want if you help enough other people get what they want.

—Zig Ziglar

ANDY STICKEL NARRATES

"I'm getting hundreds of leads a day," the voice on the phone said. "Andy, turn off the ads. I can't keep up with them!"

The voice belonged to an immigration lawyer and one of our clients—we'll call him John. Not too long before this phone call, John had been getting his few clients the old way. He put up ads here and there which said, essentially, "Hey, I'm a lawyer. Hire me." Occasionally, he put something on Facebook and relied heavily on referrals.

As we explained in Chapter 5, we call this "hope and pray" marketing. John was hoping and praying someone would see his ads and hire him.

After consulting with us, John started doing marketing the New Way. He created free content that provided real value to people. His lead numbers shot through the roof as he experienced firsthand the power of the New Way of marketing.

Give people value up front and they will flock to you.

It worked for John. This strategy constantly put his face and his firm in front of thousands of people and gave them real value, information they could use to improve their lives—for free.

Today, John has a successful immigration law firm with 60 employees. He has so many leads he has the luxury of picking and choosing from them to find the best ones that fit his firm. He's getting *more money* and *more freedom*. That's a goal every lawyer should strive for!

John's video content strategy falls under the category of Awareness Marketing. He was putting out content to people who were still in the research stage of marketing. They weren't looking to hire anyone yet. They were simply researching answers to their questions. John's content provided helpful answers to their questions and built their awareness of his firm at the same time. When, at the end of their research, they determined they needed a lawyer, guess who they elected to call? Immigration attorney John, that's who.

Once you've developed a solid intake system to sort through leads—a process we'll teach you in Chapter 9 and one which you'll hone during your Demand Marketing work—the next step is building your Awareness platform. One of the best ways you can do that is by posting content with practical value to your clients on social media.

You may have just let out a huge sigh. Why social media? Here's why: As of 2021, a whopping 72% of the population actively engages with social media.[13] That's the vast majority of the country. This is not some fringe corner of the internet. It basically *is* the internet. That 72% is going to include your ideal clients. You may not personally be a fan of social media, but—to recall a metaphor we used in Chapter 5—this is where the marlins are. It's time to learn how to bait your hook and cast your line.

The Awareness Marketing Strategy

People turn to the internet for information to solve problems, and that's where you come in. Awareness Marketing—a.k.a. *proactive* marketing—puts your solutions to your potential clients' problems in front of their faces. It gets them to see *you* as the solution to their problems. And this leads to them calling you when they have a particularly large problem.

Awareness Marketing enables you to focus on helping people by producing quality content that solves their problems.

---

[13] Anon. 2023. Demographics of social media users and adoption in the United States. Pew Research Center: Internet, Science & Tech. 11. May. https://www. pewresearch.org/internet/fact-sheet/social-media/.

It's important to note that this approach to marketing is a "long-game" strategy. Awareness Marketing isn't necessarily aimed at getting a client *today*. Instead, it strives to get your message in front of people who aren't even looking for you yet, people who don't even know you exist. That's why we call it Awareness Marketing. You're getting people to be aware of you.

This chapter is going to provide you with a guiding framework for your Awareness Marketing, acquaint you with the different ways to approach it, and then give you a whole lot of tips on recording videos—a key tactical strategy in this area.

Where do we start? With the number one goal of Awareness Marketing. Building goodwill in your target clients. All of your messaging should help your potential clients *know, like, and trust* you through helping them with their fears and problems.

ANDY STICKEL NARRATES

"Know, Like, and Trust" Through *Real* Brand Building

I was at a meeting of lawyers in Orlando a while ago. I asked the room, "How many of you have ever met me in person before or spoken one-on-one with me?" Not one hand went up. Then I asked, "How many of you here today feel like you know me?"

Every hand shot up.

They had all seen my videos. They knew what I looked like. They'd gotten used to my voice, my mannerisms, the way I stood, how I moved around the office, what my office looks like, and so on. Through my videos, all these lawyers felt like they *knew* me as a person.

And in a sense, they did. In those videos, I never tried to be someone I wasn't. I was my authentic self, always. All the lawyers in that room in Orlando were there because they knew, liked, and trusted me—solely because of the videos I'd produced. That's the most important element you want to focus on when building your brand.

The messaging you put out into the world should help your potential clients *know, like, and trust you.*

Many people (not just lawyers) think brand building is having a nice logo and making sure a lot of people know your name. But in today's world, that isn't enough. People have to know you, like you, and—this is key—*trust* you. That's the brand you want to build.

You build trust by providing real solutions to people's problems, and you build "knowing" and "liking" by doing it through a medium that allows you to convey authenticity. When it comes to content, we recommend making long-form videos that give solid information and solve problems. YouTube is the best long-form video platform currently. A 20-second TikTok video doesn't allow you to build as much trust as an 8-minute YouTube video. And, blog posts don't allow potential clients to get to know you personally—and they're more competitive. They're a good step in the right direction, but they won't get you as far as longer-form YouTube videos can.

Also, it's much easier to repurpose long-form videos into short-form videos. This is why it usually works better for an attorney to commit to making long-form videos and then to hire an editor to chop up those long-form videos into short-form social media content for your TikTok, Instagram reels, YouTube shorts, etc.

We also recommend backing up your long-form video strategy with a Facebook and YouTube ads strategy. This is really what pours fuel on the fire. We'll get into this soon.

Make a lot of videos. Dozens, even hundreds. This is how you're going to give your target viewers the ability to feel like they *know* you. Simply by consistently producing content, your viewers will start to pick up on all those details that make someone recognizable—the tone of your voice, the style of your presentation, the look of your office, your familiar facial expressions, and so on.

And don't be afraid of being your weird self, either. That's what will help your audience *like* you. Your authentic quirks can become an endearing part of your personal brand. For instance, the attorney Patrick Slaughter, who we've mentioned before, is a huge Disney fan. He and his wife go to Disney World and Epcot Center in Florida regularly—sometimes three times a week. On his videos, he had a poster of *Aladdin* in the background for a long time. One day, he replaced the

Aladdin poster with a poster of *The Lion King*. He got all kinds of questions in the comment section from his viewers. "Hey, where did the *Aladdin* poster go?" Patrick's Disney obsession had enabled him to build rapport with his audience without even realizing it. It became a signature part of his personal brand.

You can do the same. Let your interests show! Embrace your quirks. People are drawn to that. Those signs of your humanity will help viewers decide they not only know you, they also *like* you. Now, how do you accomplish the *trust* factor? We've already spilled the secret on this one. Your content should help your target clients solve real problems.

By establishing a personal brand that inspires people to *know, like, and trust you*, your marketing has sticking power. When people need a lawyer, they won't just google for a generic attorney. They'll come to you because they feel like they *know, like, and trust* you. That's the golden opportunity you have with social media marketing, and YouTube marketing in particular.

With that established, let's take a deeper dive into the two main avenues through which you can do Awareness Marketing. Similar to Demand Marketing, you can either *buy* your way in or *build* your way in—only this time, instead of Google, your context is social media. One approach uses ads and the other approach requires a longer investment of your time as you build organic traffic and followers:

- **BUY with Paid Advertising.** This involves paying for ads on Meta's platforms like Facebook and Instagram or other social media sites like YouTube or TikTok.

- **BUILD with Organic Marketing.** This involves putting up posts and videos on social media sites. Over time, you build prominence on the site through likes, shares, and followers.

The real key is in the combination of both of the above. That's where the magic happens.

Definitions are simple, but for all that, there are a number of misconceptions around these forms of awareness marketing. Let's do some myth-busting around those misconceptions right now.

Awareness Marketing Myths

Myth #1: Organic marketing is cheaper. Organic marketing is cheaper monetarily—after all, you can post a TikTok video for free—but it requires a large expense of your *time*. How much is your time worth? Given how much time this approach requires, it may not be the cheapest way for you to get leads. You might decide investing monetarily in ads is the best initial approach.

Whether you're doing organic social media marketing or paying for ads, you're going to be paying *something*. Paid advertising gets you faster and more targeted results, but it's more expensive. With organic social media marketing, the expense is your *time*. You'll need to look at your marketing budget and decide which approach is best for you at any point in your firm's growth.

Myth #2: The goal of organic marketing is to get lots of likes and views. Actually, getting a lot of likes and views is *not* necessarily what you should be striving for in your organic marketing. What you should focus on most is getting your message in front of a niche group of viewers.

To understand this, imagine you're a personal injury attorney standing in front of an audience of 400 people whose family members were all affected by a traumatic brain injury. Now, imagine you are standing in front of an audience of 100K people—but *none* of them have any connection to TBIs at all.

Which audience would you prefer? Which audience would you rather try to convince to hire you? The answer should be obvious. You want the smaller group with higher relevance.

It's the same with views versus followers. Views represent the vast unfiltered mass of people clicking around online. That's the 100K. *Followers* are the refined group of people who have a stake in what you're offering. They're the 400. They'll be your source of leads when it comes to organic marketing and that's the audience you want to target your messaging toward.

Myth #3: Your videos need to look highly polished. Your videos should be *good*—but that doesn't necessarily mean slickly produced. A good video doesn't need perfect lighting or an expensive camera lens. It simply needs to be coherent and full of quality content. It should offer people knowledge they can use to improve their lives. And believe it or not, a video that seems more "homemade" can also feel more authentic to viewers—and therefore more likable and trustworthy.

Myth #4: Social media ads are a waste of money. Actually, ads are probably your best source for leads when doing Awareness Marketing from a cost-to-acquire standpoint. We ran one of the largest talk shows in the legal industry and have talked to a lot of lawyers who have blown up on social media. Around 90% of them tell us they get *most* of their cases through their paid advertising, and their content supports their paid advertising efforts. A much smaller percentage gets their cases from their followers on social media.

What's going on here? First, we tell you social media followers are the key to getting leads, then we tell you paid advertising is the key to getting leads.

The truth is, it's both.

John, whose story opened this chapter, generates cases through a *combination* of paid advertisements on Facebook and organic social media marketing.

Our advice is to follow his example. Use the one-two punch of paid advertising combined with organic social media marketing.

Okay, so *how?* Let's break it down.

BUY Your Way In: Effective Forms of Paid Social Media Marketing

Paid advertising is the ideal way to get your lead abundance engine pumping because it automatically creates frequency and consistency, putting your ads in front of viewers. Even so, a lot of our clients push back on running social media ads because they think it produces mostly crappy leads.

This does happen—we warned you it happens. Many of the new leads you get from doing Awareness Marketing will not be worth your time. This is why we recommend getting an intake system in place that will help you filter all those leads. That's a critical step to help you cross The Abyss between Steps 4 and 5 on the Lawyer Legacy Staircase.

But a large number of crappy leads doesn't change the fact that *you're getting tons of leads.* Buried in those bad leads are good leads. *Excellent* leads. You just have to dig through the crap and find them. If you can combine social media outreach with a strong intake system, you'll see booming business. In fact, those crappy leads are the best thing that could ever happen to you because they serve as a business moat, keeping all your competition away from you. Allow us to explain.

Our business partner, Ethen Ostroff, has built a high-volume personal injury law firm off of social media and social media alone. In his first eighteen months, his social media ads generated him approximately 24K leads. Out of those 24K, he signed up over 1,900 cases. If you're doing the math, that means around 92% of his leads were bad leads—cases that he didn't accept. But it also means that he ended up getting over 1,900 cases that he *did* accept. And here's the truly crazy part. When you factor in all the costs associated with running these ads, it ended up costing him approximately $259 to acquire a case—which is a *fantastic* cost per case. Those are stunning numbers. They are life-changing numbers!

The problem is, most lawyers focus on the 92% that *don't* turn into cases, so they miss the 8% that turn into really, really inexpensive cases. That's the best thing that could ever happen to *you*, because that means there's no competition—everyone else gave up on this "junky" advertising territory a long time ago. Use that to your advantage and let them *think* this form of advertising doesn't work.

Platforms like Facebook and Instagram, owned by Meta, can source some of your best and cheapest new cases. The solution to overcome the bad traffic and poor leads isn't to simply stop running ads—it's to implement an intake system that can effectively *sort* the good leads from the bad.

In Chapter 9, we're going to show you exactly how Ethen manages to process 24K leads to find those 1,900 cases. (We'll give you a hint right now—he's not the one doing his intake.) For now, we simply want you to understand that paid ads on social media can help generate some of the cheapest new cases your firm will get in the next year.

Note that this method did not work for Ethen's entire practice. Ethen got amazing results for part of his practice, but using the same method did not get him results in other areas. Similarly, you may have to find which parts of your practice will benefit from campaigns based on Ethen's strategy. Just know that if you couple paid advertising with an effective intake system to find the good leads, it can work miracles for you.

Types of Social Media Paid Ads Strategies

Most effective ads for law firms will be paid advertisements on the types of platforms owned by Meta, such as Facebook and Instagram. Anyone who has ever scrolled through Facebook pages will see ads. All those ads are paid. They come in three varieties.

1. **Retargeting.** Facebook keeps track of ads you look at. Using this information, an attorney can buy an ad that follows users around the internet, showing up on other sites that the user visits. If someone shows an interest in your firm, now you can reinforce that interest by repetitively hitting them with more ads.

2. **Direct Response Lead Generation.** These are the ads that Ethen used. They direct someone to an immediate call to action as part of the ad, like "Click here to talk to someone on our team." Use the Qualify, Educate, Activate script we'll discuss in a moment for these.

3. **The 25-Cubed Strategy.** This is a more advanced form of the first type. When someone watches 25% or more of one of your videos, Meta directs them to a second video. If they watch 25% or more of that video, Meta directs them to a call to action. The reason this works is because people have very short attention spans on social media. If someone watches a significant portion of one of your videos, that's like them raising their hand. If they watch 25% of another video, there's a good chance they have a problem they think you might be able to help them with. This form of paid ads enables you to focus on people who have the problem you're discussing in the videos—people who are potentially great future clients.

We recommend using all three strategies. Ethen and John did, and they both achieved great success in their social media lead generation.

So, what's the first step in creating an ad?

First, select the right audience and topic by asking the following four questions:

1. What types of cases do I want to attract?
2. Who are my ideal clients that have these types of cases?
3. What specific or small problems do these ideal clients have?
4. What do these clients want to avoid at all costs?

By asking these four questions, you're able to create compelling content that resonates with your ideal potential clients. This is the key to getting them to stop scrolling and to watch your video.

Then, film a video using the Hook, Story, Offer format.

First, hook the viewer with a compelling introduction related to their small problem or something they want to avoid at all costs. For example, you could start with, "If you've been in a car accident that wasn't your fault, here's how the insurance company will try to trick you into paying you less money."

Next, tell a short story that fulfills the promise you made in the hook.

Close the video with a short call to action, or offer. Make sure the offer sounds more like they are talking to a friend, rather than a pitch. For example, you could say, "If you have any questions about a car accident, give me a call and I'll tell you exactly what to do" instead of the stuffy, "Call me today for a free consultation."

With this format, you can come up with an endless number of ads.

And, as we mentioned with Google Ads, make sure you are only targeting the right demographics and geographic areas of those who are most likely to hire you.

Here are some additional tips to make this process super simple, and ensure you get it right the first time ...

- Dress down. People want to relate to you, not feel like you're some superhuman.

- Film in front of a clear, simple background. This allows for simpler editing.

- Use your iPhone with a ring light. This will ensure you don't overthink the film setup and further build authenticity.

- Use simple captions on your video. Someone should be able to see what you're saying in the video even if they don't click on it and hear it.

- Don't forget you'll appear less energetic on camera, so increase your energy when filming to avoid appearing boring and dull.

BUILD Your Way In: Effective Forms of Organic Marketing

The "free" form of advertising on social media involves you building up a profile which attracts followers. Some lawyers love the idea of organic marketing. They might even think,

I'm going to become a TikTok star! The idea of amassing followers and making viral videos can be appealing. But it's a harder, longer slog than your favorite Instagram influencer makes it seem.

If you decide to go with organic marketing, you will save cash, but you spend time. Your results will come much more slowly than if you were to use paid ads. You can achieve in two weeks with cash what it would take you six months to achieve with time. It also takes time to produce videos and to keep up with the comments and DMs from followers, which is an important step to increase your profile's visibility.

So, before we get into paying with time, we recommend you take a good hard look at what building a social media following will entail. Your time is valuable. Consider whether or not using your time to make online videos is the best use of your limited resources.

If you *do* decide this route makes the most sense for you, then get comfortable because we're about to give you a whole heap of advice on how to do this well.

Types of Organic Social Media

There are a number of ways you can engage in social media marketing. Given how fast the technological landscape changes, there will likely be new forms to add to this list all the time. Here are some of the main platforms we see lawyers using to build their organic social media following ...

- YouTube (long-form videos)
- TikTok (short-form videos)

- Instagram

- Facebook

- X, formerly known as Twitter

If you're consistent and post quality content, you can be successful on any of these forums. However, we recommend one above all others because of its longevity, prominence, and usefulness. YouTube.

Long-Form Videos > Short-Form Videos

We recommend YouTube as your dominant content platform for a very simple reason. Videos on YouTube live forever. They will be there tomorrow, and they will be there 50 years from now.

This is not true of other platforms. TikTok videos, YouTube shorts, and Instagram feeds typically fade into oblivion.

On the other hand, YouTube videos can make an impression far beyond what you might have expected, simply by remaining there and being part of your larger library of videos. In fact, I once got a call from a lawyer who said, "Andy! Guess what? I took the Andrew Stickel challenge. It helped me raise my firm from six figures to seven figures."

"What are you talking about?" I asked. "I've never heard of the 'Andrew Stickel Challenge.'"

"I went through your videos on YouTube and picked out the 60 ones that I thought would help me the most. Then I watched one video a day and immediately implemented the points that video covered." I was blown away. This lawyer had invented a "challenge"—simply based off the videos I'd posted—and by following the advice, his firm blew up. This wouldn't have been possible with any other video platform currently available.

> **Quick-Hitting Hack:** Intrigued? Andy later turned this into a book called *The Andrew Stickel Challenge.* If you'd like to get a copy of this or view the 60 videos, visit the QR code below.
>
> (You'll find all the other bonuses from the book here or you can go to **yourdreamlawfirm.com**.)
>
> **Scan this QR Code to Unlock This Bonus**

YouTube videos don't just help you get business and raise awareness. They can be useful for intake as well. For example, David Buckley, a personal injury attorney, told us a story about when he got a lead on a big case. A DoorDash driver had injured a pedestrian. That pedestrian was looking for legal representation. Buckley was the fifth attorney the victim had interviewed, but he didn't retain Buckley right then.

After the interview, Buckley sent him an email. "Thanks for talking to me. I'm sorry about your situation. Here's a video I filmed a few months ago that could shed light on your case and give you more information." He included a link to a pertinent video he'd made and posted on YouTube a while ago.

This was a video that wasn't particularly popular—it had fewer than 100 views. But it was exactly the information that the potential client needed. It addressed a very specific issue the guy was dealing with in his legal action against DoorDash. And guess what? He hired Buckley the next day. That little video with hardly any views snagged Buckley a million-dollar case.

That's the magic of putting out an enormous number of videos. You never know which one is going to lead to something big. It's like fishing. Put out one line, you may or may not get a fish. But put out 500 lines and you're almost guaranteed to catch a fish.

Does that mean you should *never* do short-form videos? No. You can still do short-form videos to try to capitalize on the TikTok and Instagram audiences—but you can make these short-form videos *from* your longer ones. Make long-form videos, then use a cheap virtual assistant editor to chop them up into shorter videos around two minutes or less. Then post the short *and* the long. It's harder to stitch together a collection of short videos into a long video. Much easier to go from long to short.

When we interviewed social media influencer Gary Vaynerchuk at one of our events, he explained a brilliant way he used this technique. He introduced the "document, don't create" concept by hiring a videographer to follow him around and record what he does in a day. Then, he chopped that up into a bunch of smaller videos and posted them online. That strategy ultimately resulted in millions of social media followers for his account.

This is something anyone can do. Even if you can't hire a videographer, you can still create these documentation videos and chop them up into short YouTube videos. By employing this dual strategy of posting both short *and* long videos, you can maximize your potential for new leads.

Getting Started

You might be picking up on a not-so-subtle recommendation from us. Whether you're recording videos for paid advertising, or videos for organic social media marketing ... You're going to want to make videos.

Remember the goal of Awareness Marketing: You're trying to get potential clients—people who aren't even looking for your firm yet—to *know, like, and trust* you. Videos are simply the best way to accomplish all three of those goals.

For the rest of this chapter, Andy's going to school you like Spielberg. It's time to learn how to make a solid video, starring—you guessed it—*you.*

ANDY STICKEL NARRATES

The Hardest Video to Post Is the First

In Chapter 5, I talked about my "spamarella" epiphany: rather than send email spam to potential clients, I decided I was going to make free content in the form of videos that would actually help people. It was a brilliant idea. (That's why we've highlighted it in this book as the New Marketing approach.)

All I had to do to make that happen was get a camera, make a ton of videos stuffed full of quality content, and put them up on YouTube. Simple.

I went out and bought myself a camera. A good one. Perfect for what I wanted to do.

Then, it sat on my desk for six months.

Deep down, I didn't want to be on camera. I was terrified! I was afraid I wouldn't know what to say. I was afraid I'd look stupid. People would judge my appearance. People would judge my presentation. People would judge my voice.

Ironically, people know me today as the video guy. I've made so many videos at this point in my life that most people probably never even suspect that I had a hard time with it at first. But I did! I had a laundry list of excuses to keep from getting started.

- I'm having a bad hair day.
- I'm way too busy today.
- The lighting isn't the best today.
- My script isn't perfect.
- I'll "feel it" more tomorrow.

That last excuse is a perfect example of what I call *the Mañana Principle*, which simply says, "Whatever I need to do, I'll do it tomorrow." Lots of people practice this without knowing it. I certainly did. I invoked the Mañana Principle constantly.

The problem is, there's always another tomorrow. If you constantly say you're going to do something tomorrow, you'll never do it.

What finally got me to turn *mañana* into today? It was my desire for success. I genuinely believed that my idea would help me take my business a huge step forward. Eventually, that desire for success outweighed my fear of the camera. So, one day I picked it up … and made my first video.

I edited it, then I posted it on YouTube. Finally, it was freaking done.

Done is better than perfect, especially at first. Once I finally did that first video, I realized it was surprisingly easy. Not only that, it was *fun*. I was an instant convert. I started making more videos. I went into overdrive creating content.

You'll likely experience the same hesitations initially, but tell yourself that your success is more important than your inhibitions. Take a lesson from Nike, and just do it! Once you do, you'll likely experience the same rush I did at posting videos. That's going to help you build momentum—but be forewarned. The Gap of Disappointment is coming.

Gap of Disappointment

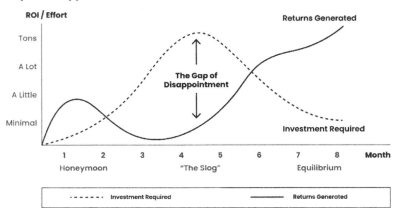

What's the Gap of Disappointment? I'll explain. When you start off creating content, it's exciting. You feel gung-ho about doing a new project and getting your face on the internet. You have no shortage of ideas, and you have plenty of natural enthusiasm. And *because* you're excited, it's easier for you to put in the work to create posts or videos. The thought of people watching, responding—possibly even sending you new business—is highly motivating.

That enthusiasm increases once you actually post the video, because people engage! You get likes, comments, even shares. People in your network aren't used to seeing your stuff, and they'll make a point to look at it because it's different and new. Typically, they'll reward you with some form of affirming engagement. And every time somebody comments, likes, or shares, you get a little dopamine hit in your brain. Granted, there's no new *business* from your posts—at least, not yet—but all those dopamine hits create their own ROI for your efforts. What a high!

That ROI, combined with your own enthusiasm, propels you to make another video. You make another video or post. And another.

And another.

But as time goes on, the novelty starts wearing off for you. Making videos or writing new posts starts feeling like a chore. You have fewer ideas. You're busy. You don't want to interrupt your workflow by filming a video. You're having a bad hair day.

At the same time, the novelty *also* starts wearing off for people in your network. Your videos don't get as many views because people no longer see you as the shiny new object. They're no longer liking, commenting, or sharing the way they used to, which means you're no longer getting a psychological return on your investment. Your dopamine-hit ROI plummets just when you could use that external motivation the most.

That's the Gap of Disappointment. It's the stage that requires your maximum effort and yields the minimum results. Guess what happens to most people when they hit the Gap of Disappointment?

They quit. Nine times out of ten.

What happens if you don't quit? What happens if you push forward through the Gap, slogging to stay consistent with your posts?

Eventually, the ratio flips again. You get better at making posts or filming videos, so it requires less effort from you. Your library of content increases, working for you even when you're not "working." And, over time, more people find their way into your network who are genuinely interested in the content you're sharing, because it provides value to them. When that happens—*that's* when you're going to really take off. That's when the ROI produces cash returns, not just dopamine hits. That's what's on the other side of the slog.

And that's what happened to me. I got gratifying results from my first couple videos. I got noticed. I accumulated comments, likes, and shares, which made me feel awesome. People *wanted* to see what I was doing. I put out more content. I was on a roll!

Then, a few weeks in, things dropped off. I stopped getting comments. "Likes" were scarce. No one was sharing my content anymore. I was suddenly singing to an auditorium full of empty seats and it was discouraging. My "dopamine hits" ROI measurement was next to nothing.

I had run up against the Gap of Disappointment.

Luckily, I knew what this was and more importantly, I knew what it *meant*. The concept of the Gap of Disappointment comes from Rand Fishkin, author of *Lost and Founder: A Painfully Honest Field Guide to the Startup World*. He explains it in a similar way I've just done and he also makes this crucial point: The most successful people in the world all need to go through it.

Here's the crucial thing to know about the Gap. It's *temporary*. And you'll eventually get through it, so long as you keep doing what you're doing. Creating videos will start getting harder because it won't be new anymore and it'll feel like you're doing it for nothing. But it's *not* for nothing. Each piece of content you create is out there, working for you for years.

I kept pumping out content. Free content. Eventually, the sheer amount of content I had out there made me impossible to ignore and the Gap began to reverse in my favor. If a lawyer was looking for a particular topic, there I was. I had made the content that addressed that lawyer's concerns a month, or a year, or five years ago. Instead of me putting in tons of work for little ROI, I got to the place where I got an *incredible* ROI from minimal effort.

The Gap of Disappointment doesn't last. And guess what? You can use it to your advantage, because *the Gap of Disappointment is where most of your competition will throw in the towel.* It's when they say, "Screw this. It isn't working." They give up. And that's when you win because you *didn't* give up and now you have no competition.

The Gap of Disappointment afflicts every business startup and every business that wants to up its game. That's super important, because if I didn't know about it, I would have quit. The crucial thing to remember is to *not let it stop you.* Work through it and you'll come out on the other side stronger and better equipped to take your business to new heights.

Suck Long Enough to Get Good at Something

I don't want you to think I was making fantastic videos from the start. Are you kidding me? I was *awful.* I was stiff and obviously uncomfortable in front of the camera. My delivery was halting and even confusing. Those first attempts were too long and unfocused.

It didn't matter. I learned from each video I did. I kept going, producing content constantly.

After a while, a funny thing happened. I got good. Even though I sucked at making videos when I started, I made so many of them that eventually I learned how to make good ones. Once I did that, they weren't hard at all. I had the knowledge I needed to make them an easy task. As of this writing, I've got over 1,600 videos on YouTube.

Most people don't want to suck at things. That's understandable. We all want to feel competent and like we know what we're doing. That feels *good.*

But it's a trap. When would I have started making content if I waited to be good at making content? Try *never*. I would *never* have started because the way I got good was by *making crappy videos.*

You need to do the same. Commit to making content and *start making content now*. Even if it's terrible. Even if it's embarrassing. That phase won't last. Stick with it long enough and you'll get good. That's how you win.

The key is showing up on a consistent basis. This is true of both paid and organic marketing. Start placing ads and/or start making videos. And do it on a *consistent* basis. Every day is ideal.

The truth is, you probably *do* suck on camera. If you're not used to doing videos, it's going to feel uncomfortable and weird at first. But remember, most people aren't going to see your first videos. Consider them your training ground. After watching them, you might realize that you want to pick a corner of the house that has better lighting, or boost your energy, or be more animated. Use those early videos to learn how to make better ones and to establish the habit of making those videos.

Just remember, you're not trying for an Academy Award here. *You're building the habit,* **which establishes frequency and consistency.** That's the crucial point. You're getting in the habit of posting regularly. And as you do, you will become more comfortable with the camera, and your true personality will shine through.

The world is littered with false starts and aborted projects. If there are 100 people in a room who say they're going to make a podcast, statistically, only one of them will make it to episode 21. It's true of TikTok videos, blog posts, Instagram reels, everything. The vast majority of endeavors hardly get started before they crash and burn. That means if you make it to 21, you're in the top 1%. Live your life to get to the next 21!

The only way to fail is to quit. But if you stick to your plan and just execute day after day, you're going to come out on top.

Quick-Hitting Hack: How do you generate topics for all these hypothetical videos and posts? Easy. You don't have to. You just have to pay attention to what's already there.

- Find videos that are already out there in your subject area and then record your own riff on the topic.

- While you're at it, read through all the *other* related videos that YouTube pulls up in your topic alongside the first video you looked at. Pay attention to the number of views. Which topics are people most interested in? How could you put your own spin on that?

- Look up videos in different topic areas, unrelated to your niche, and see what's trending. For instance, I noticed that a YouTube video entitled, "Six Figures Your First Year as a YouTuber. True or False? You Decide," had attracted close to 350K views. Clearly, there was a lot of interest in that topic. So, I made my own video and titled it, "Six Figures Your First Year as an *Entrepreneur.* True or False? You Decide."

> - We once heard marketing genius Dan Kennedy speak in a presentation and he said something to the effect of, "I've never had an original idea in my life, and I don't plan to ever have one." In other words, all he does is collect ideas and then reshapes them in a new way. For instance, if he's doing a marketing campaign for a restaurant, he looks up a great real estate campaign and applies the ideas in a new context. You can do the same thing. "Steal like an artist."[14]

Video Content Tips

Once you've gotten over that initial hump of getting started, you're ready to build your library of video content. Here are some strategies to generate video topics, be strategic in your approach, and achieve the all-important *know, like, and trust* impression on your viewers.

It's Not About You. It's About *Them*.

We don't recommend you employ a scattershot approach and try to attract everyone in your potential client pool with the same content. On the contrary, Awareness Marketing targets *specific* people. Remember everything we've said in this book already about focusing on a niche group of viewers. Your marketing content should solve the specific problems of each distinct type of target client.

---

[14] *Steal Like an Artist* is the title of Austin Kleon's excellent book which unpacks this idea further.

We've given you lots of ideas already about how to target niche groups of people, but we want to hit a key point here about speaking to that particular audience. Remember that *it's not about you.* Your target clients don't care if you accidentally film your "bad side" or cough in the middle of a sentence. All they care about is whether or not your information is helpful. Here's a quote we love from Frank Kern: "You don't have to worry about being cool. You just have to worry about helping other people."

With that in mind, consider a few key points when you're preparing to record content for your target clients. Your videos should address at least one of three things:

1. What does this target client want?
2. How do they get it?
3. What will their life be like after they get it?

The focus, always, is on them. Not you. When you remember that you're catering to *their* needs, you can keep your focus where it belongs. On them. Not on your level of photogenicness or cool factor. Viewers don't care if you are cool or not. Keep your focus on your target audience and simply deliver the information.

Focus on Frequency, Then on Quality

Let's say you want to start up a new workout routine. You schedule your gym workouts three days a week at different times: 11 a.m. on Monday, 5 p.m. on Wednesday, and 7 a.m. on Friday. How long do you think you'll keep up with that schedule? Probably not very long. There are too many gaps, and it's also a little confusing remembering the time for each day.

On the other hand, what if you went to the gym *every day* at the same time? At 6 a.m., Monday to Friday, without fail. You'll most likely stick to that schedule. Working out will become habitual. You may not be great at first because you might be out of shape, but remember, *done* is better than perfect—especially in the beginning.

That's the kind of schedule we recommend for making your content videos for your organic marketing campaign. Make a new video every single day, at the same time every day. Eventually, it will become a habit.

Organic marketing, as we said, takes time. I didn't get a single lead until four months of posting videos daily. But I kept going, every day and *eventually*, all those videos started bringing in leads.

When that starts happening—and only then—you need to start thinking about quality. Why? Because you will most likely plateau on your leads. To push past that plateau, you might have to up the polish and look of your videos. This is the quality part, which comes *after* the frequency part.

We recommend hiring a virtual assistant and editor right away to outsource your editing and content management. These professionals can help you maintain your schedule and consistency. Eventually, you could choose to hire a professional videographer to boost the polish of your videos. But focus on frequency first, polish second.

As we write this, the ideal schedule we've found for an attorney to follow is to post two 5- to 10-minute videos per week on YouTube, and one short-form video per day on TikTok, Instagram Reels, YouTube Shorts, and LinkedIn. Remember, you can make those short videos from your longer videos.

A caution here: the digital landscape is constantly changing. The above paragraph may be completely outdated by the time you read this. You need to constantly monitor online trends to see where your message will have the most impact.

The Goal Is Their Attention

Oprah Winfrey has a huge worldwide audience. I often ask my clients the question, "If you were offered a chance to be interviewed by Oprah, would you do it?"

Just about every lawyer I ask says, "Yes! I would do it."

Why? What good would it do for your business? You'd be in front of a completely unfiltered audience, just there for the attention.

Is this a bad thing? Absolutely not. Whether or not it's Oprah asking you to be on her show, you should be an attention hog! Should you be interviewed on someone's podcast that has 25K subscribers? Yes! Should you go on TV to be interviewed by your local news as a legal expert? Hell, yes!

Get the attention. That's brand building. That's people getting to know you, becoming aware of you.

Another tactic to snag viewers' attention is to tie your videos to something with local appeal. For example, say the NFL team in your market is contending for the Super Bowl. Do some videos that incorporate those games. You could discuss the three most common places people get arrested for DUIs after a game. You could talk about the fact that players with CTE often have completely undamaged helmets and connect that to the fact that a car can be relatively undamaged in an accident, but the person inside could be seriously injured. Talk about your views of the game or the players or the coach— even the cheerleaders or the food at the stadium. Then at the end of it, say you're a lawyer.

The possibilities here are endless. Let your imagination go wild. The holy grail of marketing is attention. You want to command people's attention so that when they need a lawyer, they will think of you.

Types of Videos

What topics should you cover in your videos? Here are just a few ideas to get you started.

Start by Answering FAQs

Every client that we interview has the same questions for us. These questions are so predictable that we get bored answering the same ol' FAQs. It eats up valuable time!

We're guessing you can relate because most lawyers encounter the same situation.

Here's where your YouTube videos can help. Make some quality content that answers all the FAQs you know you are likely to get during a consultation with a potential client. Record what you would say during the in-person interview. Then, before you meet with your potential client, send them an email linking to the videos that answer all those questions.

As we've been saying all along, make sure you give quality content in these videos. Answer the FAQs in detail. Don't hold anything back. Give thorough and pertinent information. YouTube videos that answer common FAQs can even replace you in the intake process. Give your team access to these videos so they can tell leads, "Hey, our attorney has already answered this question. Here's the video."

One more advantage of making all these FAQ videos is that it allows your personality and knowledge to scale up. Once you put 100 videos online, and keep adding to that, it's impossible to run from yourself. The real you will come out. Everything in your brain will be public. That's a good thing. Your potential clients will begin to *know, like, and trust you* before they ever set foot in your office.

PSA Marketing

Most of us have seen cringe-worthy posts on our personal Facebook feeds by a friend who just joined another multi-level marketing company selling essential oils, workout gear, or some other product they're trying to hock as a side gig. The person making the posts often seems desperate. It's awkward for everybody.

Luckily, there is another way.

People are hesitant to put themselves out there in front of their friends and family, but before you build a following, *that's* your network. So, how do you market to your personal connections without feeling cringey? The solution is Public Service Announcements.

PSAs enable you to share good info and there's nothing cringe-worthy about them. They don't try to get you to buy something. All they're doing is providing information. Good, solid information people can use to improve their lives— that's exactly the type of content you should be producing in the New Way marketing approach.

This format is a goldmine for your own content generation. Make YouTube videos that *don't* include a call to action to contact you.

For example, here's a good solid script from a personal injury attorney:

"Hey guys, as you know, I'm a personal injury attorney and I want to tell you something that will save you lots of money because I see this over and over and over again. Everybody needs to pull out their insurance policy and make sure they have *uninsured motorist coverage.* It's usually only about $20, but you can't afford not to have it. Let me tell you why. We had a potential client come into our office who got rear-ended by someone without insurance. Now, she has $20K in medical bills. But because the person who hit her doesn't have insurance, this person is on the hook for that twenty grand. If she had uninsured coverage, her own insurance company would have covered those costs. So, everyone with car insurance, take a look at your policy. Make sure you have uninsured motorist coverage."

The PSA-style video ends with two clinchers. "Do me a favor and share this video with everyone you know. It's crucial information. And if you are having trouble figuring out your own policy, give me a call. I'll look at your policy and give you a free review."

"*Share* the video and *call me* if you want help." These are two huge marketing pitches, and yet this script isn't cringey! It doesn't feel like a desperate attempt to drum up business or lure people into a multi-level marketing disaster. It just gives good solid information. It's a PSA—something people will feel good about forwarding to friends and family, thereby expanding your reach and your visibility.

If you decide to do these PSA-style ads, be casual. Make them selfie-style, just you and a cell phone held in front of you. You don't want it to look like an ad. It should look more like a friend just sitting with you, telling you something useful. You can share helpful information about clients you've worked with personally, or even ones you've just heard about from other colleagues. Be mindful of changing any confidential information, obviously, and focus on the interesting, relevant details. Here's another example:

"If you're dealing with any legal situation, *do not* post anything on social media. Even a seemingly innocent selfie can be taken out of context and used against you in legal proceedings. I just heard of a woman who was fighting for custody over her kids, but she posted a selfie with a pornographic picture in the background. It wasn't taken at her house, and she didn't even realize it was in the background, but the selfie was used against her in court as evidence that she wasn't providing a good environment for her kids. So, do yourself a favor. If you're going through legal proceedings of any kind, *don't* post videos on social media, *don't* post pictures—just take a break from posting things for a while. If you think this message would benefit anyone else, please share it, and if you have any questions, send me a DM."

The key is to make the content relevant to a large group of people. With PSA-style videos, you're not after a niche audience here. Millions of people own cars and have auto insurance making that topic a good selection for a PSA.

To come up with your own script, think about something everyone should know that is related to your practice. Explain it in simple, clear terms that everyone can understand. Here are some examples:

- If you're a tax attorney, do a PSA about how the IRS really works.

- If you're a medical malpractice attorney, do a PSA with tips on how to navigate your medical insurance negotiations.

- If you're a labor lawyer, do a PSA explaining the value of belonging to a good trade union.

By providing useful information that can improve people's lives, you won't come across as a desperate salesperson. Instead, you'll leave the impression of a competent, smart, helpful expert. And guess what impression that will leave on viewers? Say it all together now … They'll *know, like, and trust you.*

Heck yeah, they will!

Misconception Education

We talked about this when we looked at Ethen's approach to making videos. It's the second item on his list of three and it's worth highlighting here.

You can gain a lot of trust just by correcting people's misconceptions about the law. Just because something is common knowledge to you, doesn't mean it's common knowledge to the general public. For example, telling people they don't have to pay a lawyer up front for a personal injury case is misconception education. They pay only if they win. That's huge! To someone hearing this for the first time, it's like getting access to inside information.

John, the immigration lawyer we mentioned in this chapter's opening story, has explained that one of the disheartening things about the immigration law field is how long a case takes to get through the system. Cases can be stuck in administration processes for years.

So, here's what John did to correct misconceptions around immigration law. He made a video that informed people that they could *sue* the federal government, forcing them to take their case out of administrative processing and move it forward. Most people don't know this. John told them. He built an enormous amount of trust with just that one bit of information. Then, he backed that up with a call to action. "Click this link and download a free guide on how to sue the government and get your case moving forward."

He built trust by busting the misconception most people have that you just have to wait for your case to go through the process. When you record videos about misconceptions in your own field of law, you'll get people's attention and secure their trust.

Call to Action

Nearly always, your videos should end with an invitation to contact you. This is the third item in Ethen's format and one of the most important elements to include. A call to action.

Notice in the examples above, both Ethen and John had calls to action. Ethen asked people to fill out a contact form to connect with his firm and John asked people to download a free guide to find even more information than his video presented.

Both approaches can be effective. Note that John's call to action was more likely to engage people who weren't quite ready to contact a lawyer. This means he might be a little more successful than Ethen in getting leads from their respective videos.

There are many ways you can encourage viewers to engage with you, your firm, and/or your website. Think about what kind of call to action you want to include, but make sure you do include one. This is how you're going to turn your videos into leads!

How to Be Top Dog

We've given you a lot of tips on how to approach Awareness Marketing, both through paid ads and through organic social media marketing. And we've given you an in-depth tutorial on making videos that land with viewers, bring you new leads, and help people *know, like, and trust you.*

We're going to end this chapter by showing you why all the effort will be worth it.

One of our first employees at SMB was a guy named James Helm. Hardly anyone knows him by that name anymore. In the Philadelphia area, he is known far and wide as Top Dog, the owner of Top Dog Law, the highest-volume personal injury practice in his market.

When James first struck out on his own, he did a lot of Instagram videos—but those didn't initially get him much attention. What he did next was pure genius. He teamed up with local influencers—local celebrities and comedians. He recorded videos with them. This was an unconventional way to "*earn* his way in," but it worked. The collaborations turned into extremely funny videos—people all over town found them hugely entertaining. They gave James the added bonus of boosting his profile through the celebrities' large followings.

James became a local celebrity himself and amassed hundreds of thousands of followers, all concentrated in the Philadelphia area. But initially, all of his Awareness Marketing was in the organic marketing category. James was playing the long game. Those early videos weren't about getting cases in the next week or even month. His focus was on getting attention and building awareness about his brand.

Once he got that big following, he pivoted to paid ads. He embraced ads on Meta's platforms big time. That's when he became unstoppable. Today, he does 50% paid ads and 50% organic marketing, and he continues to dominate the market.

The lesson here is that when you're doing Awareness Marketing, paid and organic ideally should work together. You don't have to choose one or the other. You can choose both. And keep in mind what "both" entails for you. Your money *and* your time.

A lot of lawyers come to us wanting to get started in social media. The first question we ask them is, "How much money are you going to spend on ads and what days of the week are you going to be posting stuff online?"

Money and time. Those are the two expenses lawyers need to be thinking about if they hope to succeed on social media. Top Dog did it with 50% wallet and 50% calendar. You could do the same, or you could mix it up a little. Each lawyer needs to find a balance that works.

It's up to you, but don't neglect one for the other. Paid and organic work together beautifully to bring you an abundance of leads—more leads than you could get in 100 years by using "hope and pray."

Once you get those leads, what do you do about them? As immigration lawyer John and Ethen Ostroff can tell you, you don't want to get buried under an avalanche of bad leads.

We've been beating this drumbeat for a while now, and it's finally time to discuss how to get a fundamental piece in place for both your Demand and Awareness Marketing campaigns. You need to have a flawless intake system to handle the crush.

We'll show you how to do that in the next chapter.

Chapter 8 | Takeaways

1. The goal of Awareness Marketing is to get potential new clients to *know, like, and trust* you. The best way to do that is through recording video content.

2. You can pay for Awareness Marketing either with your money or your time. Buying your way in will get your results fastest, through using paid ads. Building your way in through doing organic social media marketing is cheaper monetarily, but requires a lengthy commitment of your time and energy to post content frequently and consistently. You'll likely need to put in months of effort before you start seeing a consistent ROI.

3. Many people feel hesitant to record and post their first video, but once you get started, you'll build momentum. The most important thing to remember is to post regularly and not stop when you hit the Gap of Disappointment, which is the point when most of your competitors will bail.

4. When recording videos, make sure your content *helps* your target viewers. You can do that by considering the needs, questions, and desires of your target audience.

Worthwhile video topics include answering FAQs, PSA-style content, misconception education, and videos that tap into topics with local appeal. Remember that most of your videos should include a call to action that invites engagement from viewers.

CHAPTER 9

INTAKE & SALES

FIND YOUR RIGHT FIT CLIENTS AND TURN THEM INTO SIGNED CASES

"Success is almost totally dependent upon drive and persistence. The extra energy required to make another effort or try another approach is the secret of winning."

—Denis Waitley

Picture this ... A loud pounding on your firm's glass door causes you to look up from your conversation with your administrative assistant. There's a woman on the other side of the door, kicking it loudly with her boot. Her arms are full of file folders—maybe 30 of them. She's even gripping a file folder with her mouth. She gives you and your assistant an angry, exasperated look and makes a muffled protest through the file folder in her mouth, then kicks the door again. Your assistant hurries to let the woman in. As soon as she's in the reception area, she drops the file folders onto the floor in a heap. Papers scatter everywhere. The woman scowls at you.

"Took you long enough," she complains. "*You* can reorganize those damn files!"

Behold, the nightmare client. The client you would *never* want to take on in a million years. What do you do with her?

A growing firm can reject this woman and send her elsewhere. But a firm practicing "door law" can't. They have to take her on as a client. They have to take on *anyone* as a client.

That's the curse of "door law."

What's door law? Door law should scare a law firm owner more than a werewolf under a full moon. It's the practice you fall into when your intake system is so bad you take any case that comes through the door, whether it's a good fit or not. Doesn't matter if the person who comes through your door is foaming at the mouth, whacking people with their umbrella, or throwing their files in the air. You can't afford to slam the door shut on anyone. You need them all just to survive.

This is the worst practice you can be in, and it's no way to run a law firm. We've sought to cure you of the door law curse by teaching you strategies for effective Demand and Awareness Marketing so that you get heaps of good leads.

BUT—big, fat BUT—your marketing efforts will come to nothing if you don't have an intake system to sort through and handle them all. If you've generated all these new leads, you need to know how to sort through them and convert them to signed "right fit" clients.

Your intake procedure should be set up in such a way that it does the following:

- Provides a **great first impression** of your firm.

- Sorts through the abundant leads your Demand and Awareness Marketing bring in to **weed out** any unqualified cases.

- From the remaining pool of qualified cases, identifies a smaller number of **right fit clients.**

- Impresses and **secures the trust** of those right fit clients so they convert into signed cases.

So, how do you set up a system that does all of the above?

We bragged about one of our partners, Ethen Ostroff, in the previous chapter. You might remember that Ethen was able to use Awareness Marketing to seriously scale up his firm's business because—and *only* because—he had a honed intake system to filter out bad leads.

So, how'd he get his intake system to such a flawless, efficient place?

Ethen began working for a large personal injury law firm some years ago, overseeing marketing and intake. This firm did over $100M in fees. Even then, it was a major player. But in spite of its success, soon after coming on the job, Ethen saw a lot of problems.

For one thing, receptionists were involved with intake. This kept them from what should have been their real priority. Dealing and interacting with existing clients.

Attorneys were spending a lot of their time picking up the slack for receptionists who had been pulled away from their true jobs. They also ended up doing some intake when they should have been devoting their energies and expertise to their casework. In fact, a lot of attorneys in this firm were working nights *and* weekends, just trying to keep up with their cases.

Everyone's time was being wasted, people were frustrated, and morale was low.

To top it all off, the firm wasn't even getting enough of the cases they wanted. They were agreeing to take on small personal injury cases, like a soft tissue injury in a fender bender. A case like that is not worthless, but it's peanuts compared to what a serious accident would be worth, such as a tractor trailer wrongful death case which would be significantly more valuable. They weren't getting enough of their ideal cases, which meant they were losing out on income.

Ethen came up with a model that would enable his intake team to quickly sort through leads so they could maximize their attention on the cases they wanted. As a result, efficiency improved, and they were signing way more cases for the same marketing spend.

So, how'd he do it?

Ethen's Model: The "Cases I Want" Score

When Ethen gets a lead, they typically include a short description of the problem the client is facing. Maybe a person filled out an online form, plugged their information into a "call to action" link, or left a voicemail. In any case, there's a small amount of information to work with.

Based on this information, Ethen directed his intake team to assign each lead a ranking score with one of four labels. He calls this the "Cases I Want" score. You can use any sort of ranking system to assign scores, but we'll explain using the numbers 0, 1, 2, and 3.

- **A 3 is a case you definitely want.** It means that something in the description aligns with the cases you're most interested in getting. For instance, if you're running a car accident campaign as a personal injury law firm, the lead might include the phrases "rear end" and "broken arm." That's a clear 3. If you're running a RoundUp class action lawsuit and the lead description includes "non-Hodgkin's lymphoma," that's another clear 3. Your intake team should zealously follow up with all 3s, reaching out maybe 15 to 20 times. Ideally, the person calling the 3s is a trained closer. (More on this when we discuss Specialized Roles later in the chapter.)

- **A 2 is a lead you need more information about.** If the lead comes in blank, with *no* description—perhaps the person only left their name, number, and email—it's a 2. There's nothing to indicate their case *wouldn't* be a good fit for your firm, but there's also nothing to indicate it *is* a case that you decisively want. Your intake team should still follow up with 2s to gather more information. However, they might focus less of their time and effort here compared to the 3s, following up around eight times, rather than 20. Your 2s can be contacted by VAs or an intake specialist.

- **A 1 is a case you probably don't want**. A lead gets assigned a 1 if something in the description contradicts the criteria you're looking for, either because they don't have a case or because they don't fit your criteria. For instance, a lead contacts you about the RoundUp class action lawsuit, but they note in their description that they have lung cancer. There's no evidence that RoundUp causes lung cancer, which means that's probably not a case you want. Their data doesn't fit your criteria. Or, take the car accident campaign example. A 1 would be assigned to a lead description that says, "rear-ended but no injury." That's likely not a case you want—if there's no injury, there's no case! However, your team should still follow up with 1s to get them to orally confirm the contradiction. It's also valuable to follow up with 1s because, even if they're not a lead you want right now, they might be a lead you want one day. For instance, a criminal law firm might assign a 1 to a person who writes, "I have a question about a DUI. I got pulled over and given a breathalyzer. I passed, but I want to know what would have happened if I didn't." There's no case there, which makes it a 1—but this lead might eventually be in a situation where he could use your legal help, and it's worth your time to invest in that relationship. 1s can be contacted by a VA or intake specialist as well, but VAs wouldn't be the ones to decide if a 1 lead should be changed to a 0.

- **A 0 is a lead you *definitely* don't want.** Nothing is a 0 until a potential client orally *confirms* that they don't fit the criteria you're looking for. What's an example of a 0? Your team calls the RoundUp lead who confirms they have lung cancer and, by the way, they also chain smoke cigarettes. Now, that's a confirmed 0. But let's say you call the "rear-end, no injury" lead, which had been scored a 1. That potential client gets on the phone and says, "Actually, I didn't *think* I got injured, but now I'm experiencing a lot of neck pain and my doctor thinks it's related to the accident." That 1 now gets scored a 3. This is why you should always follow up with 1s to get oral confirmation of their contradictory status. And ideally, the only person who decides a lead should be a 0 is someone you highly trust to make that decision. If you had a VA contact the 1 and they think the lead should be changed to a 0, the VA should fill out an "under review report," to be evaluated by a trusted member of your team who would make the final call.

This "Cases I Want" ranking system enabled Ethen's firm to create segmentation within their intake process. As a result, they were able to aggressively follow up with the cases they wanted and allocate their resources accordingly. They also had clarity about how to follow up with the 2s and 1s, focusing on gathering information, rather than giving a big pitch. The ranking scores also gave them clarity about which team members to assign to which leads. The closers called the 3s. VAs handled the 2s and 1s. And a trusted team member evaluated the 0s. We'll talk about this more when we describe Specialized Roles later in the chapter.

You might be wondering when the potential client speaks with an attorney in this "Cases I Want" system of follow-up? Well, it depends on your intake team. Ethen's VAs got to the point that he could trust several as closers, meaning most people signed up with the firm before they ever met with an attorney. However, smaller firms might choose to involve an attorney sooner. For instance, as soon as it's determined that this is a case you want, that might be the time an attorney gets involved, or you might elect for all in-person consultations to occur with an attorney. However, bigger firms might be able to handle intake entirely with their own separate intake team, enabling attorneys to exclusively focus on casework and never involve themselves with intake.

If you are a flat fee based law firm, you can have an intake specialist or VA whose primary responsibility is to get the person on the phone and "sell" the paid consultation.

In either case, once you have the criteria for your ranking numbers, you can determine the plan for follow-up and assign the right team member to reach out, according to your intake structure. Will it be someone on your intake team, or an attorney? If it's a case you want, allocate your team members accordingly to give that lead the best impression of your firm and ideally secure their case.

We were so impressed by what Ethen developed that we adopted his system for our own clients. The beauty of Ethen's approach is that it doesn't just work for personal injury firms.

Any attorney, no matter what their specialty, can use this system to get them more of the cases they truly want.

In this chapter, we'll reference Ethen's system and go into greater depth about how you can make it work for your law firm. First, though, we've got to deliver some bad news.

Your Current Intake System Is Holding You Back

We're willing to bet there's a good chance your intake is subpar. Why? Because *most* firms have a weak intake system.

Dan Newlin is a notable exception. He heads one of the biggest personal injury firms on the planet. He operates out of Florida and typically has *18K* active cases at any one time. He's a huge deal.

Guess where he has his office?

It's *right* next to the intake room. He even has a door from his office into the intake room. He does this because he knows that room is the heart of his firm and he wants to keep a close eye on his intake team to make sure they are operating efficiently and effectively.

Think of intake as the filter on a dam. On one side of the dam are all the cases, including the ones you want, pushing against the dam. On the other side is your team, ready to review and accept the cases that are right for your firm. Letting too much through will overwhelm your team. Not letting *enough* cases through leads to stagnation. It's the filtering system that determines just how much should pour through the dam at any given time.

That's intake. A good intake system allows you to secure the cases you want—and that's how you grow your firm.

#1 Intake Goal: Right Fit Clients

Let's get one thing straight from the start.

The whole point of intake is to convert the highest possible percent of right fit clients who contact your firm into signed cases. These are your dream clients. They are lucrative cases that fit your firm's experience and expertise. They are cases you live for. The "3s" in the "Cases I Want" scoring system.

It's always great to get a *lot* of cases, but beware of door law. Let's say you have 100 leads, and you sign up 65 of them. That's a good ratio, but how many of those cases are ones you really *want* to sign? As Ethen realized when he got a closer look at his personal injury firm, taking too many "poor fit" cases can lead to burnout and low morale across your firm. That's the problem with an intake system that allows too *many* cases through.

What if there were 10 right fit cases in those 100 leads but your intake only found two of them? Does having two right fit cases out of 100 still sound like a great signing ratio? Obviously not. That's the problem with an intake system that can't convert *enough* leads into cases.

Somewhere in the middle, there's a happy medium. An intake system that finds 10 out of 10 of those right fit clients.

So, how do you create your criteria to determine your 3s, 2s, and 1s? The guidelines are pretty straightforward.

- **Step 1.** Review your ideal case buckets to determine your right fit clients. Remember, you identified your ideal case buckets in Chapter 3. These are the cases that will ensure you meet your annual plan targets. Your ideal case buckets will inform your marketing campaigns and, accordingly, will pull in corresponding leads.

- **Step 2.** Identify the criteria that would characterize a "3" in one of these buckets. For instance, if you're a personal injury law firm and you've led a marketing campaign to represent high-value car accident cases, a 3 would mean there was an injury, hospital time was required, and the client was not at fault. As a small firm, your criteria might be broad. "It was a car accident which resulted in an injury, no matter how minor." But let's say your firm grows because of your excellent marketing and you get a deluge of leads. Now, the criteria should become more selective to weed out smaller cases, which you can now refer to other firms. "It was a car accident which resulted in injuries requiring hospital time and rehabilitation." With more selective criteria, cases you used to score a 3 might now be ranked a 1. The subjectiveness of this scoring system enables you to change your criteria, depending on how selective you want to be.

- **Step 3.** Write clear "yes" or "no" screening questions. In your lead form or in the beginning of the call, potential clients should be asked straightforward screening questions. "Were you involved in a car accident?" "Was the accident determined to be your fault?" "Did you sustain an injury as a result of the accident?" "Did you require hospitalization as a result of the injury?" These screening questions will enable your intake team to clearly assign a 1, 2, or 3 to each lead. As your criteria for what constitutes a 3 evolves, your screening questions should evolve as well.

- **Step 4.** Train your staff to evaluate the criteria. Conduct training to ensure your intake specialists know how to recognize and delineate between a 3, a 2, and a 1. You also want to make sure a trusted person understands what would shift a 1 to a 0.

- **Step 5.** Follow up with your leads according to their ranking. Leads ranked as a 3 should get the bulk of your resources and attention. They should also be contacted by a person who specializes in closing with clients. The 2s and 1s should be followed up with as well, but primarily for the purpose of gathering more data.

Remember, depending on where you are on the Lawyer Legacy Staircase, your approach with these ranking numbers will look different. At a lower step on the staircase, your main focus is simply getting more leads. The problem at that point is that you don't have enough! A 3 at that point may be any case that fits your broad legal categories. However, higher on the staircase, you need to get more strict about your criteria. Once you have an adequate number of cases, shift your criteria from quantity to quality.

The problem that Ethen faced with a large and successful firm was that they weren't getting enough of the *right* cases.

Quality is better than quantity when it comes to intake. As your firm grows, design your intake to find those home run cases and filter out the others you would only take because you had to—not because you wanted to.

So, your number one intake goal is to convert the highest possible percentage of "cases you want" into signed cases.

That's your main intake *goal*. Now, let's talk about your number one intake *principle*.

#1 Intake Principle: Don't Give Up, Follow Up

If you only walk away with one insight from this chapter, it's this principle: The fortune is in the follow-up.

We taught you this principle first in Chapter 6, but it deserves another hammering here. Follow-up means everything when it comes to securing your right fit clients and it involves texting, emailing, and calling your leads—particularly the 3s.

Relentlessly. Every day. Multiple times a day.

Don't give up on the 3s until they either tell you to stop, or they sign with your firm. Follow up is your key to turning leads into clients.

Here's a tale of two attorneys we worked with, which is 100% true. Each of these attorneys hired us to run a Facebook ad campaign for their firms, and we got each of them 300 leads in one month. Attorney A—let's call her Alyssa—didn't turn a single one of those 300 new leads into a client. Attorney B—we'll call him Bernard—managed to convert 75 of those leads into new cases.

It was the exact same campaign—identical copy, ads, targeting, practice area, etc.—and resulted in the exact same number of leads. But these two attorneys got entirely different results.

We called Alyssa. "What happened?" we asked.

Big sigh. "I couldn't get anybody on the phone. Nobody answers the phone when I call." Made sense. We hung up with Alyssa.

We called Bernard. "How did you get all these cases?" we asked. "A different attorney got the same number of leads, but she told us no one answers the phone when she makes calls."

Bernard said, "Yeah, nobody answers the phone. I have to call them multiple times before they answer the phone. That's why I also text and email. I'm relentless about it."

Bernard had figured out a crucial piece about growing his business. It's not as simple as just *getting* new leads. You also must *convert* those leads into actual cases by relentlessly pursuing them and offering them real value for free in your marketing, as we've discussed at length in other chapters. We're going to give you follow-up strategies later in this chapter.

Identify and convert your right fit clients. That's your main intake *goal*. Your most important intake *principle* is to follow up, give value, and don't give up.

Now, let's get into the nitty-gritties of actually doing the dang thing.

Strategies to Level Up Your Intake System

Your intake system should accomplish four things. Can you name them without looking?

1. Provide a **great first impression**.
2. Weed out unqualified cases (the 1s and 0s) and **identify right fit clients** (the 3s and vetted 2s).
3. **Follow up relentlessly** with the 3s, those right fit clients. The nature of your follow-up with the other leads will be determined by their intake score.
4. Get your right fit clients to **know, like, and trust you** so they convert into signed cases.

Let's do a deeper dive into these four key strategies now.

1. Create a Great First Impression

There are a few specific ways you can ensure your potential clients' first impression of you is one that leaves them wanting more. Hint: They're the same strategies that make you feel good when *you're* the one phoning someone as a customer!

No Calls to Voicemail

When you call a plumber, do you want to get voicemail? Of course not! When your toilet is overflowing, you want a plumber *now*. It does you no good to hear "Hi, I'm Joe Plumber. I'm not available right now, but leave your name and number and I'll get back to you."

If you hear that message, you're going to hang up and call the next plumber on your list. You are *not* going to leave a message and wait around to see if Joe will call you back. No one wants to leave a voicemail when they have an urgent problem.

Guess what else people hate? Phone trees. How much do you love calling your bank? Do you enjoy being told to "press 1," then "press 1" again, then "press 2 and 8 and 9" and so on, as your life drains away on a useless phone tree? No. Of course you don't. No one does. So, if you hate calling your bank, then why would you subject people calling your law firm who are ready to give you their money to the same miserable experience?

When someone calls a lawyer, 99% of the time it's because of something bad happening in their life. They've been charged with a DUI, been arrested, been served divorce papers, been injured in an accident, whatever. Except for the rare exception, it's never about anything good and it's *always* an emergency to the caller. People are impatient if they're feeling the stressful urgency of a legal problem. These people want to talk to someone. They want human interaction.

Are they going to wait for you to call them back if you're not available? No way. Are they going to have a good first impression of your firm if they have to navigate a painful phone tree? Highly unlikely. If they're directed either to voicemail or a phone tree, it's likely they'll call some other lawyer until they get a real live human on the phone.

One of our clients is a criminal defense attorney in Long Island. When we examined his phone logs, we saw call after call that lasted exactly one minute. There were hundreds of them. We wondered what was going on, so we called him.

We saw the problem immediately. After 60-seconds on the line, we heard the beep that preceded his "leave me a message" script. Since his log was littered with one-minute calls, we had ample proof that potential clients were hanging up as soon as they were asked to leave a message.

We switched him to an answering service. His one-minute calls went away and people started leaving their information with the person answering the phone.

No one wants to talk to a robot or be told to leave a message. Have a real live person answering your phone. Ideally, that should be a trained receptionist, and if they're not available, you should have an answering service in place.

> **Quick-Hitting Hack:** Want to kick it up a notch? Train your person answering the phones to use a **pre-frame**, i.e. a tailored pitch that will help shape the potential client's positive first impression. Here's an example to illustrate what we mean.
>
> - *No pre-frame:* "Hello, this is [XYZ Law Firm]. ...You got a DUI? ... Okay, what's your name and number?"
>
> - *Pre-frame:* "Hello, this is [XYZ Law Firm] ...You got a DUI? I'm so sorry to hear that, but you made a great decision calling this firm. DUIs are the number one kind of case we handle and it's very likely we'll be able to help you. Attorney Smith is one of the most experienced DUI attorneys in the city!"
>
> Even if your receptionist or answering service is obviously being paid to say those lines, it doesn't matter. It still pre-frames your firm with a positive impression and helps persuade the potential client they made the right decision to call you. That favorable first impression will make them much more likely to book a consultation and eventually hire you.

We do understand that in a busy office, there will be times when the stars all collectively cross and the call is sent to voicemail. Your phones should be managed so this is an extremely rare occurrence. However, since it may happen, we think a simple message like this is appropriate: "Hi, this is attorney John Smith. I'm not able to answer this call, but leave your number and I will get back to you *within five minutes.*"

Now, you and I both know that you're not going to be able to get back to everybody in five minutes. It's just not going to happen. But the *expectation* of a quick return call might be the only thing that actually gets the potential client to leave their name and phone number with their information. After a short window of time—probably longer than five minutes but less than an hour—you can call them back. If it was longer than five minutes and the client points that out, apologize profusely. "I'm so sorry it took me an hour and not five minutes." But guess what? If you have the opportunity to apologize, *it means you have the potential client back on the phone with you.* If they don't have the expectation of a quick call back, they're probably not going to leave their information at all.

Better to act first and beg for forgiveness later. Wouldn't you rather endure making an apology than losing out on a potential case altogether? Even if some people get mad at you for taking longer than five minutes, you're still likely to gain more leads through this method than you would if people assumed you'd take forever to call them back and hang up without leaving their information.

Obviously, though, it's best to not need to beg for forgiveness at all. Given that five-minute promise, this voicemail recording should really be your last resort. Your best bet is to have a dedicated person or team answering your phones.

> **Quick-Hitting Hack:** Think that a five-minute call-back promise is a bit unrealistic? Here's a sobering statistic you need to know. Between 35% and 50% of sales go to the vendor who responds to a potential customer *first*.[15] That means *you need to be the first attorney to call back a lead.* If you wait too long, the caller will move on and hire someone else. Our recommendation is to call back as soon as humanly possible—within 15 minutes, or ideally, within five. Don't let that client slip away.

It's much, much better to invest in a real person answering the phone. So, what's the most affordable way to do that? By employing virtual assistants.

Employ Virtual Assistants

Virtual assistants (VAs) can be a lifesaver. They will answer your phones and make sure you don't lose any leads. They're also affordable, usually functioning as low-cost contract workers.

In fact, the only way that Ethen Ostroff was able to revolutionize his firm's intake system was through employing VAs. Prior to his intake system overhaul, it was the firm's receptionists and attorneys who were handling conversations with leads.

---

[15] "The Digital Evolution in B2B Marketing." Marketing Leadership Council, in partnership with Google. 2012. CEB. https://www.thinkwithgoogle.com/_qs/documents/677/the-digital-evolution-in-b2b-marketing_research-studies.pdf (accessed: 14. December 2023).

Given the volume of leads coming into Ostroff's firm, the receptionists were falling behind on important administrative tasks and the attorneys were taken away from their case work. Not to mention, their answering service was botching the name of their firm and turning down right fit clients because their exact situation wasn't on the "list" of accepted cases. Also, the answering service was not able to follow up with any leads who they didn't get into contact with. The result? Many right fit client leads fell through the cracks. Attorneys and support staff felt burnout and frustration. And administrative tasks were often left incomplete. It was impossible to grow the firm further without dealing with the intake issues.

When Ethen overhauled the system, he determined that VAs might be the solution—and they *were*. By the time Ethen's overhaul was complete, here's what VAs were doing:

- VAs answered *all* calls.

- They pre-vetted all leads, following a very specific set of instructions that he created.

- In most cases, VAs also were able to send over paperwork and sign up the case, assuming they met a preset list of criteria that he'd set.

- They took over some of the more routine administrative tasks that had been falling through the cracks.

Ethen's first VA hire was a friendly and competent VA named Clifford. He spoke fluent English with barely a trace of an accent. Ethen trained him on the intake criteria, set him up with an intake dashboard (more on that soon) and gave him all the instructions to do administrative tasks. Soon, Clifford was sending paperwork out to 95% of the firm's leads without involving an attorney, and there was *no* drop in the firm's case volume. Subsequent VA hires were given the same training. The result for Ethen's firm was *no* reduction in new cases, happier attorneys, happier support staff, and better results for their clients because the attorneys could focus on the actual casework.

In spite of all the significant benefits of using VAs, a lot of people have false beliefs about VAs. They remember the last time they called Hewlett Packard to get technical support for their printer, when they were funneled to someone in a noisy customer service center who couldn't understand them and spoke with a thick accent. But there are plenty of VA services out there who provide a great customer service experience. For instance, if you work with VAs based out of South America to handle some of your client communication, you'll see they're highly effective and, when they do speak with a subtle Spanish accent, it's an accent many U.S. residents are already familiar with. And, if you're hiring VAs for high-detail work, we've found the Philippines is a better place to source talent from. But both work great!

When you're just starting out, you want to keep your answering service for a bit, and strictly have your VAs start by following up with leads you already did not convert. As they follow up with your leads, listen to their call recordings and coach them until they're ready to handle their own inbound calls. Once they're ready and trained, you then set up your phone system to direct all calls first to the VA, and then have your answering service as a backup (if the VA is busy on another call when the next call comes in). Over time, as your lead volume increases, you will see the differences in results and you will likely expand from there.

But how can you make sure you hire a VA who can communicate well and does great work? First off, you can evaluate their ability to communicate effectively when you interview them by asking them questions that they can't google. You might ask, "What do you like to do for fun? Tell me about your family. What are your favorite vacations?" By doing that, you'll get a sense of their English fluency and ease of communication. Only advance with VAs who have strong communication skills.

Secondly, your VAs will perform at the level of *clarity* you provide to them. You need to provide crystal clear instructions. We use a screen recording software called Loom to train our VAs, which enables you to show how to complete tasks on your computer, click by click. If you've hired a VA with great communication skills and provided clear instructions, there's no reason why they won't be successful.

Quick-Hitting Hack: Worried that you may not be able to trust your VAs? Provide yourself reassurance on this point by installing security software on your VAs' computers, such as Black Talon. We also get our VAs HIPAA certified to ensure compliance and confidentiality.

Other people don't like the idea of VAs, because they assume people will want to speak to an attorney when they initially call the firm. This is a false belief. If you were calling a brain surgeon's office, would you expect to talk to the brain surgeon? Of course not! He's not there to answer the phone. He's there to perform surgery. That's why other people answer the phone.

The same principle applies to lawyers. If a potential client calls a firm and the *attorney* answers the phone, that client will likely feel instant concern. "Why isn't this lawyer working on cases? Why is he spending his time answering the phone?" Most likely, that client will form a *negative* impression from that intake experience and look for a firm where the attorneys function as experts, not receptionists.

VAs can provide the availability you need to ensure no calls go to voicemail and—provided you pick a good service—they can give your potential clients a great first impression of your firm.

Quick-Hitting Hack: Scan the QR code below to watch a video about ways to effectively employ VAs as part of your firm's intake. The video also smashes a few other false beliefs about VAs!

(You'll find all the other bonuses from the book here or you can go to **yourdreamlawfirm.com**.)

Scan this QR Code to Unlock This Bonus

Change Your Hours to 24/7

Go to your computer or phone outside of normal business hours and open a Google search window. Now type in "personal injury attorney" for your town.

You're going to see a bunch of firms pop up. Many of them will have a big red "CLOSED" notice next to their names.

Now, say you're a person with a typical 9-to-5 job. You're probably not going to be calling a lawyer during your work hours. You're more likely to call on the weekend or after 5:00 p.m. when you get home. But when you Google "personal injury attorney," half of the firms say "Closed."

Are you going to call a closed firm first? Doubtful. You'll probably get an answering machine or a frustrating phone tree.

Instead, you're going to call one of the firms that *is* open. One of the firms that never closes. One that takes calls and does intake 24 hours a day, 7 days a week, 52 weeks a year, without fail. Firms that do this capture all kinds of cases that other firms, tied to regular business hours, miss.

So, part of your Google Business Profile must show that you are open all the time. Make sure this is true of your firm. One of our clients switched from regular hours to 24/7 hours. The *first* weekend he remained open, he got a new client. That 24/7 shift can be a game changer for any firm.

This 24/7 strategy is especially useful for firms just starting up. Many of the big fish in your pond will keep regular business hours. The way for you to swim with the big players is to snag all those cases they are missing on weekends and evenings. You do that by simply being open all the time. How do you do that? By employing Virtual Assistants, of course.

2. Weed Out Unqualified Cases & Identify Right Fit Clients

As Ethen discovered when overhauling intake in his law firm, it doesn't work to have attorneys handling intake. Most lawyers spend decades of their careers on the phone, taking calls. This is a terrible way to run a law firm. Even worse, it's a terrible way to spend your life!

Growing your firm will require that you completely remove yourself and the other attorneys from intake and give that task to someone who can give it their full attention. Do not succumb to the temptation to take those calls simply because you think you're better at taking those calls. Even if you are, that's irrelevant.

You're a *leader*, not a phone person. You can't be on call all the time. You must look to the future of your firm and work on long-term strategies for building it up. Let's talk about who to get in that intake seat and how to train them to perform even better than you could.

Specialized Roles

Some lawyers see their phones are getting answered and they're happy with that. "A human being is answering the phone. That's enough to create a good impression, right?" Wrong. You need to have the *right* person handling the phones at the *right* time.

Smaller law firms will typically have just one person handling their intake, due to smaller lead volume. In those cases, that person should receive training in each of the areas noted below, so they know how to adjust their communication, depending on whether they're handling administrative calls or sales conversations.

However, once your firm's lead volume increases, you're going to want to have specialists handling your intake. Ideally, a law firm should have three distinct people employed to answer the phones.

1. Your **receptionist** deals with *administrative* calls. For example, they might handle calls from insurance companies, schedule and reschedule court dates, and handle any client fires. A good receptionist should be detail-oriented. They keep meticulous notes, consistently communicate with signed clients, and are on top of any issues that might cause problems in the firm. Many lawyers give intake to their receptionist, but this is faulty task allocation.

2. Your **intake specialist** should handle initial calls with all new leads and assign them a 3/2/1 score according to preset criteria. It's the intake specialist

who performs that all-important task of vetting clients. They will aggressively pursue the 3s and also follow up with the 2s and 1s to weed out the leads your firm *doesn't* want and book consult appointments for the ones you *do* want. That's it. They don't do administrative work. That's for your receptionist. They also don't close. The intake specialist role is one that can be effectively carried out by a competent VA.

3. Your **closer** is the person who gets the lead to sign with the firm. In a smaller firm, it would be the attorney. For larger firms like Ethen's, it's a specifically trained intake closer on the team. A skilled, trusted VA could work their way up to this role. Whoever is assigned to be closer, their job is to *persuade* the lead. They are salespeople, through and through. These are the people who should be speaking with the 3s, i.e. the "Leads You Want," and any vetted leads from the 2 category who are passed up from the intake specialists.

Note that sales expertise increases as the number on the list gets bigger. Your receptionist has the least amount of sales mojo, your intake specialist has a little more, and your closer must have a lot of sales savvy.

The method of assigning numbers to leads also enables you to track the efficacy of the people serving in each role and be strategic about assignments. For instance, if you notice that one of your closers has a particularly high conversion rate turning 3s into signed clients, you should direct your highest priority leads to that person. They're killing it! On the flip side, if one of your closers shows great judgment but has a low conversion rate, you may want to shift that person into evaluating the "under review" 1s. Let them focus their time into determining which clients are a definite "no." If one of your intake specialists consistently persuades 2s to book consults, take a look at their call recordings and study their success. By systematizing your intake, you can ensure you get the right people in the right seats and consistently evaluate their performance.

We see many lawyers get confused about these roles and try to have one person serve all three objectives. However, each of these tasks requires a different skill set and it's extremely rare to find a person who is excellent at—and has the bandwidth—to successfully manage all three. That's why you should allocate appropriate tasks to distinct people and keep the roles separate. Remember, you can hire a Virtual Assistant to handle one or more of these roles if you're operating with a smaller staff.

Quick-Hitting Hack: As you scale, pay attention to your *intake breakpoints.* In other words, where during the intake process do you tend to lose potential clients? Does the receptionist do a good job booking appointments, but then the first in-person interview tends to lose them? That's a sign the problem is with the interviewer. Or, do you send potential clients a survey to get their case details and never hear back? That's a sign the survey might be scaring them off from further engagement. Study your metrics about where the cases fall off, so you can tighten things up constantly.

There is one exception to the specialized roles hierarchy. Personal injury firms sometimes combine the intake specialist and closer roles because clients do not pay up front. The intake specialist can say, "Look, there's no risk here for you. You don't pay up front and you can fire us any time you want. Are you ready to sign with us?"

But if you're not running a personal injury firm, make sure the roles are clearly separated. Even if you *are* running a personal injury firm, intake should not be handled by receptionists, case managers, paralegals, or attorneys. You need to have specialized and dedicated people whose *only* job is intake. If all those other people are doing intake, the quality of their other work will suffer. Managers will be forced to pick up the slack left by their subordinates, people will get resentful, they'll be working extra hours, morale will suffer, and clients will be neglected and ill-served.

You don't want that to happen. You'll get a bad reputation and negative reviews. Don't dilute the skills of your people by having them do tasks they are not suited or trained for. Save intake for intake specialists and let everyone else do the job they are trained for and good at.

And on that note—let's talk about how to train your intake specialists and closers so that they can nail those conversations consistently.

Intake Sales Training

When training your intake specialists and closers, consider **what** they should communicate and **how** you can give them practice.

Intake specialists should work with effective, well-written scripts. This is the **what**. They should know how to introduce themselves on a call, how to extract the relevant information from the potential lead, and how to end with a compelling recommendation to book an appointment for a consult.

"Great! It sounds like there's a really good chance we can help you fight this DUI. The next step is to come into our office so that we can show you exactly how we can help you beat this case. Let's do Friday at 3:00 PM. Does that work for you?"

Make an appointment as soon as possible. The bigger the gap from when they call and when they come in for a consultation, the *less* likely they are to come in for the consult, and the *more* likely they are to hire someone else. Speak confidently. Remember that anyone with a legal problem wants to be led by a capable person who can help them through it!

The intake script should not be random or haphazard. Give intake specialists a specific and effective script that they follow on every call.

Part of the script should consider cases where the lead is not ready to sign. For instance, if the client says, "I need to think about it," your intake specialist should *never* then say, "Okay I'll call you back." Instead, they should say, "I appreciate that. If I was in your shoes, I would want to think about it too. What specifically do you need to think about, and how can I help you think through that right now while we're still on the phone? Can we work through this together?"

We call this "objection handling." Your team needs to be trained on closing lines and objection handling. Those are some of the considerations regarding **what** they need to say.

How about **how**? Your intake specialists need to practice their scripts *before* they get on the phone. They need to rehearse. Does an actor figure out on opening night how to deliver their lines and where to stand on stage? Of course not! That would be crazy. They rehearse for hours and hours before they ever perform for an audience.

The same thing applies to your intake specialists. Practice makes perfect. The last place your team should be practicing is on the phone with a lead you've already paid for.

Rehearsal should not just happen once. It needs to be an ongoing task, a requirement of their employment. At our company, we do daily role playing and we do sales training every single week. We built scripts and training for every scenario in our online sales university.

The difference between professionals and amateurs is professionals practice more than they play, and amateurs play more than they practice. Given that you're dealing with professionals, you should make practice a cornerstone of your intake training.

Intake Dashboard

But how do you know which VA is a rockstar, and which one is letting good leads fall through the cracks? How can you track your closers' conversion rate? How do you know if the follow-up is happening in the right way, with the right regularity, for the 3s, and 2s, and 1s?

Two words. *Intake. Dashboard.*

Most lawyers today have case management software to track their cases. Nothing wrong with that. However, a lot of lawyers think their case management software can also handle their intake.

Most of them can't.

You need a software for intake that plugs into your marketing sources and tracks every lead on a minute-by-minute basis. An intake dashboard has functionalities that focus exclusively on marketing and intake. It would track information like:

- Ensuring leads are followed up with every other day until contact is made

- Specific outreach reports

- Logged call reports

- How much time elapses between receiving a lead and converting them to a signed client

- Which lead sources yield the most signed clients (highest ROI)

And so on! An intake dashboard will answer all these questions.

Bottom line: Don't skimp on getting a good intake software for your firm. You need a way to stay on top of your leads and your intake process and to hold your team accountable.

Quick-Hitting Hack: Scan the QR code below to get our most up-to-date recommendations on intake dashboard software. We've also provided a link to see a virtual walk-through of Ethen's dashboard.

(You'll find all the other bonuses from the book here or you can go to **yourdreamlawfirm.com**.)

Scan this QR Code
to Unlock This Bonus

3. Relentlessly Follow Up

Once you've identified your right fit clients, you need to chase after them until they sign! Remember, 3s should be contacted around 10 to 15 times by your closers, and 2s and 1s should be followed up with by your intake specialists between 5 and 10 times.

Here's how.

3 Times, 3 Ways: Text, Call, and Email

Remember Attorney Alyssa and Attorney Bernard, who had us run the exact same ad campaign, only Bernard got 75 new cases out of it and Alyssa got none? The difference was in the follow-up. Bernard operated with the motto "3 times, 3 ways." Every day, for three days, Bernard reached out to his leads. First with a **text**, second with a **call**, and third, with an

email. He did this every day for three days in a row. By using multiple forms of outreach on multiple days, Bernard was able to execute a relentless follow-up system that secured 75 new cases for his firm.

Ethen's model bumps the relentlessness up another notch, because instead of three days in a row, his intake team follows up with the desirable three cases *fifteen days in a row,* via text, call, and email. The intake protocol for following up with the 2s and 1s is less frequent, but no less strategic. Through this repeated process of follow-up, Ethen's firm has an incredible rate of securing the cases they want.

A few tips for maximizing the effectiveness of your follow-up ...

- When you send a text, make sure to include your full name. "This is John Smith, from ABC Firm." iPhones record this information and use it to inform caller ID. When you call from that same number, the screen will say, "Maybe John Smith." People are far more likely to answer a phone call from someone whose name they recognize than a random number. If they see "Maybe John Smith," they're going to think, "Hey—that's the law firm I reached out to," and are more likely to answer.

- Double dial! Robo callers don't double dial, but humans do. Specifically, humans who have an urgent need to discuss a matter with the person they're calling. If your potential new client sees a repeated call come in from your number, they're more likely to understand it's important and will pick up.

- Stagger your calls. If you're trying to call Jane Doe at 10:45 AM every day, but that's the time she goes to CrossFit, you're not going to succeed in reaching her. Instead, try her in the morning, then in the afternoon, then in the evening. You're more likely to find her in a free moment if you change it up.

- In your text, ask for a good time to call. This feels like a "human" request and, if they respond, they're far more likely to take your call later when you reach out at their requested time.

- In any form of follow-up, ask them to provide you with a few additional details about their case. This will not only make them feel seen and validated, it will also trigger their curiosity and is more likely to elicit a response from them. Plus, asking a question makes it more likely that you'll get a response.

Can you do all of these things? Can you, Law Firm Owner, follow up this consistently, this relentlessly? No. You can't. Nor should you—you have more important things to do. That's why we recommend you delegate intake to a stellar VA or two whose entire job is devoted to following up with leads.

We want to spotlight two more strategies for follow-up because of how truly effective they are. Using the "magic hours" and texting. (Wait—didn't we just talk about texting? Yes, but you have no idea yet how powerful texting can be.)

Take Advantage of "The Magic Hours"

When is the best time to call your 3s? When are you most likely to reach the 2 and 1 leads, to get the clarity you need about their cases?

Here's a hint. It's *not* when people are at work, between 8 a.m. and 5 p.m. It's during the magic hours, between 5:00 p.m. and 9:00 p.m., and on the weekends. Those hours in the evening and on weekends when people are off work account for a big portion of the new cases Ethen's firm brought in.

Embrace Texting

Maybe you've been slow to embrace texting because you prefer a good old-fashioned phone call. But if texting isn't already a regular part of your follow-up approach, it *should* be. Phone calls may go unanswered, and emails often get deleted. But texts get read. In fact, one study found that texting gets *800%* more response than email.

Think we're making that figure up? We're not. Studies have found that texting produces engagement rates *six to eight times* higher than email marketing when used for redemption, data collection, and brand awareness.[16]

Everyone has their phone with them these days. What's more, they don't like to answer their phones. Too many scam callers. But most people, especially Millennials and Gen Z–ers, will pay attention to texts. They read them and they respond to them.

---

[16] Anon. SMS has eight times the response rate of email: study | Retail Dive. https://www.retaildive.com/ex/mobilecommercedaily/sms-has-eight-times-the-response-rate-of-email-study.

So, be sure to include texting in your follow-up campaigns. And remember to use the new way of marketing when you do. Give them *value for free*. Your messaging in those follow-up messages shouldn't just be a plea for the lead to sign with you. Give them information that will be valuable to them and demonstrate your expertise.

Another powerful way to embrace text messaging is for your intake specialist to send selfie style video texts to your prospective new clients. That'll get their attention.

4. Get Your Right Fit Clients to Know, Like, and Trust You

In every touchpoint with your potential clients, you want to establish yourself as an expert in their eyes. That's crucial in building their trust. We've talked about how to create a positive first impression, and your subsequent communication needs to go even further. You want to *dazzle* them. Let's talk about how to help your clients *know, like, and trust you*.

KLT Materials

Any person who contacts a lawyer usually has some stressful stuff going on. Take a criminal defense law firm, for example. When someone gets arrested, they typically have a few burning questions.

- Am I going to jail?
- Will this be made public and ruin my reputation?
- Will this be on my permanent record?

These are not insignificant concerns, and they generally come up during the first consultation with a criminal defense lawyer.

In our opinion, talking about these concerns during a first consultation is too late. Those questions should be answered *before* the consultation. How can a lawyer do this? Simple. When you get the call from an arrestee, you send them a video you've already produced that answers those three questions and more.

It's the same value-for-free concept we've been hammering throughout this book. Solve their problems. Give them useful, free information before they even talk to you.

By doing that, you've given them something that will make them know, like, and trust you. That's KLT material. Those clients will be *much* more likely to hire you because of the goodwill you created with them.

> **Quick-Hitting Hack:** Scan the QR code below to watch a video for more details about creating Know, Like, and Trust material.
>
> (You'll find all the other bonuses from the book here or you can go to **yourdreamlawfirm.com**.)
>
> **Scan this QR Code to Unlock This Bonus**

Equally useful are testimonial videos. Make some content where previous clients talk about dealing with some of the same issues as the caller and have gotten good results from hiring you. For a family law firm, you might feature a video about a father who went through a custody battle, or a woman who needed to get spousal support. Any client with a good outcome would be an ideal candidate for this type of video.

Make enough videos so that you can match the content to the caller as closely as possible. People like to see themselves in these testimonials. Film satisfied clients who fall into a range of demographics, so that you can send potential new clients a video that they immediately connect with. This will give them reassurance that you know what you're doing. "Oh wow, they've done this exact thing before for someone who seems a lot like me." Yes, this will require amassing a large collection of these so you can send the right video to the right person. Think of your video testimonials as though they were pieces of a puzzle. The more pieces you have, the more readily you can fit the exact right piece into your client's uniquely shaped need. That's how you'll help clients feel like they know, like, and trust you!

All of the above principles can also be embedded into your email newsletter system. Imagine if every client who ever contacted your firm was automatically sent an email every other day with something valuable and related to what they reached out to you about. And, let's take this up a notch. What if you sent *every* person who *ever* contacted you an email every single week on local, interesting news (talking nothing about the law)? It would ensure you stayed top of mind. You'd generate referrals on autopilot from leads you generated in the past. Gosh! The opportunities are *endless* for follow-up.

ANDY STICKEL NARRATES

Conduct a World-Class Consultation

I learned how to run a world-class consultation from, of all things, a home building company. A number of years ago, my wife Chelsie and I were building a house, and we were considering several different contractors. We went to an in-person meeting with one particular home builder and they completely nailed the consultation—to the point that we ended up signing with them.

First off, when we arrived, we saw an 8x10 sign holder with a sign that said, "Welcome, Andy and Chelsie." It wasn't impressive—just a printed piece of paper in a plastic sign holder that was probably ordered off of Amazon. But the personalized gesture still made us feel special as soon as we entered the office. The second thing they did was give us a free gift. It was small—a multitool keychain—but it sparked our feelings of *reciprocity*. Reciprocity means that when someone does something for you, you feel compelled to do something for them. It's ingrained in us from an early age and it means that even a small gift makes us feel inclined to return the favor somehow.

After establishing a great impression, they brought out the kind of "Know, Like, and Trust" materials we just described in the previous section. They reinforced the fact that they were offering a *great product*, which meant our positive feelings about them were supported by data.

There are other psychological tools that can help you put your best foot forward in a consultation—including, ironically, admitting weakness. When your clients come to you, they've most likely got their guard up because they're expecting a sales push. They're concerned you might simply be trying to secure them as a client to get their money. However, if you admit a shortcoming right up front, that will help them trust you more—for instance, being clumsy, not being a morning person, laughing at your own jokes, or admitting to a harmless guilty pleasure. It implies authenticity and vulnerability, enabling them to feel safe with you.

When discussing their case, focus less on what they will *gain*—that can sound too much like a sales pitch. Instead, address what they stand to *lose*. People are much more motivated to avoid losses than they are to acquire gains. When you explain what you intend to do to help your client, focus on how you'll help them *avoid* losing money, or *avoid* losing a relationship with their child, or *avoid* losing their license. A discussion around loss aversion acknowledges the fears the potential client most likely carried into the meeting. And don't be afraid to get descriptive when describing their problems. One of our mentors aptly pointed out that whoever can best articulate the problem is automatically thought to have the best solution. If you thoroughly demonstrate you *understand* their problems and can help them overcome those fears, they'll be more likely to trust you to handle that case.

Whoever can best articulate the problem is automatically thought to have the best solution.

On that note though, make sure you present *a clear plan* to demonstrate how you will help them. If you bring up fears, but don't provide a clear plan to help them overcome that fear, they'll ignore your subsequent messaging and they won't leave the meeting feeling trust in your firm.

If you combine your competency and knowledge with attention to the details—making the potential client feel special, providing a free gift, strategic messaging, and a plan of action for their specific case—your consultation will truly be world class.

Quick-Hitting Hack: What about leads who blow off a scheduled consultation and never show? Check out Andy's video with tips to ensure clients have a 100% show-up rate to your scheduled consultations.

(You'll find all the other bonuses from the book here or you can go to **yourdreamlawfirm.com**.)

Scan this QR Code to Unlock This Bonus

After the Consultation

But what happens if they leave the consultation *without* hiring you? Hey, the game's not over yet. This is your opportunity to employ "by the way" marketing.

What is "by the way" marketing? It's a highly effective form of following up with potential clients, which involves dropping a bit of golden wisdom into one of your communications. You do so with an innocuous little lead-in. "By the way…"

One of the best times to do this is after a potential client has walked away from you. Our friend Lance Fryrear, a criminal defense lawyer in Seattle, is a dedicated practitioner of "by the way" marketing. Here's how he does it.

Let's say Lance meets with a potential client for a consultation, but the lead doesn't hire him during that meeting. Lance will send a follow-up text to the lead that says, "Thanks so much for coming in and meeting with me today. *By the way,* I happened to notice that the judge handling your case is [Judge LastName.] That judge has a very specific preference for how cases before him should be handled. [Here is what that preference is.] Just wanted to make sure you were aware so that you have the best chance possible at winning your case. All the best!"

Lance's little "by the way" wisdom gives his leads information that could have a huge effect on their case. He offers them sterling value in his follow-up messaging and demonstrates his *expertise* in doing so.

Guess what his conversion rate is, after sending one of these "by the way" follow-up messages? We don't know the exact number, but we can tell you it's pretty high.

And *by the way,* you can use your library of YouTube videos for this type of messaging. If a potential client leaves your office and you know you have a video that's relevant to their situation, send them an email with a "by the way" link to that video.

It's a form of follow-up that they'll be eager to engage with and will often be received well enough that you gain a new client.

The Threshold

Think of intake as the threshold of your firm. It's the difference between potential clients remaining *outside* in the cold versus coming *inside* as a signed client where they'll be well taken care of. Your intake process includes everything that helps right fit clients cross that threshold, starting with the first impression you make, extending to your screening process, involving a relentless follow-up system, and then dazzling them with experiences that help them know, like, and trust you—so they *sign*.

What comes next? After generating lots of new interest through your honed marketing and then securing new clients through your excellent intake system—now, it's time to talk about how you attract, manage, and retain the staff to handle your new business.

Chapter 9 | Takeaways

1. A good intake system should accomplish four things: 1) establish a great first impression on potential clients, 2) screen potential clients to weed out unqualified cases and identify right fit clients, 3) employ relentless follow-up, and 4) help your right fit clients feel that they know, like, and trust you.

2. Use a ranking system to organize your intake and employ strategic follow-up according to their respective rankings. A 3 is a case you definitely want. A 2 is

a case you need more information about. A 1 is a case you *probably* don't want. And a 0 is a case you *definitely* don't want.

3. Your number one intake *goal* should be to sign up a high percentage of your right fit clients. The number one intake *principle* is that the fortune is in the follow-up.

4. Create a great first impression by ensuring people can easily get a hold of a human being connected with your firm, any time of the day or night. Do that by ensuring no calls go to voicemail, employ Virtual Assistants, and change your hours on Google Business profile to 24/7.

5. Your intake person should not be your receptionist, or administrative assistant, or another attorney. It should be someone who exclusively handles intake conversations. Most firms will also want to train a separate employee(s) to handle the closing conversation. Having specialized people in these roles is a huge component in identifying right fit clients. You're not going to start there when you have a small team, but over time, you will get there.

6. Relentlessly follow up with your right fit clients by calling during the magic hours and texting them.

7. Seal the deal with your right fit clients by helping them know, like, and trust you. Provide helpful videos to them ahead of time, ensure their initial consultation with you is a great one, and provide client testimonials. Remember to provide free, value-rich content even after the consultation, such as "by the way" marketing.

PART 3

SELF-MANAGING TEAM

How to Recruit and Lead a Team of A-Players and Deliver a World-Class Experience to Your Clients

FREEDOM ENTREPRENEUR

SELF-MANAGING TEAM

INTAKE

LEAD GENERATION

PROFIT + FREEDOM

REVENUE

CHAPTER 10

HIRING A-PLAYERS

GET THE LIFE YOU WANT BY HIRING THE PEOPLE YOU NEED

"Talent wins games, but teamwork and intelligence win championships."

—Michael Jordan

BILL HAUSER NARRATES

The skunky smell of stale pot hit me as soon as I entered the office. That's when I knew I had to rethink my hiring practices.

Today, SMB Team has over 100 full-time W-2 employees and more than 70 full-time equivalent freelancers. But turn the clock back to 2018 and it was a very different picture. Then, it was just me and a computer. That was the whole business. I spent most of my time making cold calls selling Google ad campaigns for lawyers and then frantically trying to figure out how to deliver on what I was selling.

This is where most businesses stop. One person tries to run a business. The Small Business Association tracks these things, and they have found that 85% of businesses are solo endeavors. These business owners believe it is too complex and risky to hire someone.

No business can grow under those circumstances, but the fear of hiring stops almost all entrepreneurs. They remain solopreneurs instead.

For me, the need to hire someone became clear when I entered all my revenue into a spreadsheet and realized I had enough money to hire someone else to do the client work. That would allow me to concentrate more on selling and working on high-level strategizing for the business.

I put up an ad on Indeed offering $48K a year for someone to run the Google ad campaigns for my clients. And let me tell you, this may have been one of the most nerve-wracking things I ever did as a business owner. I was proposing to give *half* of my revenue to this new hire. I was terrified it was the wrong move.

But when I looked back at the goals I had written out for my first year in business, I saw, "make $450K a year." Was that possible? I believed it was. Was it possible as a solopreneur? No way.

That meant hiring someone was the only way to go.

I interviewed applicants and found someone I *kinda* liked who *kinda* had the experience I wanted. The key word here is *kinda*. I wasn't going for top candidates at that point. I wasn't reaching for A-players.

But I did learn to hire. (Kinda.) I trained this new person on all the tasks they were supposed to do and tried to explain all the stuff I had been doing intuitively. I learned how to build processes to help my new hire.

Over the next two years, I hired more people, using the same *kinda* process, until I had a staff of about a dozen. Things should have been going well ... but they weren't. One morning, I walked into the office and found one of my first employees with tears in his eyes. His pupils were dilated, and the whites were bright red. Dude was high as a kite. First thing in the morning.

The realization was like a bucket of cold water thrown over my head. For the first time, I started seeing the dysfunction I'd been trying to ignore. It wasn't normal for employees to constantly create drama in the workplace. It wasn't normal for employees to blame each other for their mistakes. And it was *not* normal for employees to come to work high on drugs.

But without meaning to, I had inadvertently created a culture of mediocrity in which that kind of ridiculous behavior *was* considered normal. Why? Because I hired people who were *kinda* okay at their jobs, which collectively meant my business *kinda* sucked.

There was one main reason I had tolerated this for so long. Fear. I was afraid of *firing* people. I didn't want to let anyone go. I thought if I fired an underperforming employee, the rest of the office would have to pick up the slack and that would cause a new set of problems.

But clearly, I had to bite the bullet and fire some people. I also had to get more disciplined in hiring. I completely revamped my recruiting process, implementing background checks, reference checks, and personality index tests. I also made sure every candidate read and understood the company's vision statement. I created clear job descriptions from a core values perspective rather than from a task perspective. And—this was big—I gave new hires a stake in the company by offering bonuses based on performance.

I stopped worrying about getting a *lot* of candidates applying for positions and instead began to concentrate on *quality* candidates instead.

With these new systems and principles in place, I executed a talent rebuild. Over the next eight months, I fired 80% of my employees. During that time, I also increased my staff because for every person I fired, I hired two more. (If you're wondering how I was able to afford that, it's because I was profiting next to nothing at the time. I reinvested every spare dollar into rebuilding the team.)

The difference was dramatic. My new hiring practices pushed away low-quality candidates and attracted excellent candidates who were high-performers and drama-free. Finally, I had a crew of A-players. And I was able to *keep* them by offering them a piece of the pie. When Andy's team joined us, we became even stronger.

SMB Team is now light years away from where it started, with just me and my computer. In fact, *Fortune* magazine named us one of the top 100 small and midsize companies to work for in the United States. That's a hugely gratifying result, and all the more so because *Fortune's* survey mainly interviewed employees of my company.

This success happened because we hired the right people and worked hard to retain them. And listen. Any firm can do this. *You* can do this! The effort is worth it, and the success that comes from having a dynamic team of A-players will help you achieve the life of your dreams. Hiring A-players is the secret to getting better results for clients, more freedom in your life, and improving your staff retention.

You want to become an expert at hiring? Then get ready to feel stupid.

You Don't Have Time to Be the Smartest Person in the Room

What constitutes an A-player? These are people who are highly skilled at what they do. People who have an abundance of skills, knowledge, experience, and are highly motivated. In fact, these people should be *smarter* than you. On top of this, they should live and breathe your core values—they have to embody your standards in all areas.

Tough sell? A lot of lawyers who want a successful business constantly strive to be the smartest person in the room. Every room. All the time. They must have the last word. That's why they became lawyers!

But there's a problem with that attitude. *It will scare away smart people.* When A-players work for a pontificating, micromanaging leader, they quickly determine there won't be room for them to develop their own talents. After all, if the firm's owner thinks they know everything, what can an outsider bring to the firm? Those A-players will take their knowledge and expertise somewhere else where they can be valued.

Even if you really *are* the best and the brightest (which is probably not the case), sell some of your IQ points. Embrace your inner dunce. It's not the best lawyer who builds incredibly successful firms but the best *delegator*. You must learn to excel at running a business, and learn to *delegate* lawyering, intake, and all other elements of running a firm to your team. That's the difference between lawyering and businessing.

We like this quote by Richard Branson: "A business is a group of people working together to solve a problem."

But not just any people. You want the *best* people on your team.

To make this happen, you need to do three things.

1. *Attract* A-players to your business.
2. *Win them over* so they decide to work for you instead of a competitor.
3. *Keep* your all-stars and enable their growth.

We're going to talk about the first two points in this chapter and devote our next chapter to unpacking number three.

Hiring is a skill, just like any other skill. You can learn it! Our goal in this chapter is to teach you the fundamentals of hiring so you will have the confidence to do it and do it well.

Attract: Culture Is Crucial

A lot of lawyers downplay the idea of culture in their firm. "Culture?" they say. "Are you kidding? I'm busy. I've got case-work! I don't have time for culture."

This kind of thinking will lead to mediocrity, because without culture, you don't have a team. Your employees will end up working at cross purposes to each other instead of being a team working together in harmony.

Culture also gets a bad rap because so many companies tout their mission, culture, and core values—yet no one actually seems to believe in the mission or practice the values. As a result, the "culture" is mostly defined by hypocrisy.

Listen, your firm *will* have a culture, and it will either be a good one or a bad one. Either it will be an intentionally cultivated environment that excites and nourishes A-players—or it will be a negative byproduct of neglectful leadership, where everyone does their own thing and no one feels inspired.

Company culture is simply the collective understanding about how people at a business operate together, and it stems from the top. You, as the leader of your firm, must define a culture for your team and make sure every employee understands and follows that culture.

You need to say, "This is *who* we are, here's *why*, and here's *how* we're going to achieve that vision."

Before you hire anyone, define your culture. Decide what you want your firm to be about and hire people accordingly.

When people first encounter SMB, they often say our culture is "electric" and they want that same feeling with their firm. Well, this didn't happen by accident. We *made* it electric. We made it dynamic, energetic, and smooth-running. We did this by defining and implementing a culture of ethics and productivity, and we did it by hiring A-players.

When you hire A-players, you not only confirm the value of your culture, but you also put the B- and C-players on notice. They soon realize they are underperforming. After some coaching, some of them will rise to that challenge and transition into A-players. Others will not.

That's when you *must* fire the underperforming B- and C-players. You do this for the benefit of you, your firm, your high-performing employees, and your culture. A-players drive everything. They will make your firm world class if you let them.

Your culture is shaped both by the people you hire and the people you fire, but culture is also what will *attract* those A-players to your firm in the first place. There are two cultural elements in particular that deserve your close attention. Core values and—yes—marketing.

Core Values

One of our core values, early on, was to do whatever it took to please a client. If that meant staying at the grindstone until midnight or later—so be it.

We had one employee who lived this value to the max. He was hard-working and did an excellent job. He was always ready to put in extra hours. He took on whatever we threw at him. That is—until he couldn't anymore. One day, our exemplary workhorse had a breakdown in the office. He sobbed and yelled, expressing incredible anger at all of us. He was completely burned out, simply from following our core value of pleasing the client at any cost.

As soon as we saw that, we realized our "do whatever it takes" core value wasn't healthy for our people. We removed that value from our culture and began rethinking the ones we still wanted to uphold. We didn't want what happened to him to happen to anyone else.

Let our mistake serve as a cautionary tale. Choose your core values wisely. After shelving the "do whatever it takes" value, we opted for a healthier evolution we call "Three-way Winners." With every client we take on, we look for three things. A win for the client, a win for the finances of the company, *and* a win for the team.

Let's look at how this might play out in a particular case. Imagine we have a super profitable client that's happy with the work we're doing. That's two of the three. Happy clients and favorable financials. But this client is a pain in the ass to work with. He's abrasive, bullying, and insulting. He communicates sporadically, badmouths us to other firms, and is just generally unpleasant to be around. In other words, he is *not* a win for the team.

Do we keep this client? No. We let him go because our core value dictates what we want from working with a client and this client was not delivering as a win for our team.

In our "do whatever it takes" days, we would have put in the long hours and weekends to please this pain-in-the-ass client.

But that approach drives resignations. Employees get fed up and leave for other employment. We know this because we lived it. That's why we've come to understand the Three-Way Winner approach is the best for our long-term excellence and sustainability—even if it means we fire a client. And if we do resort to firing a lucrative client because they conflict with our Three-Way Winner value, that sends a message to the entire team that our culture and core values are real.

This is also true for firing employees. Culture is established by who you fire, not who you keep. Culture shaping terminations are so important, in fact, we've devoted an entire section on it in our next chapter.

Bottom line: The values endorsed and exemplified by your firm's leaders will play a big role in shaping the culture of your workplace. *You* must decide what's right for *your* firm. And remember that core values are not necessarily carved in stone. It's okay to revise and change them as needed, based on what you see happening in your firm and your employees.

Core values are the materialization of what you stand for and a driver of your culture.

How can you tell if your culture is solid? One sure way to know your culture is working is when you don't have to hide anything from your team. Just today, we told our team that we made $25.8M last year and only profited 3% of that because we're reinvesting in hiring, product development, and marketing so aggressively. We also told them that our goal this year is to profit over $9.5M, and that we want them to share in the wealth when we hit those goals with our new bonus plans.

We were completely open and honest about what was going on with our financials. Our team already knows we're scaling fast and investing in growth because transparency is also one of our core values.

Once you have your core values that define what your firm will be, make your team live and breathe them. You can't just write them down and post them on your website. You must bring them to life.

How? Conduct seven-minute morning huddles every single day of the week with your whole team. We have a very specific structure for these huddles, where we go through the company's numbers from yesterday, share short departmental updates, read our client wins from yesterday, and last but not least, go through our "core value gratitudes." In about two minutes max, we have three team members each call out another member of the team who lived one of our core values yesterday. They bring up stories about how when so-and-so was working with client X, they demonstrated a core value. These are regular practices we do at SMB Team that help ingrain our values into the fabric of the culture.

Make the awareness of core values part of the everyday culture at your firm. You want to get to the point where your team embodies your culture and core values just as much as you are. You and your team should be celebrating them constantly.

What's the second key element to attract A-players to your culture? As a marketing firm, we're a little biased on this next one …

Client vs. Candidate Marketing

Yes, marketing. You don't just market to get clients, you market to get good *candidates.*

We hear this complaint from our clients far too often: "I can't attract great people."

Now why would that be? Simple. Great people want to work for a great firm. They want to work for a place that's doing great things. Are you doing great things? If you aren't, you are not going to attract A-players.

A lot of law firms concentrate on what we call client marketing. They build their website, do Google Ads, design a first-rate intake system, and so on, all designed to get quality clients through the door. There's nothing wrong with that. We spent chapters of this book explaining how to do that well. And while your client marketing should help you attract A-players, you need to do *candidate* marketing. This means marketing your firm to potential candidates. You need to show that your firm is exciting. If you're just treading water, what A-player is going to want to work for you?

Compare a word-of-mouth law firm that just takes clients based on referrals, versus the firm that's on the front page of newspapers and is the lead on local TV stations because they just did the biggest ever backpack giveaway to homeless kids in their city. Where do you think top candidates are going to send in applications?

Your online content can also help you attract great candidates. Grant Cardone is a phenomenally successful entrepreneur and self-proclaimed billionaire. He puts an enormous amount of content online. When he was a guest on our weekly talk show, he explained why he does this. It is not, as some might think, to attract clients. His main reason for all that content is to attract *candidates.* He markets himself and his company so that people see his company as a place where things are happening, where the future is exciting. A-players want to be part of such an organization.

Every potential candidate researches your firm before they apply for a job. They would be crazy not to. After all, they are considering devoting 40 to 60 hours a week of their lives to your firm. When someone types your firm's name into Google, what do they see? How about Glass Door or TikTok or Instagram or any number of other sites? You want to be there with dynamic content. Show people what they'd be signing up for by working at your firm. Are you changing the world? Are you *about* to change the world? If you've got videos showing how you're living into your vision as a firm, you'll attract the kind of candidates who are excited by that vision.

One of our clients—we'll call him Chris—runs an estate planning firm who needed to hire an attorney. His job ads weren't pulling in stellar candidates, but he had put up so many TikTok videos that a highly qualified A-player ended up contacting him after seeing all his online content. This candidate wanted to be on a moving train, somewhere that was hurtling toward the future. Chris' massive online presence convinced him Chris' firm was the place to be. And this new hire was a dream come true for Chris.

There's huge added value of having an awesome online presence. A-players want to be a part of big things. If you do big stuff and create buzz, you will attract great candidates. It's just that simple.

If you want a small firm full of B- and C-players who just come in and turn off their brains and click a mouse all day, don't bother with any of our suggestions. Don't work on your culture. Don't work to make your firm an exciting place to be or an organization that contributes to its community. But then don't complain about not attracting A-players. Your firm is set up to repel them! And if, by luck, you do snag one, they will not stick around for long. They will go somewhere more exciting.

Impress the high achieving candidates! Give them a good reason to apply. Have a vivid vision. Be bold. Tell them all the exciting things you're going to be doing over the next three years. Are you doubling and tripling your business every year? Say that! Are you becoming market dominant? Shout it from the rooftops.

Here's what you want a potential A-player to understand about your firm. "If you are on board with working for a visionary and fast-growing firm, JOIN US. Just want to punch in and punch out? Don't bother. There's no room for you here." That kind of line will repel the people who'd prefer to skate through their workday, but it will excite and compel the people who work at the highest level.

Your firm's culture and vision are the first step in attracting great candidates. Now, let's dial in the marketing further as we get into the language of your job ads and your approach to interviews. You want to hire these star candidates? Then it's time to bust out the proverbial box of chocolates and flowers. You need to woo them, wow them, and win them over.

BILL HAUSER NARRATES

Win Them Over: Job Ads & Interviews

Let's continue our tour of Bill Hauser's Museum of Mistakes so you know what *not* to do. Both Andy and I agreed we'd be very candid in this book about our missteps and bad calls, so you don't have to make the same mistakes we did!

For instance, some of the early job ads I posted for SMB. Great example of a bad misstep! Those ads were very one-sided. They were all about *us*. They were generic job ads that said something to the effect of "the successful candidate must have a certain amount of experience, be responsible for certain tasks and outcomes, put in a certain number of hours," and blah blah blah. It was all about what a potential hire could do for *us*.

Those ads brought us—want to guess? Mediocre candidates. B and C-players, all the way. Out of 100 applicants, maybe only two were worth interviewing. Barely.

At first, we didn't see that the ads were the problem. Our response to getting all those sub-par applicants was to say, "The job market sucks." And we really believed this. We convinced ourselves that there were no good candidates. If there were, why weren't they applying for our jobs?

Our eyes got opened to the reality of the situation when Andy and Bill picked up *Who: The A-Method of Hiring*, an eye-opening book by Geoff Smart and Randy Street. That book taught us to think of a job ad as a sales pitch. You're trying to *sell* a potential hire on how cool it is to work for your company.

Once we absorbed the information in that book, we saw that our ads were all wrong for attracting A-players. Our ads didn't sell anyone on devoting 40 to 60 hours per week to our business!

We revamped how we wrote our ads to include personality-based questions and benefit-oriented copy. Basically, we *marketed* our own company in the job ads, using standard persuasive copywriting.

Say we were looking to hire a salesperson. We wanted a high charger, a quick start, someone able to deal with uncertainty. So, how should we convey that in a persuasive ad?

Like this:

> *Do you hate micromanagement? Do you love dealing with unpredictable circumstances? Are you good at thinking on your feet and creatively problem-solving during the sales process? Do you want to be part of an environment where there are uncapped commissions? Do you want to make more than the CEO makes, just by performing well? Would you like to have five weeks of paid time off per year?*
>
> *If you said yes to any of these questions, keep reading. If not, go to the next job ad.*

Attract top people by telling them the great benefits they will get from working for you. Remember, in any job ad, you are asking someone to dedicate their working life to building *your* dream. Why should they want to do that? Give them a good reason. Make that prospect compelling.

Job Titles

And don't forget about the title of your job ad. That's probably the *most* important part to get right since that's what will prompt the A-players to open your job ad in the first place.

If you're hiring a paralegal, do you just put "paralegal" as the job title? No! Give it more pop, more pizzazz, more panache. Convey what the job actually is by adding something compelling and specific. "Paralegal for a Fast-Growing Family Law Firm." Just that simple tweak separates you from the rest of the swarm. It tells applicants a lot more than just the word "paralegal."

We've actually tested this theory. Once, when we were looking to add to our sales team, we placed two ads on all the job boards. One ad was for a **Sales Consultant** for a fast-growth lawyer marketing and coaching company. The other ad was for a **High Ticket Closer** for a fast-growth lawyer marketing and coaching company.

Everything else about the ads was the same. The rest of the copy was identical, and we devoted identical budgets to each ad.

The **Sales Consultant** ad brought us ten times the responses compared to the **High Ticket Closer** ad. Does that mean that we stuck with the Sales Consultant job title? Absolutely not. When we looked at the applications for Sales Consultant, only about 5% of them were qualified. On the other hand, 80% of the responses to the High Ticket Closer ads were qualified. That was a dramatic and decisive difference.

Remember, you're not writing your ads just to get large numbers of applicants. You want to write your ads in such a way that you attract the most *qualified* applicants. You may have to experiment to find out what job title works best. In our case, "Sales Consultant" was too broad a term. A shoe sales employee could see that and apply for it. Most shoe-sales employees, however, would not apply for something labeled "High Ticket Closer." That second job title scared away almost everyone who was not qualified, and it made sorting through the applications a lot easier.

When we hired our EVP of Coaching, the job ad said "EVP of Coaching of a $100M Lawyer Coaching Business." We included in the job ad what's in it for them and then that it was mandatory that they had already scaled a coaching program that did over $100M in revenue. We direct-messaged one person using that job ad. We got one application. And, that person is now in charge of our rapidly growing coaching program.

Compare your job ad to all the other ads on Indeed. If your firm doesn't stand out from the pack in its hiring ads, then the ads aren't doing the job. Ask yourself this question: "If I was an A-player, would I apply for this job?" If the answer is a clear "No way!" then you've got some work to do.

We made our job ads stand out from everybody else's job ads by telling the job seeker what's in it for *them,* not what they could do for *us,* and we made sure the titles of the job ads were compelling and specific. We turned our ads into awesome recruiting machines that began to attract super-performing A-players.

First-Round Interviews: Stand Out as a Company

You've followed our advice and created distinctive ads that bring in star applicants. You've screened out the people who won't fit into your firm.

Now you're up against the first-round interview. You and the applicant are both nervous, and you're both feeling each other out. How do you win them over?

This is where you *must* stand out as a company. If the recruit sees that the job ad was just some creative copywriting and your firm is pretty lackluster in reality, they're not going to stick with you. They're certainly not going to join your company. They are going to see you as just average. And why would a star applicant choose to work with an average firm?

Here are a couple of ways to make yourself stand out from the pack.

- **Make sure the person conducting the interview is the most exciting, core-value fit person on your team.** They should be passionate about your law firm—someone who absolutely *loves* the culture you've created. They should be enthusiastic and excited. This will make the applicant say, "Whoa! This is awesome. This company has a different vibe than all the others I've seen."

- **Sell them on the vision.** Describe where your firm is going, how they can contribute, and how they'll be rewarded if they perform at a high level. Make them excited about potentially working for you.

- **Give the applicant a task for the second interview.** At SMB Team, we tell them to read our vivid vision and create a 60-second video on how they intend to make that vision come true. We use a simple app called myinterview.com for this. If the applicant cannot do this, weed them from the pool. This task is designed to scare away people who are not invested in your vision or core values. It's designed to attract the high-performers who love to be held accountable and will share your growth goals. This is the most important part of the process.

On that note, let's talk about tools you can use in between interviews to further evaluate your candidates. These sorts of tests or activities will turn off lazy candidates, but high-performers will be excited to engage and show you what they're capable of.

Between Interviews: Relevant Tests

Would you hire an opera singer for the world's biggest stage without ever hearing them sing? Would you just accept their claim that they could hit the high notes and do the arias flawlessly?

Of course not. That would be idiotic. You would ask them to sing before signing them for the show.

Same thing with hiring. You need to know that the person applying for your job can do the job. You do this by giving them tests. This is a vital piece of the interview process.

If someone is going to be doing a lot of writing in the job, give them a writing-based test as part of your hiring process. If the job requires a lot of Zoom calls with clients, you need to have them do a Zoom-based test. Basically, tailor their tests to their duties.

One caution here is to not give them these tests too soon. We made this mistake early on. In our job ads, we asked people to read our vivid vision before they even applied. Eventually, we realized we were asking too much, too early. It made more sense to get them excited about the vivid vision during their first round interview, and *then* ask them to reflect on it. Similarly, once you've gotten them excited about your firm during that first interview, that's when you could give them the written test or the Zoom test or whatever other test you've devised.

By the time you're done with that first interview and those tests, you should have a great idea of which candidates will be the A-players who could help take your firm to the next level. In your final interviews, continue to pull out the stops to win them over.

Quick-Hitting Hack: Want to dive deeper on this topic? The book we mentioned earlier, *Who: The A-Method For Hiring* by Geoff Smart and Randy Street, will give you plenty of additional information in building your hiring process out past the first interview.

Poaching and In-House Recruiters?

Now we're about to contradict everything we just taught you, but hear us out. Once you get to a certain level as a firm, it might make sense to stop running job ads altogether. Instead of waiting for the A-players to find you, *you* go out and find *them*.

For instance, create a list of your five biggest competitors, go to LinkedIn, look up their employees, then reach out directly to your dream hires. This is called poaching.

Learning to poach people from other companies is one of the five highest value skills Bill has ever learned as a CEO. Give them a reason to leave their current position and come work for your vision. When you learn this skill, you will never again say, "The job market is hard!"

Another approach is hiring an in-house recruiter. We came to this insight one day after reviewing our expenses in our QuickBooks account and saw that we were spending hundreds of thousands of dollars for job ads on LinkedIn and Indeed. It was a shocker to both of us. We didn't think we were getting a good ROI on that money, so we decided to hire someone in-house whose job it was to go out and *find* the exact people we wanted.

Today, we don't run any ads. Our in-house recruiter finds people on LinkedIn who are open to new opportunities and who have the experience we want.

Do we recommend all law firms go this route? Not until you are spending over $60K per year on job ads or outside recruiters. Also, if you are slow growth and not bringing in a lot of revenue, hiring a recruiter probably is not the right approach for you.

But if you are bringing in $1M or more a year, it would be worth your time to consider the benefits of an in-house recruiter. It could be just the advantage you need to rapidly grow your team.

SMB Team plans on building a legal recruiting business in the future.

Speaking of dollars and cents, let's talk about the biggest thought still on your mind. How are you going to be able to afford these all-star candidates? Let's do the math.

Hiring Math

Pop quiz! Remember the 20/40/10 rule? The first 20% goes to marketing, the next 10% to personal development—and the biggest number, 40%, goes to … what?

Not "what." WHO. Your people!

A lot of law firm owners look at their revenue and say, "I don't have the money to hire new staff." But what they're missing is the fact that hiring staff is not an expense. It's an *investment*.

The smart law firm owner looks at their revenue and says, "I don't have the money to hire staff. That means I'm not generating the income I should be generating. That means *I need to hire someone to help solve the problem of that shortfall.*"

The right new hire will add to your revenue, not drain it. Here's how you can be strategic and ensure that every new hire helps grow your firm.

For a growing law firm, we believe every hire should produce a 5:1 return on investment (3:1 at the lowest). In other words, if you're paying a lawyer $100K, that lawyer should be bringing in $500K in revenue.

This would be true of other revenue–producing roles as well, such as a dedicated intake person. For instance, if a smaller firm finds a good intake person, well-trained in sales and able to answer all the firm's phone calls, that hire will have a direct impact on the firm's bottom line. Their contribution is invaluable! If you're paying that intake person $50K a year, they should be bringing in $250K in increased revenue. That's a healthy ROI that will grow your firm.

Now, what about non–revenue producing roles, such as your HR manager or your receptionist? In those cases, lean on your KPIs (Key Performance Indicators). Track that employee's contribution against measurable standards that the employee understands and can strive toward. For instance, what are the top three responsibilities of a receptionist at your firm? State them clearly and track them diligently.

Remember the "Cost of Goods Sold" indicator we mentioned first in Chapter 4 when talking about Profit Metrics? That's another KPI to reference. If Adam takes five hours to complete a task and Beatrice takes one hour to complete the same task *at the same level of quality*, then you have some key information about how to compensate and manage them appropriately. Beatrice might get a pay bump to start coaching other people like Adam on increasing efficiency, thereby leading to higher profit margins.

Both revenue-producing hires and non-revenue-producing hires can add to the quality, efficiency, and profitability of your firm. The former generate income. The latter handle the work of that increased revenue.

A common mistake law firms make is to hire a lot of administrative people because they are generally much cheaper. But if you do that, you're going to be unbalanced with people doing tasks all day that aren't attached to an increase in cases or average case value. Your revenues won't grow and your firm will stagnate.

Hire in the right order. Revenue producers first, non-revenue producers second. That's the hiring math that leads to success.

Okay, now let's talk about how *much* you're going to hire them for.

A-Players, At What Cost?

Bill Gates once said, "A great writer of software code is worth 10,000 times the price of an average software writer."[17]

Bill Gates knew what he was talking about. Most firms focus on the salary of an A-player (the price) rather than the exponential increase in value that they will get from that A-player (the value).

The lesson here is simple. You must pay top dollar to get top performers.

---

[17] Hastings, Reed and Erin Meyer. 2020. *No Rules Rules: Netflix and the Culture of Reinvention.* Random House, p.. 78.

Office Team conducted a survey asking 2,800 workers what would make them pack up and leave their job for a new one. They found that 44% said they would leave for more money.[18]

High salary is the single best employee retention tool you have. It's definitely not the only one—more on that in the next chapter. But money is a major piece of the pie.

Still—those top performers will more than compensate for their cost. Here's a story to illustrate. At our firm, we had two employees doing the same job. One was making a salary of $75K and the other was making $85K. A total of $160K. They were both B-players. They did an *okay* job at best. We made the decision to let them go and ended up hiring someone else in their place—except, instead of looking to hire two new people, we decided to look for one stellar person and offered a much higher salary than what we'd paid the B-players.

We found her. This woman was *great*. She did twice as much work as the two B-players put together, produced better content, did not need managing, and was an excellent culture fit. In other words, she was an A-player. We had to pay her $120K, and she was worth it in so many ways, not the least of which was how much *time* she saved us. And if you're a quick study, you'll notice that her higher salary was still $40K less than the combined salaries of the two B-players. She made us more, and she cost us less. That's some winning hiring math.

Are things going smoothly in your firm? If they are, you can get lulled into complacency. If it's only ever smooth sailing, you most likely aren't growing. You could be stagnating.

---

[18] Ibid, p. 79-80.

If you want to grow, you need pushers and shovers. You need people who go above and beyond, who think around corners and are committed to finding growth opportunities. They need to have a bit of the disruptor in them. They need to be proactive, hungry for the next thing, and ready to help take your firm to the next level.

In short, you need A-players, and you need to pay for them.

In the long run, as we showed with the earlier example, hiring A-players ends up being cheaper than keeping B- and C-players on your payroll.

There are other advantages to hiring A-players. Often, they will spur your B- and C-players into becoming better employees. The low performers think, "Dang, this new gal is making me look bad. I'm going to have to up my game to compete." A-players can raise your team to higher standards.

Your A-players can also help you weed out the underperformers. If someone on your team is criticizing a good A-player, you know they are *not* A-players themselves. They're intimidated by someone good and not interested in improving. That's when you know it's time to let them go.

If you're asking yourself, "Is this employee an A-player?" your answer is "No." You know an A-player when you see one. High-performers are their own advertisement.

But also keep in mind that as your business grows and you are able to afford higher and higher salaries, your definition of an A-player will change. An A-player at $120K per year is nothing compared to an A-player at $300K per year.

In sum, don't be afraid to pay for top talent. Incredible people lead to stellar profit. They're the best way to grow your firm.

Quick-Hitting Hack: Confession time. Most of the A-players we've hired in the past year were people we poached from other companies. Why did we resort to that? Because we learned that most A-players are not currently unemployed, looking at job postings. No way! They're working somewhere—because people are chomping at the bit to hire them!

The same is true in your case. One of the best ways you can get A-players for your firm is to approach great employees who are not happy at their current place of work and invite them to consider working for you. LinkedIn is a good place to start. Consider shooting an A-player a message and say something like, "We are so impressed by the work we see from you. Would you ever be open to considering a change in employer?" Then, describe a few key selling points about your firm: the salary, the culture, the nature of the job, and the impact they could have working at your firm. If they get back to you and say, "No thanks, I'm happy," that's fine. You leave it at that. But often, people will be open to a dialogue about working with you.

Some people feel squeamish about this because they feel it's unethical. But you're not forcing anyone to do anything. You're simply offering an opportunity. They're free to turn it down. If they say yes, they weren't happy in the first place. Keep in mind, for this to work, you need to be able to offer these A-players a *better* work environment. This is yet another reason why it's so important to have great culture at your firm, and to offer better salaries than what people could find

> elsewhere. This form of direct outreach can be a great way
> to recruit A-players—and it doesn't even require putting up
> job ads!

Now, let's address your final two questions. Which position is
most important to hire for first? And ... How do you make
sure your new hires pay for themselves quickly enough to
justify the expense of their salary?

Figure Out Who You Need in Which Seats

Where did we begin this book? In Part 1, we helped you
form your annual plan, broken down into clear quarterly
boulders and the 5 Law Firm KPIs. Now, that annual plan
gets connected to people. Each of those quarterly boulders
should be assigned to members of your leadership team. Any
obvious gaps in the talent necessary to hit those five law firm
KPIs becomes your focus for hiring.

Just like the five KPIs, there are five key functions in a business.
Vision, Operations, Marketing, Intake, and Client Experience.
Your leadership team should have at least one owner for each
of these five key roles. If you are a solo, that means you are all
five roles right now. If you have a team of five, that means you
can have two people on your leadership team. That could look
like you owning Vision and Marketing and your office manager owning Operations, Intake, and Client Experience. When
you get to a team of over 20, it's time to have one person in
charge of each of the five functions. This is around when you
enter the Abyss, and why getting through it can be hard. You
need leaders in each seat who can drive strategy and execution.

But, when it comes to recruiting, you just have to start by being crystal clear with the type of person you want and exactly what outcomes you want them responsible for.

Spell Out Responsibilities

Once you've assigned goals and roles to specific people, you need to make their roles crystal clear. Each person should have a clear set of responsibilities and goals, which should all tie directly back to your annual plan. Remember the five KPIs from Chapter 4? Make sure you have at least one person assigned to lead each of the five areas.

At SMB, we set up this alignment and accountability through job scorecards—and we use these scorecards as a component of our hiring process. Before a person joins our staff, they have clear expectations about their role with us. Then, during our weekly one-on-one meetings, we use the scorecards so they know how they are performing to their numbers.

Here's an example:

Role Scorecard Template

Role Name:
Preferred Experience Level:
Final Hiring Decision Maker:

Ideal Hire Date:
Salary Range:

MISSION: The mission of this role is to produce amazing content on youtube, gather amazing client reviews, and strive to massively increase customer experience (NPS).

	OUTCOMES	WHY THIS MATTERS
1	**MARKETING:** Create client update process that keeps clients updated & reaches 50 NPS score with 50% client response rate by January 15, 2024.	Clients need to be updated more to increase NPS score. Remove anxiety about "not doing enough"
2	**MARKETING:** 60 Youtube videos created & published by January 31, 2024 that are used to attract new clients & create evangelists of current clients.	Hard to reproduce marketing strategy. Lead Generation. Lead abundance. Better NPS.
3	**MARKETING:** 30 NEW 5 star Google reviews by January 31, 2024	Branding. New lead gen. SEO growth.

Each scorecard has a job description and a maximum of three outcomes, which represent that role's contribution to the annual plan. The outcomes column is not general or wishy-washy. It states *exactly* what's expected. In the case of the marketing role described, that means 60 videos, 30 five-star reviews, and so on. Using this scorecard, everyone—both the employee and the employer—knows where they stack up in meeting the annual goal.

Allow us to reiterate a key point. You don't just use the scorecards *after* people are hired. You present it at the interview. In fact, it's part of your recruiting process! You say, "Do you understand you're going to be measured against these numbers and receive bonuses if you exceed these three outcomes? Do you understand that if you don't hit these three numbers, you're not going to remain employed at this firm?" You're asking them if they're okay with being held accountable to a high standard—which, trust us, is very revealing.

You would not *believe* how many B- and C-players this simple tactic scares away. But the A-players are excited by it. They see those numbers and hear about those bonuses, and they think, "Hell yeah. Bring it on!" Those are the people you want.

Remember, these scorecards have to be clear and specific. They need to say *exactly* how much is expected of the recruit. If you don't have that clarity, you will attract low performers. However, with that clarity, not only will you attract A-players, but they'll also pay for themselves very quickly by helping your firm increase its value.

Quick–Hitting Hack: Scan the QR code below to access the template we use for tracking KPIs across our business, along with the bonus plan, which rewards people for hitting them. This document helps you assemble all those job scorecard results into a big-picture map for your firm. Think of it as your company's scorecard. It helps you see all your key metrics in one place, like new cases in the door, closing rate, client experience (NPS score), efficiency metrics, and so on. It also shows your people how much money they stand to make if they hit their piece of the pie. Stay on top of these numbers to motivate, track, and ensure the health of your business. That's your job as the head of the firm!

(You'll find all the other bonuses from the book here or you can go to **yourdreamlawfirm.com**.)

Scan this QR Code to Unlock This Bonus

BILL HAUSER NARRATES

Individual Accountability is Key

Now, what happens if someone *doesn't* hit their goals? In fact, what if your entire team falls short? Do you just fire everyone and start over?

Of course not.

I struggled with this issue early on when I was still trying to figure out how to set the right quarterly goals. I *had* goals for my company and communicated them to my team—but they didn't work. The team lost their attachment to the goals because they were written up as a goal only *an entire team* could accomplish. That meant no single person could achieve them—there was no specificity about what *each person* needed to accomplish. It was hard for anyone on the team to recognize if their collective efforts were getting them where they needed to go, which meant motivation never kicked into high gear. Once I realized this, I instituted *individual* goals. I gave each person on the team their own set of goals that they could achieve. That changed everything! People felt individual ownership over their goals and, because of the bonus incentives, they saw the direct impact their success would have on their paychecks. Motivation was suddenly no longer an issue.

That didn't mean I abandoned the team goals. It wasn't an either-or thing. The individual goals helped build momentum toward the team goals, and the team goals helped build communication and collaboration among individuals. Each type of goal was necessary, and together, they were sufficient. Likewise, a healthy firm should have both team and individual goals.

And don't leave out the bonus incentives! People's salaries should be sufficient compensation for doing their jobs—that's a given, and a necessary piece to have in place if you're going to hire A-players. But bonuses should also be a component of rewarding people who hit their targets.

At our firm, we base bonuses on the three KPI goals listed on the individual job scorecard. We have A, B, and C targets for those numbers, correlating to dollar amounts.

- A: Your number exceeds the previous best number in this category by 20%.
- B: Your number is the best ever in this category.
- C: Your number exceeds the average of the three best results ever in this category.

The higher you are on this list, the higher your bonus. We've seen bonuses spur people into even higher rates of productivity and achievement. So, when you're figuring out how salaries fit into that 40% you've allotted to payroll, don't forget to set a pot of money aside for bonus incentives.

Quick-Hitting Hack: Some famous people disagree with us about bonuses, BTW. The book *No Rules Rules: Netflix and the Culture of Reinvention,* by Netflix founder Reed Hastings and Erin Meyer, recommends a system paying A-players high salaries and *not* offering any bonuses. Clearly, we've rejected this advice at SMB Team and have tied all of our positions to bonuses. This works for our culture and our firm. We think it helps keep our employees accountable and motivated. But it's important for you to know that there are other ways of doing it. Hastings makes a great argument for his approach and it's one that might appeal to you more than ours. If you decide to go his route, be prepared to fire people if they don't meet your expectations. But keep this key insight in mind: whether you use bonuses as incentives or not, A-players are worth the money. You get what you pay for.

Buying Law Firms

A lot of this can seem tough and overwhelming. But what if I told you there is a way to hire a dozen or so A-players at once, with one decision? It might sound impossible, but it's not. It's called buying a law firm, and it works amazingly well.

If you really want to ramp up your business fast, consider buying an already existing business.

You not only acquire a competent and seasoned staff, but you also get all of the internal processes, systems, intellectual property, and marketing assets they've built. Even better, you avoid the time necessary to build all that on your own, which can represent years of savings.

There are lots of law firm owners that would happily sell you their business because they hate running it. They don't want to be a CEO and they are ready to get out. That's a prime opportunity for you.

We know this from our own experience. The year that Andy's company merged with SMB team, we went from $5M a year in revenue to approximately $15M the next year, we went to nearly *$26M*. Bringing Andy's company into SMB was the best decision Bill ever made as a CEO. It created a synergy that allowed for multiplier growth and a team of over 13 people to come onto SMB in a matter of weeks.

Number Three

We told you earlier in this chapter that, to operate a firm with a high-performing team—a team with the best, *best* people—you needed to do three things.

1. *Attract* A-players to your business.

2. *Win them over* so they decide to work for you instead of a competitor.

3. *Keep* your all-stars and enable their growth.

We've discussed how you can hit those first two requirements. We also gave you information about the hiring math related to salaries, monitoring KPIs, and ensuring accountability.

But what about number three?

There's no point in bringing on top people if you end up losing them again within a year. That's why number three gets its own chapter. We're going to teach you how to effectively lead, manage, and retain your quality staff so they can shine for you for years to come.

Chapter 10 | Takeaways

1. The best way to grow and scale your firm to get the lifestyle you want (more money, freedom, and impact) is by building a team made up of exclusively A-players.

2. Attract star performers to your firm by developing your culture. Hone your core values. Create your vivid vision. Engage in your community and online so that potential candidates can see you're doing exciting things.

3. Get A-players' attention through effective job ads. The title should be more specific and compelling than a mere job description. The job ad should focus less on what you want a candidate to do for *you,* and more on

what your firm can do for *them*. Your job ads should help your firm stand out as distinct—the kind of place that would attract an A-player.

4. During your first round interviews, excite the candidates about your firm by thoughtfully selecting an enthusiastic, core-values-embodying all-star to conduct the interview. Talk up your vivid vision. After the interview, send the candidate any relevant tests that will help you determine your top applicants and weed out underperformers.

5. An A-player should be able to produce a 5:1 ROI. If their salary is $100K, they should be able to produce $500K worth of value within a year. For non-revenue producing roles, evaluate their ROI via KPIs tied to their role results. Each individual should have clear, measurable outcomes they're directly responsible for. We recommend awarding bonuses for team members who hit their targets.

CHAPTER 11

~~MANAGING~~ LEADING A-PLAYERS

UNLEASH YOUR ALL-STARS BY DELEGATING AUTHORITY, NOT TASKS

"The key to successful leadership is influence, not authority."

—Kenneth H. Blanchard

BILL HAUSER NARRATES

We've reached another stop on our tour of "Bill's Hard Won Wisdom From Mistakes Made During SMB Team's Early Days." Welcome!

When I first started SMB, I hired two employees who had almost no experience building landing pages. So, before they started work, I created a step-by-step manual in which I broke down every single granular detail on everything they needed to do to build a landing page.

425

Then I trained and managed them on that document. It worked! Under my guidance and the guidance of that manual, they built great landing pages for clients.

In fact, that system worked so well, I created similar step-by-step manuals for our sales, our marketing, and pretty much every piece of our operation. I did that for the first two years of the business. The whole business—every single detail—came out of my brain. Everything.

Let me tell you, that set up made me feel like I was this incredibly smart guy. I was the guru of SMB's business model! Everyone and everything had to go through me. I felt indispensable and because of that, I thought I was so incredibly amazing that the business could not function without me micromanaging everything.

And that sucked.

At the end of those two years, I realized I was spending all my time—time I would never get back—basically running the business myself because I had to communicate every single detail of every single process to my team. I couldn't take a vacation or even a day off. Fatigue and burnout set in. I felt like crap at the end of the day. Work was tedious, unstimulating, and soul crushing. And I was beginning to sense that it wasn't just me feeling that way—it was also all the employees I was micromanaging.

I got to the point where the thought of sitting in front of another Google doc and manually typing out a system for intake or follow-up or interviewing or anything else made me want to gouge my eyes out.

I thought, "There has to be a better way."

I was right. I found that better way in *Who Not How: The Formula to Achieve Bigger Goals Through Accelerating Teamwork* by Dan Sullivan and Benjamin Hardy.

This is the key insight I got from that book. Instead of trying to teach others how to do systems, why not hire people who are smarter than you who are already experts at those systems?

This was the point of our previous chapter. Get your A-players. Find a salesperson who already knows how to close clients. Find a marketing person who's already a genius at Facebook Ads. Find a web designer who can do landing pages in their sleep. Why? Not just so your business can thrive—but also so you can *stop micromanaging everyone.*

It seems so obvious, but sometimes we don't see the obvious because it's hidden by our egos. When you hire A-players, as we explained in Chapter 10, you can delegate all those tasks that take up way too much of your time *while* making your business better. Instead of micromanaging, your task as a leader is to ensure that your high-performers are motivated to *sustain* their high performance.

Today, Andy and I pay a full-time employee six figures to run our ads. Why? Because this person knows how to run Meta ads on Facebook and Instagram way better than we do. All we had to do was tell them our vision and goals and say, "Here's the password. Go to it."

How much could you and your firm benefit from something like this? Think about all the time you would get back in your life if you could delegate all or most of the tasks you are doing now. That's what you're paying for when you hire A–players. They can make your life and your business better! But even with highly talented A–players dominating your team, you still have to manage them.

I like to use the analogy of a marathon runner here. You can have the best long-distance runner in the world, but if they're going in the wrong direction, they're never going to get to the finish line.

Your job as leader is to provide direction and coaching. You need to point every member of your team toward your firm's goals and vision and *then* let them do their magic.

Getting your team running in the right direction is incredibly important to your firm because without that direction they'll fall short of their goals—and *your* goals. This is terrible for A–players. They want to win. That competitive edge is what makes them A–players!

Your newly hired all–stars don't need to be micromanaged. They need to be *unleashed*. Your focus as a leader is to make your ultra-talented team happy so they can make your clients happy. To do that, they need clear direction from you. We're going to talk a lot in this chapter about how you can build a culture and clarity that keeps your A–players motivated and pumped to do great work.

But before we get there, we need to draw a very clear distinction between two different management styles that will define everything about how you run your firm.

Systems-Focused? Or People-Focused?

To manage your team properly, you need to make a decision. Are you going to be a *systems-focused* law firm, or are you going to be a *people-focused* law firm?

Systems-Focused

In a systems-focused firm, you manage your people through tightly architected systems. You use task lists and check off boxes. Everyone gets clear marching orders along with clear instructions about how to march. The management method I outlined in this chapter's opening story gave me a systems-focused business: I micromanaged every single action each employee took.

I ran it like a franchise operation—like a McDonald's restaurant. Every McDonald's runs exactly the same as all the other McDonald's. They have identical procedures for opening, cooking, cleaning, customer service, and so on. They can hire people at the lowest possible wage and plug them into the system, because they don't need to be particularly talented—they just need to be able to follow the *system*. If a manager holds them accountable to that system, they'll get results.

Here's the problem with micromanagement: it kills momentum and stifles A-players. That's why you don't see a whole lot of talented people working long term at fast-food franchises.

Systems-focused operations may get the job done, but they don't leave room for growth.

It works for people with little prior experience, motivation, or skill—for that reason, it might be appropriate if you're still in the first or possibly second level of growth in your law firm.

But once you get those A-players? You need to shift away from a systems-focused form of management. It will damage people's self-esteem and stifle their creativity. Their growth will be contracted and then, guess what? Your entire firm's growth will stagnate.

We're not saying systems as a whole are bad. Any effective organization will have identified best practices for certain repeatable tasks. That's a sign of organizational health. For that reason, we've provided tips on how to optimize your systems in the second half of the chapter.

However, using standard operating procedures for certain tasks is different from running your entire firm in a micromanaging approach. Micromanagement will not bring out the best in people. It will always lead to a low-performing team. That's the problem with a systems-focused company.

People-Focused

Not McDonald's then. How about Netflix?

Netflix is the perfect example of a people-focused company. In a people-focused firm, team members aren't assigned tasks—they're assigned *authority*. People are given the freedom to achieve their objectives in their own way, within the context of a company's vision.

Netflix's people-focused approach is entirely appropriate given their creative focus: they produce new movies and TV shows. Would you set up a systems-focused operation to produce creative content? Absolutely not. You can't have people follow a manual, then come up with groundbreaking ideas and compelling new shows. To do that, you need highly creative people who are given the freedom to invent, explore, and fabricate something new.

That's why Netflix hires A-players: people good at writing, directing, makeup, costumes, and all the other creative components of making movies, and lets them do what they do best. They don't micromanage those people. They don't even *manage* these talented folks because A-players can manage themselves. Instead, they *lead* them.

You should do the same in your law firm. Take our approach with our videographers, for example. We don't micromanage their lighting, setups, or framing. We tell them what we want from a video, and they make it happen. We coach. We do not boss.

If you want to lift your firm to higher profit and become dominant in your market, you need to consider becoming more of a people-focused organization. Ditch any impulses you have to micromanage. Instead, unleash the creative potential of your A-players.

Three Principles for Running a People-Focused Law Firm

Here are the three most important concepts you need to embrace when transitioning to a people-focused law firm.

- **Level 5 Leadership.** This is a concept explained in the book by Jocko Willink and Leif Babin, *Extreme*

Ownership: How U.S. Navy SEALs Lead and Win. Level 5 Leadership balances professional will and personal humility. You must provide your team with perfect clarity on where you want to take the firm (your professional will) and at the same time let them know you need their help getting there (your personal humility). Be as open as possible. Don't keep anything about your vision a secret. And don't keep your shortcomings a secret, either. Let your team know exactly where you need help.

- **No Micromanaging!** We'll keep beating this dead horse because we know this habit dies hard. Allow us to repeat: micromanaging is detrimental to you, your team, and your firm. You must move away from it. To do that, build a culture of trust. Tell your team you trust them to keep the interests of the firm foremost in their minds and actions. If they don't, you will call them on it. If there is one thing to micromanage, it is the strategic priorities of your law firm—that's it.

- **Context, Not Control.** Leadership in a people-focused firm requires letting your people know where you are going as a firm and when you expect to get there—but not *how* you get there. That's up to your team. You are not controlling their actions. Instead, you provide abundant *context* so they know how to align their efforts with your clear vision, along with accountability to motivate their self-managing acceleration.

If you follow the advice we gave you in the previous chapter, you *can* trust your team. It's full of A-players! These are people eager to do good work and manage themselves in the context of your culture. People who need nothing more from you than effective leadership.

So, how do you provide that effective leadership? Two words: clarity and culture. Those should be your two main priorities in leading high-performers. You need to provide *clarity* about your vision, quarterly boulders, role expectations, and deadlines so that each A-player knows *exactly* what to do, by when. (That's a fuller description of what we just identified as "context.") And you need to foster a *culture* that consistently aligns with your core values, one that celebrates wins, supports people through mistakes, and shows *intolerance* for anyone who flouts the core values.

Let's start with culture first.

Cultivating Culture

We talked about cultivating culture in our previous chapter as a vital element of attracting A-players to your firm. But we need to hit on different aspects of culture building in this chapter as well, because you can't recruit based on your culture and then drop it once the A-players are actually working there. Culture is vitally important in both recruiting *and* management and retention. Let's hit on some key culture building elements that specifically impact high-performance management—er, rather, high-performance *leadership*.

Culture-Shaping Terminations

For the leader who's serious about cultivating a culture that fosters high performance, one of the most important ways you will build trust among your team is through your firing choices.

Yes, that's where we're starting this section on culture. Firing. Termination. Get them off the bus. *Let them go.*

Here's why this matters. We had a high-performing salesperson at SMB who was crushing her job. Let's call her Shari. She consistently closed a high number of deals.

The only thing was, she didn't keep track of her outgoing calls. We needed that data for our performance evaluations, so we asked Shari to pay attention to this. She didn't. One Monday morning, we told her she needed to track her outgoing calls for one full week. Shari promised she would.

Come Friday, she told us she didn't do as she'd promised.

This violated one of the core principles of our culture. Three-way winners. Shari was prioritizing her convenience at the expense of the team. If we had looked the other way at Shari's blatant disregard of an explicit expectation, we would have eroded the culture of trust we were working to build. All of our other employees would have seen we weren't serious about enforcing our values or role expectations. "Bill and Andy talk a good game, but when it comes down to it, they don't do what needs to be done. It's just yip yapping from on top of a mountain." Not only would they have lost trust in us, their leaders, they would have lost trust in one another and questioned why they should bother achieving their own role results.

You can't have a viable culture if you just say, "Here's what we stand for," and then do nothing about it when someone shows blatant disregard for your core values.

It was not a tough decision for us to fire Shari. She was gone that afternoon. We kept our word to the firm and the team to maintain our culture.

The hardest situation we've run into is when someone is a top performer, but constantly creates drama and toxicity. This sucks. And, while it seems like the right call is to let them perform and "shield their toxicity from the team," this is the wrong call. We have tried to turn these situations around too many times to count. It's always been a mistake to hold on to the drama-creators. The tension they create is not worth their performance.

Why would we share a story about firing someone when discussing culture? Because *your culture is formed by your firing decisions.* Remember that. It's crucial. To maintain your culture, you can't accept bad attitudes, drama, or broken promises, even if the people exhibiting those behaviors are high-performers. Get rid of them.

Your culture is formed by your firing decisions.

This won't be easy. Firing an employee is probably the worst part of leading a business. We've had to let people go who violated our culture even when we loved them. But maintaining consistency in this area is necessary if you want a healthy team of high-performers. Consistency aligned with your values is how a healthy culture is built and maintained.

That's why intolerance for breaching your values should also be also addressed on a smaller level. At SMB Team, if we see someone violate a core value—even if it's not a fireable offense—we immediately call them out on it. We don't wait for a meeting; we pull them aside and address it point blank. We call this radical transparency and all team members participate in holding each other accountable.

These call-outs are not an excuse for anyone to be a jerk, and we emphasize growth rather than shaming. For example, if Ali calls out Brandon, Ali needs to offer a constructive alternative to Brandon's behavior and communicate that in a polite way. But we do call people out, regularly. This radical transparency is part of how our team recognizes that we're serious about living according to our values.

"Firing and call-outs ... Bill and Andy, aren't there any more *positive* ways to shape a culture that fosters A-players?"

Absolutely.

Culture Shaping Habits

One of the best ways to foster a high-performing culture is through practicing culture habits. At SMB, we conduct morning huddles every day of the week without fail. We invite team members to recognize other members of the team and express gratitude for exhibiting one of our core values.

We also hit on our core values by celebrating awesome clients. Throughout the year, we bring up stories at meetings about how Client X demonstrated a core value in our work together. The values get reinforced again at every quarterly meeting when we review the core values and our vivid vision.

Quick-Hitting Hack: Scan the QR code below to watch a video of our daily huddle so you can experience the camaraderie, energy, and overall awesomeness our team brings each morning.

(You'll find all the other bonuses from the book here or you can go to **yourdreamlawfirm.com**.)

Scan this QR Code
to Unlock This Bonus

We make the awareness of core values part of our everyday culture. It becomes habitual—second nature. The values are in our heads *all the time*. And that's what you want for your firm as well. You want to get to the point where your team is living and breathing your core values as much as you are. Your high-performing culture will rise out of that consistent values emphasis.

The point of all of this is to make your culture such an integral part of your team that everyone believes in it, participates in it, and keeps it strong.

On to the second key element to leading your team of high-performers. Enhancing clarity.

Enhancing Clarity

Imagine a football team where every player is a quarterback. In fact, they are the *best* quarterbacks in the league. No other team has a quarterback as good as any of theirs.

Is this team going to win the Super Bowl?

The answer is obvious. No. To win a Super Bowl, you need kickers, running backs, and blockers. A team of quarterbacks—no matter how good—will not be able to play like an all-star team.

Now, let's say you have a well-diversified team—stellar kickers, running backs, tight ends, fullbacks *and* quarterbacks—but no one has studied any plays. What's more, even though *you* have a clear idea of who's supposed to play what position, your players *don't*. The wide receiver thinks he's supposed to play fullback. The coach for special teams thinks he's supposed to work with the offensive line. No one knows their job description. Is *this* team going to win any NFL Titles?

Once again, that's a resounding no.

The same is true for your law firm. You might have A-players on your roster, but your team will collectively fail if any of the following are true ...

- Every single one of your employees is a top trial lawyer. *Fail.* That's a team full of quarterbacks.

- You've got a diversified team but no one has clarity over their specific objectives—in other words, no vivid vision or quarterly boulders. *Fail.* You've got no plan to get the ball down the field—no one's learned or memorized any plays.

- You've got a diversified team who has learned good plays, but no one is clear on their job description. *Fail.* That's like Tom Brady trying to fill in as kicker.

This is why *clarity* is so crucial for the success and high performance of your team. We've spent a lot of time in this book already talking about the importance of your vivid vision and quarterly boulders, and we've also spent time talking about how to get the right people in the right seats. That takes care of the first two bullets.

So, let's focus now on the third. Ensuring that everyone on your roster clearly knows and understands their roles and responsibilities.

Clear Roles

"No offense, Bill and Andy, but I can skip this section. My people understand their roles and responsibilities."

Hang on—if you think you've provided that clarity, check yourself. How do you know? Do they have a job scorecard, or some sort of comparable, current description of their role expectations that's regularly revisited? Or are you basing your answer on the job ad they answered two years ago that is probably obsolete by now?

If you're flying seat-of-the-pants style on this part of your firm, it's time for you to put together an organizational chart. That's the best possible way of making sure everyone's role is clear and there are no overlapping roles.

Rather than taking your current team and putting all their positions in a chart, we recommend starting from scratch. Begin with a blank chart and position the job titles *you need* with the top three to five responsibilities assigned to each job. Make it clear who reports to whom. Only then should you slot in names for each position. Once you have clarity about who is truly necessary to complete the work of your company, you should also have greater insight into what each person's top priorities should be.

We also agree with Gino Wickman, who, in his book *Traction: Get a Grip on Your Business,* recommends you have a person on staff who oversees the implementation of your firm's vision. This person takes responsibility for integrating that vision across all departments in the firm and provides clarity over who takes ownership over each quarterly boulder. This is known as an "integrator."

Whenever I'm evaluating a law firm that has come to us, I look at their organizational chart. Who's in charge of sales? Who's in charge of marketing? Who's in charge of operations? Who's in charge of finance/admin? Who's the visionary? Who's the integrator?

We often get a deer-in-the-headlights look from clients when we ask these questions. "What do you mean?" they ask. "*I'm* in charge of everything."

Small law firms often require the CEO—that's you—to function in all five of those roles. This may be okay for a small firm, but it doesn't scale. You need a separate person for each of those roles if you want to grow your business.

What too many law firm owners don't realize is that, just as they delegate tasks, they also need to delegate *authority*, especially in these five areas. Remember? That's the hallmark of a people-focused firm.

Commit to divorcing yourself from these roles and take your place as a full-time visionary. If you don't, you'll constantly feel like things are hard, complicated, and just plain overwhelming. No one can do all these roles well simultaneously and still create a high-earning firm.

So, here's how you start delegating authority. Decide which role you want to divorce yourself from *first* and take the steps necessary to make that happen. Find the right person to take over that role. Once they're onboarded, repeat the process with the other roles.

You need freedom to step into your role as a full-time visionary. You won't have that freedom until you delegate authority to others in those five key departments.

This section is about enhancing clarity, so let's dial that down even more. The people you've delegated authority to need to clearly understand the parameters of their authority. What's under their jurisdiction and what's not? That means *you* need to clearly understand the parameters of the authority you've bestowed. One tool we use to provide that clarity is the Employee Maturity model.

Employee Maturity Model

Often when we talk to a client, they tell us they have a "marketing director." But we've found that, in many of these instances, the word "director" is a misnomer. Most lawyers don't have directors. They have people who function as *managers* who take direction from the head of the firm and act on that direction.

We're recommending you get directors in place who function in the true spirit of the word. They can create, guide, and *direct* their teams independently, in the same way a movie director would steer the artistic vision and interpretation of a writer's script. All a director needs to execute is the necessary context and clarity of your vision.

We use the Employee Maturity Model to illustrate role delineation to our clients. It is made up of three levels. Director, Manager, and Individual Contributor.

- **Directors** proactively look around corners and come up with new ideas about how to solve issues in their department. They do not wait for direction from the CEO or the head of the firm. Their role is creativity generation and holding managers accountable.

- **Managers** execute an existing strategy that has been handed to them, usually from the head of the firm or a Director. Managers do not come up with their own ideas. Their role is managing an existing strategy and managing Individual Contributors.

- **Individual Contributors** execute the instructions given to them by the Manager. They do the actual day-to-day work or provide the service. We also call these folks associate or technician-level roles.

When most firms look to scale up, they try to do it with existing staff. That often means individual contributors are scrambling to develop into managers, or—an even further reach—directors. Although you'll inevitably have some talented people who rise to the challenge, generally, this strategy doesn't pan out well. It's like asking your special teams players to start functioning as the offensive line.

To correct this, you need to either invest in training your team to *become* managers and directors, or—often a much easier approach—hire *experienced* and *seasoned* managers and/ or directors who are ready to hit the ground running from day one.

There's no third option here. Individual contributors will not pick up the fundamentals of managing and directing by osmosis. You must either train your individual contributors or recruit people who are higher up on the Employee Maturity scale.

Once you're clear on the level of authority that should be assigned to each role, you'll have more clarity on the type of tasks you can delegate.

Levels of Delegation

There are three levels of delegation. Task, priority, and authority.

- **Task Delegation.** Systems-focused companies lean heavily on task delegation, which involves tight overhead control. In essence, you give your employees step-by-step instructions on what to do, how, and when to do it. Task delegation is most often assigned to *individual contributors.* This is also the level you have to implement if you hire inexperienced people and have to hold them to a tight process.

- **Priority Delegation.** In a people-focused company, priority delegation would be assigned to *managers*. It involves communicating to the employee *what's most important* in a task or system, then allowing the person to figure out what steps need to happen to achieve the outcome you're looking for.

- **Authority Delegation.** This is the highest level of delegation and one we believe should be assigned to *directors*. Authority Delegation means you tell your director, "Here's the vision and context. Here's your team's goal. You are in charge of producing this result and have authority to create the priorities and the to-do list to make it happen."

Ineffective managers—i.e. micromanagers—never make it beyond task delegation. They treat even their team leaders as though they have to be tightly controlled every step of the way. However, to lead a high-performing team, you need to delegate priorities and authority to your A-players.

Here's an example to illustrate. Let's say you've hired Linda to oversee your marketing department and you've given her the title "marketing director."

An example of task delegation would be you telling Linda, "Our website needs to be updated to include these photos. Please get them up on the site." You're telling Linda exactly what you want her to do, as though she's an individual contributor. In this case, you're treating Linda as a marketing assistant, rather than a marketing director. If "assistant" is her job title and her role expectations, that's fine—but if you hired her to be a director, you either over-titled her, or you're micromanaging her and she's going to get tired of that, real quick.

In priority delegation, you would say to Linda, "We need to scale up our Google Ads campaigns to bring in more X case types. Dive into our campaigns, talk to some experts, and figure out the best moves to optimize our campaigns." You're getting closer to the target now. Linda is exercising more autonomy and making some decisions. However, this is more high-performance *management* on your part than *leadership*. You're still giving Linda her marching orders. If you've hired an A-player to be a director, you need to go one step further and empower her with the authority to lead.

In authority delegation, you only need to tell Linda one thing. "We need to get 200 leads per month at $40 per lead. Figure out how to do that."

You can run your firm with any of these three levels of delegation, but note what happens at the authority level. You don't have to micromanage anyone. Your directors can do the tasks and build the systems on their own, thereby freeing you to act solely as the company's visionary.

A lot of lawyers think scaling their business is going to be hard because they can't figure out how to manage (cough, cough, micromanage) all those new employees.

But in a people-focused company full of A-players, *you don't have to micromanage* if you practice authority delegation. Sure, if all you are doing is task delegation, then you're going to be buried and scaling your firm will be impossible. Don't do it.

Instead, commit to authority delegation. It's one of the key factors to successfully scaling your firm.

Here's one final tip on authority delegation. Please be aware of the difference between delegation and abdication. Abdication is when you fully mentally abandon something after you assign a responsibility to someone. Abdication is when you give someone no context and tell them to do something.

For authority delegation to work wonders, you first need to make sure everyone on your team is clear on your Vivid Vision, Quarterly Boulders, and the 5 Law Firm KPIs that are most important to your Annual Plan. Then, you need to provide as much context as possible to each person on your team, so they can *think* the way you think.

And, when you do it the first few times, people are going to make mistakes. It's your reaction to those mistakes that are make-or-break. Do you use the mistakes as coaching moments or as opportunities to scold the person you delegated to? Your reactions will show your team your true character as a leader.

Lastly, once you delegate something, you can never take it back. That's unless you want to demoralize your team. Let them learn and fail. And coach them to success. It's a little pain now for a lot of freedom and happy people in the future.

If you do all that (and you have a team of A-players), then authority delegation will be transformative for your life, your firm, and your future.

> **Quick-Hitting Hack:** In Chapter 1, we provided you with some tools to help you identify what to get off your plate through delegation and what—if anything—you want to keep. Generally, you want to keep your dream life in mind and delegate accordingly. If you love casework and the thought of handling another case makes you giddy like a kid in a candy shop, keep some casework for yourself. If you find it to be burdensome—delegate it all! Do you enjoy being on camera and being the face of your firm? Make that part of your essential job description. If being on camera makes your skin crawl, delegate that to the marketing department.
>
> Think about what you most love doing and claim those tasks for yourself. Then build a team around you to handle everything else.

BILL HAUSER NARRATES

You Can't Delegate Caring

There's one thing you absolutely *can't* delegate, and that's *caring*.

We don't mean caring, like Care Bear hugs. We mean caring, like, *This firm's success is up to me and I'm going to do a damn good job because I care so frickin' much.*

How does this relate to your law firm? When lawyers start delegating tasks, they can get very comfortable. They see all these competent people around them handling all aspects of the business and they can fall into a trap. They can think these smart people *care* about the business just as much as they do.

This is rarely, if ever, true. Your team might be incredible, but they have no incentive to care about the business as much as you do. It's not their business. This means that if you don't stay on top of the business, it's going to spiral into stagnancy. Your culture *and* clarity will suffer.

Here's what this means for you. *You can't abdicate running the business.* You need to show your team that your attention is on *everything* in your firm, and you are not mentally tapping out.

The best way to do this is to make big commitments and follow through on them. Make big marketing commitments, big hiring commitments, and big spending commitments. Basically, be the commitment machine of the firm.

A couple of years ago, I set a goal for a marketing event. I wanted us to bring in $2M, but ticket sales were lagging far behind. I went to my marketing team and asked them what was going on. Why were we behind on this?

They said, "We thought $2M was a stretch goal."

No, it wasn't. That same week, I booked Alex Rodriguez to speak at our event. He cost almost $200K.

As soon as the marketing team saw this, their eyes went wide. "Oh, wow, the $2M goal is real! Bill's serious about this. That $2M goal is no joke."

They kicked their marketing into high gear and that event became one of our most profitable and successful ever.

It happened because I, as leader of the business, committed to a big goal and backed that up with my own actions. It made the rest of the team step up and commit as well.

That kind of commitment doesn't come from your team. It has to come from you. You have to show you *care* about the success of every aspect of the firm, from intake, to marketing, to casework. You're not going to blow it off, and you're not going to let anyone else blow it off either.

When you make those big commitments, ensure your team has crystalline clarity about it through communication. An excellent way to amplify your clarity with your team is through a system used by the Navy: Plan, Brief, Execute, Debrief.

Plan, Brief, Execute, Debrief

Not only does this system work, it kind of rhymes, so it's easy to remember. Here's how to implement it.

- **Plan.** Decide what your big commitment is going to be. For the Navy, it might be taking a piece of land. For you, it might be holding a phenomenally successful seminar.

- **Brief.** Tell your team the plan in detail. When the Navy briefs troops, they're communicating things like how and where to deploy and which route to take to execute the mission. In your case, you might brief your team on who you'll get to speak at the seminar, and how your marketing team will prep the speaker so that their gifts are put to maximum effect. During the briefing stage, you need to get mental buy-in from everyone on the team. Make your caring contagious so that they care just as much about getting the plan done.

- **Execute.** The commanding officer does not execute the plan. His or her troops do. Similarly, *you* do not execute the plan. Your team does.

- **Debrief.** After execution, get your team together and share lessons learned and ways you'll improve the next time. The idea here is to learn from the execution. What went right? What went wrong? What will you keep and what will you eliminate?

If you consistently implement this system, eventually your team will get so experienced at this method of clear communication that *they* will start doing the planning and the briefing without you. This will further help your directors lead with authority and ensure you get the best out of your A-players.

Strategies for Systems in Your Firm

You can't get away from systems entirely—nor should you. Even people-focused firms employ systems at all levels of their business that should be well-crafted and adhered to. And some firms need to lean on systems more heavily if they're not ready to bring on the highly qualified staff to operate as a people-focused firm. Those firms need tips to effectively implement systems across the board.

What is a system? In a nutshell, it's a repeatable process that gets a predictable result.

A good example would be an intake script. That's a *repeatable* system that gets *repeatable* results. A system doesn't have to be complicated. A simple document or video that explains how to do something is sufficient.

Where some lawyers go wrong is by hiring people to implement those systems and then retreat into complete mental abandonment, figuring their hires will take care of things. That's a prime example of abdicating your responsibility to *care.*

These law firm owners wake up months later and find out that their systems—which they so carefully created and offloaded—are no longer being followed. Or that the person they hired created the wrong systems.

To prevent this disastrous result, you need to maintain accountability. Continue to care! You can do that by implementing two key procedures in your firm:

1. **Secure buy-in.** Get your team on board. You need to give them an *incentive* to believe in the importance of the firm's systems so they actually want to create, improve on, and stick to the firm's systems. This is how you can make your own caring contagious.

2. **Have your team improve your systems.** Start with sub-par systems that you create. Then hire people who can modify your systems. The people doing the work should be the ones to hone the systems, since they have the greatest insight over what's working and what isn't. Not only will your individual contributors help improve the systems where they work most

closely, but if you give them some authority in this area, they'll be more incentivized to stick closely to them. Your job is to provide direction, feedback, and guidance as they improve them.

Don't let yourself fall into the trap of waiting to perfect your systems before you hire. It's not necessary and will pose an obstacle to growing your firm. Instead, delegate some authority in this area. Let go.

Ask the skilled people you hire to improve your systems, with incentives.

What kind of incentives? Let's discuss.

Systems 101

We recommend incentivizing your team with bonuses. Cold hard cash works wonders. Always has and always will. Here are just a few instances where cash bonus incentives will help motivate stellar work.

- Reward someone on your team who writes an amazing script for intake.

- Audit a new hire for a week or a month and check to see how often they use the script associated with their job. If they use it 80% of the time or more, give *them* a bonus for faithfully using the system.

- Give bonuses to team members who effectively update and revise your systems.

All these are effective ways to make systems and procedures an integral part of your firm.

What about keeping your systems *organized* and easy to find? Remember, culture and clarity are both crucial for leading your high-performers. Here are ways you can ensure clarity around all aspects of your firm's systems.

1. **Store in One Place.** Don't have a dozen different tech tools to store your law firm systems. Choose one. We recommend Google Drive because it's accessible and easy to use, but you may have a preference for another platform. The crucial thing is not the technology, but the commitment to keeping everything in one easily accessed location.

2. **Update Regularly.** There's nothing more frustrating than trying to make an out-of-date system fit into new circumstances. That's why systems should be revisited and updated regularly. Schedule a systems review meeting with members of your team every quarter. Everyone on the team should be involved to secure buy-in. The person closest to the execution of the system should lead in updating the system. For instance, the lead copywriter updates the copywriting systems.

3. **Live by the 80/20 Rule.** Random gardening fact: Did you know that 20% of pea plants produce 80% of the peas? It's true, and the analogy applies to your firm's systems. Only create systems for the 20% of your firm's activities that produce 80% of your results. That would include answering the phone, following up with leads, setting marketing strategies, hiring people, and firing people. Do *not* spend time building a system for making business cards. This 80/20 rule appears throughout nature, and it is most certainly built into your law firm.

The ultimate goal of systems is to create higher efficiency per employee. You want a unit of your employee's time to be worth three or four times a unit of your competitor's employee's time.

Always think of your systems as machines that remove redundancy from your business. They should produce a high labor utilization rate. They exist to streamline your business and get the absolute best out of your team that you can.

Quick-Hitting Hack: If you want to learn more about the effective implementation of systems, check out our coaching video with John Nachazel.

(You'll find all the other bonuses from the book here or you can go to **yourdreamlawfirm.com**.)

Scan this QR Code to Unlock This Bonus

There's one monolith we haven't yet touched on the topic of leading a high-performing team … We haven't touched it yet because we know you hate it.

But we're going to teach you to love it. (Or at least, hate it less.)

Can you guess what we're talking about? Drum roll, please …

It's the *Meetings Monolith*.

Meetings 101

Try not to barf in your mouth. Yes, most people hate meetings. But they're vitally necessary for any successful organization. In fact, *Harvard Business Review* did a study of the most successful companies in the world. They found that the CEOs of these companies spent 72% of their time in meetings. They averaged 37 meetings per *week*. That's a lot of meetings—and they're integral to the companies' success.

People tend to hate meetings because they're generally *not done well*. Your meetings should have clear agendas, timed segments, someone to take notes, and well-defined action items assigned to specific people.

> **Your meetings should have clear agendas, timed segments, someone to take notes, and well-defined action items assigned to specific people.**

Let's take a look at all the types of meetings you should be conducting in your business.

> **Quick-Hitting Hack:** For more excellent advice on leveling up your meetings, I highly recommend *Meetings Suck: Turning One of the Most Loathed Elements of Business into One of the Most Valuable*, by Cameron Herold. Herold is the former COO of 1-800-GOT-JUNK, a waste removal company that went from zero to over 100 million in annual revenue under Herold's operational leadership. In the book, he explains the value of meetings and teaches you how to conduct a good one. As mentioned before, he's also been Bill's 1-on-1 coach for 3 years.

BILL HAUSER NARRATES

Annual Planning Meeting

As I shared in Chapter 1, one of the most important things I ever did as a CEO was plan my year. That's why we opened our book by teaching you how to envision and then actualize your annual plan.

> **Quick-Hitting Hack:** Gino Wickman's book *Traction: Get a Grip on Your Business* has a great section on running an annual meeting. I would suggest you follow Wickman's steps to the letter. That's the template we follow at SMB Team and it's proven to be highly effective.

This two-day meeting is held a few weeks before the end of the year. You and your leadership team will review all of your financials, data, and boulders from last year. Then, you'll compare that to your goals for next year.

You and your team will decide on your quarterly boulders for the upcoming quarter. You will also reset each other's roles and responsibilities to ensure full alignment with the company's goals and needs.

Make sure this meeting is not at your regular offices. A change of scenery is vitally important for open-minded thinking and decision-making.

Quarterly Planning Meeting

A quarterly planning meeting is just a mini annual planning meeting. At the beginning of the year, it's called an annual meeting. At the end of each quarter, it's called a quarterly meeting.

Quarterly meetings are only one day long and should happen two weeks before the end of each quarter. They require less data analysis and reflection since we have already committed to our annual goals in the annual meeting. This meeting is more about steering the ship in the upcoming quarter so you can stay on track to hit your annual goals.

You and your leadership team will still review your annual plan, financials, data, and boulders from last quarter to determine what's working or not working.

This meeting should ultimately generate a list of quarterly boulders along with the clear shifts you need to make to your KPIs in order to reach your annual plan.

Just like the annual, quarterlies should not be held in your office. Once again, the book *Traction* has a superb format for conducting quarterly meetings. Don't reinvent the wheel. Use their format. Just make sure you implement the specific goal-setting strategies we shared earlier in the book which are not included in Traction.

Quarterly All-Hands Meeting

Your quarterly all-hands meeting is where you update your entire team (not just your leadership team) on the progress you made towards your annual and quarterly goals last quarter. It's what we call the "Steve Jobs" presentation. This is the time to share the vision and to get the team excited about the future.

Talk about the big wins you've had and the amazing progress you've made. Secure buy-in by being an open book. Tell them how you're tracking the goals you set this year. Tell them how you're going to get to the goals for next quarter. Don't make yourself perfect. Let your team know your shortfalls and your failures.

Practice radical transparency and tell your team *everything*. Radical transparency is vitally important if you want to have a team that works toward your firm's goals with diligence and commitment.

Make sure the entire team gets briefed—not just the ones who attended, but also those who could not be there.

Weekly Accountability Meeting

Weekly accountability meetings are where the rubber hits the road and your annual plan comes to life. This is a group meeting with your leadership team where you go through your law firm's numbers and boulders to problem-solve issues that arise on a weekly basis.

Say you want to generate 1,200 leads in a quarter. That's 100 leads a week. If, in your first weekly meeting, you find you've only generated 50 leads, you'll know you're behind and will have to generate 50 more leads in the remaining 11 weeks.

That's the kind of thing you need to be looking for in weekly meetings. You're mostly interested in finding where you need to make some fast adjustments.

At the very least, you should have a weekly meeting with your leadership team. As your firm expands, every department of your firm should have their own weekly meetings in addition to the leadership meeting.

We've created our own format for weekly accountability meetings. We gather our key team members and go through the list.

- Share wins from the week.

- Review KPIs. Review the key numbers relevant to the company as a whole or department. For example, the marketing team would track the number of leads, number of new clients signed, cost per lead, cost per client, and so on. We have a specific scoreboard template that we use for this in our internal meeting software.

- Review Quarterly Boulders.

- Headlines (these are department-wide announcements that everyone on the team needs to know).

- Challenges and Opportunities. (This is where we dive into the most important issues currently facing our team; 75% of the meeting is spent here.) It's important that you only discuss challenges that, if solved, will help you reach your annual plan (not just anything that pops up).

- Rate the meeting.

Quick-Hitting Hack: Why and how would you rate a meeting? It's important for you, as the leader of your firm, to ensure that meetings are productive and helpful. For instance, if you leave the meeting feeling like it went great, but your team felt steamrolled because you talked for the entire duration, that's data you should know. That means you want to collect feedback in real time.

So how do you do it? The way we do this is with a ranking number between 1 and 5, which people indicate by holding up their fingers at the end of the meeting. Everyone flashes their number at the same time on the count of 3...2...1! That way, no one is influenced by the numbers that other people hold up. A person might hold up five fingers if they felt like the meeting productively was able to solve a major problem. A person might hold up two fingers if they felt certain people's concerns weren't addressed, or the meeting got unproductively bogged down in one section. When you see people holding up their numbers, ask a few to explain why they chose the number they did, and pay particular attention to the outliers. With the "finger feedback," you're getting information about how the meeting went so that you know what to improve on.

Daily Huddle

We mentioned this before, but at SMB Team, nothing impacts our culture more positively or consistently than our daily huddles. It's an energy meeting, designed to get everyone ready for the day.

It begins at 8:58 Eastern time every morning and ends at 9:05. Precisely seven minutes long. Not eight. Not six. Seven.

The entire team is there and the huddles are conducted by our most energetic team members. We start with some loud and upbeat music. Then we have people share exciting departmental updates.

We read customer success stories out loud to the team and talk about how we transformed their lives.

Then we transition into core value gratitudes where members call out someone else on the team for living one of our core values the day before.

The last person to offer a core value gratitude chooses someone else at random to close out the huddle with a saying that goes like this …

"If you haven't heard it today, I love each and every one of you. Today's a great day to have a great day on purpose! Everybody put your hands in. On three, we're gonna say 'Be the bar.'"

Then everybody puts their hand in. They chant, "ONE, TWO, THREE, BE THE BAR!"

There is no better way to build culture in your organization than by conducting these daily huddles. They are pure gold!

One-on-One Meetings

All of the above meetings are group meetings. But accountability happens most on a one-on-one basis when someone has clear numbers that they are personally being held accountable for.

In a one-on-one, a manager sits down with an employee on their team and reviews how they are performing based on their numbers and any boulders that they own.

If the employee is falling short, the manager supports that employee in getting back on track so they can get unstuck and hit their goals.

These meetings should happen every week or two with every single employee in the firm. Ideally, these meetings will constitute a whole lot of congratulations for a job well done. But if and when they don't, you'll need to employ one of the last tools we'll share with you in this chapter: write-ups and performance reviews.

Quick-Hitting Hack: If you'd like meeting templates for each type of meeting we just discussed, scan the QR code below to book a call with our team. We'll provide you with the templates and answer any questions you might have!

(You'll find all the other bonuses from the book here or you can go to **yourdreamlawfirm.com**.)

Scan this QR Code
to Book Your Call

Write-Ups & Performance Reviews

Imagine you're an owner of an NFL team who's paying your quarterback $40M a year. That's a lot of money—better be a good quarterback!

Now, imagine that quarterback drops the ball five seasons in a row, both literally and figuratively. He's not a good leader. He doesn't complete his passes. Your team ends up missing the playoffs each season you've had that quarterback.

Whose fault is it that the team has done so poorly?

Not the quarterback. He's just doing his best and collecting his pay. The fault lies with the owner who did not take steps to address the quarterback's underperformance or fire the quarterback for consistently failing to meet expectations.

Owners have a responsibility to uphold high standards for their teams. If the standard falls, it's up to the owner to take action.

Now, consider your law firm. What if you have someone on your team who is not performing to your standards of excellence? You have to address that and coach them into performing better. If that doesn't work, then you have to pull the plug and let them go.

If you don't, it's your fault that the firm is not succeeding. Your firing decisions are the clearest indication of your culture. By firing someone, you are saying, "This person is not living up to our standards. Therefore, for the good of the firm, I am letting them go."

Now, no firing should ever be a surprise. Before you get to that point, you should have had performance reviews and write-ups. You should have been completely transparent with that employee.

A performance review is a thorough one-on-one. It should be a well-thought-out, well-prepared-for, candid and open conversation about whether that employee is meeting, exceeding, or underperforming to your culture and expectations.

If the employee is falling short, offer action steps the employee can take to improve. Give them a chance to do better.

If your salesperson is closing at a rate below the company standard, you let them know *before* the formal performance review. "Your sales closing rate is not up to standard and not sustainable. I'm going to write you up." That's how you practice radical transparency and how you keep on top of your employee's performance.

Then, when they get to their performance review, it won't be a surprise to them when you tell them they are in trouble. They've already heard it in the regular one-on-ones.

The absolute worst thing you can do to a person is never bring up their shortcomings on the job, and then fire them out of the blue. By doing that, you put their family and their future at risk. You didn't give them a chance to improve, and everyone deserves at least that much.

Quick-Hitting Hack: At SMB Team, we have a specific tool we use for performance review one-on-ones. Formal reviews happen quarterly, and we also have weekly or bimonthly one-on-one check-ins. Scan the QR code below to view our tool and learn more about our process.

(You'll find all the other bonuses from the book here or you can go to **yourdreamlawfirm.com**.)

Scan this QR Code to Unlock This Bonus

After a set number of write-ups, the next step is termination. When termination is warranted, you must step up and do the firing. Remember, that was the first point we discussed in our section on culture. Your decisions about what you tolerate and don't tolerate have a *huge* impact on your retention and successful leadership of A-players.

There is no point in having standards if you don't enforce them. If your team sees you giving a pass to an underperforming employee, they'll see that you are not serious about upholding your standards, and then standards will fall across the firm, in all departments and with all employees.

The Final Piece in Doubling Your Law Firm's Revenue

In the last chapter, we told you how to hire A-players. In this chapter, we've explained how to lead, manage, inspire, and retain them. Are you done? No!

You can have the best lead system and people in the world. You can hire the best team ever and implement a flawless management plan. You can have an amazing number of quality leads coming into the firm all the time. All this can be going on with your firm … and yet you might still have pissed-off clients. Even if you do great case work for them!

In our final chapter, we're going to show you how to give your clients the best experience possible. We'll explain how to set up an automated system that will make raving fans of the people you represent.

Using our methods, you will learn to generate more five-star reviews and testimonials than you ever thought possible. We will show you how to build a law firm that will blow your clients' minds.

Chapter 11 | Takeaways

1. A systems-focused firm delegates tasks and holds people to tightly managed systems. A people-focused firm delegates *authority,* and provides the culture and clarity people need to excel in their roles without feeling micromanaged. We recommend you work to operate as a people-focused firm with systems to back it up.

2. Shape a culture that fosters all-stars by being consistent with terminating people who blatantly disregard your core values. Call out underperformance. Celebrate instances when people clearly emulate a core value and publicize wins.

3. Enhance clarity for your A-players by ensuring everyone has a clear understanding of their job description and role expectations. Use the Employee Maturity model and reference the levels of delegation to ensure you've delegated the right level of authority to the right person. Remember, the one thing you can't delegate is your own caring and zeal for overseeing the firm's success.

4. Hone your firm's systems by getting input from your team on the systems' development. Incentivize your team with bonuses when they do a great job at this.

5. Your firm needs meetings to ensure clear communication and consistent execution of your vivid vision. We provided a list of the types of meetings you should be holding regularly. Annual, quarterly planning, all-hands, weekly accountability meetings, daily huddles, and one-on-ones.

CHAPTER 12

HOW TO WOW YOUR CLIENTS

COMMUNICATE WELL TO BLOW YOUR CLIENTS' MINDS, GET REFERRALS, AND INSPIRE 5-STAR REVIEWS

"All customer complaints at Amazon turned into our greatest innovations and product expansions. Don't run from them."

—Jeff Bezos, founder of Amazon

BILL HAUSER NARRATES

If a heavenly paradise exists and I get to go there, I hope it's something like arriving at the Four Seasons in Costa Rica. That's where my wife Emily and I vacationed one year, and it stands out as *the best* customer experience I've ever had.

Picture the two of us pulling up to the resort, which is built on a peninsula. Palm trees are swaying. Tropical breezes are blowing. Exotic flowers are blooming. We're greeted by a concierge who hands us each a glass of champagne and then shows us a bulleted list of our preferences on a printed sheet with our names on it. He asks, "Did we get everything right?" Once we confirm yes, he guides us to set up a group text with another private concierge at the front desk, so we can contact them anytime.

Ocean waves crash on either side of us as we walk to our room. We see the glimmering turquoise of swimming pools, backed by the lush green of the jungle canopy. The grounds are stunning and immaculately maintained. Every staff member we walk past treats us like celebrities by stopping, putting their hand on their stomach, and bowing to us.

As if that wasn't enough, when we get to the room—I kid you not—we find a box of custom-made chocolates with our names etched into the top. Not the top of the box, mind you. *Our names are etched into the top of each frickin' chocolate.*

It went on from there. The Four Seasons staff paid attention to every detail, kept us informed about activities, and treated us like we were the only people at the resort. It was white glove treatment from start to finish. In fact, if there's such a thing as *diamond* glove treatment—that's what we experienced. When we got home, we told all our friends about how incredible it was and immediately started planning when we would go back. We were WOWed—big time.

Now, contrast that with the terrible customer service experience SMB Team had with QuickBooks.

Andy and I merged our companies to create SMB in 2021. Soon after, QuickBooks decided to keep about a million dollars of our money and not deposit it into our bank account. We had opened a new account for the merged company and apparently they had an issue with that.

We called QuickBooks as soon as we realized what was going on. We explained the situation over a lengthy phone call, gave them all our information, and then learned the person we were talking to couldn't help us. The person "didn't have the authority to release the funds."

We called again. This time we got someone higher up—or so we thought. After providing all our information a *second* time, we were once again told the person on the phone had no power to make a decision that would help us. Mind you, we were told they *did* have the authority at the beginning of the call.

We called a *third* time, this time going through manager after manager after manager. Not one of them could help us. No one in the organization seemed to care about the fact that a huge portion of our budget was being held hostage! No one stepped up to take care of it. Eventually we got tossed to an assistant in the president's office who told us our funds would be released in 48 hours.

A torturous 48 hours later, the funds were still not released. The money was still not in our account. Another call from us. More lack of results from QuickBooks. The situation dragged on day after day. We couldn't pay our vendors and even ended up missing a cycle of payroll. We felt like our survival as a company was at stake—and it *was.* QuickBooks' terrible customer service threatened to crater our operations. We were unable to run our business the way it was supposed to be run.

Eventually—*over two weeks* after our first phone call—Quick-Books released the money, But for those two weeks, because of their unwillingness to take our complaint seriously, we felt both helpless and furious. And we feared for our livelihoods. All we wanted was for someone capable to show up and make everything okay.

In fact, we felt very much like what a typical client coming to a law firm feels like.

People come to lawyers when they're in trouble. They're often scared and feel helpless. They need attention, competence, assurance, and communication—*especially* communication. That's why you, as a law firm, need to give them the heavenly and memorable Four Seasons Resort experience—not the QuickBooks experience from hell.

And guess what happens when you provide that white glove treatment to people who desperately need it? They become evangelists for you, sending you referrals and posting five-star reviews, just like my wife and I did for the Four Seasons. Customer satisfaction—no, client *happiness*—is the final piece you need to get in place to double your law firm's revenue in short order.

In this chapter, we'll show you how. But first, there's an important step you need to take: measure your clients' happiness with your firm.

You Can't Fix What You Don't Measure

Soon after we started SMB, we were convinced our clients were happy with our services. We knew they were getting a good return on their money and we were getting very few complaints.

That meant things were going well, right? Not exactly. About that time, I picked up *Never Lose a Customer Again: Turn Any Sale into Lifelong Loyalty in 100 Days* by Joey Coleman. In that book, he explains that any business must track customer happiness. The key step to doing this is asking your customers to rate you on a scale of one to ten, answering this question: *How likely are you to refer us to a friend?* This survey measures your net promoter score (NPS) which we first introduced in Chapter 5 as the fifth of the five KPIs.

So, I downloaded the software and sent the first survey out, fully expecting to get replies from completely happy clients. Within minutes, the first response came back. It was decidedly negative.

I was shocked. I truly thought 100% of our clients were happy with us. I quickly learned that wasn't even close to the truth. As more survey results came in, it became clear that more than a third of our clients had a negative experience with SMB and would not refer us to anyone else.

People said we didn't communicate well, we didn't follow up with them, some of our marketing advice was not working, and so on. They had *negative* things to say.

We thought our clients were happy because they weren't saying anything to us. That was our error. We mistook silence for satisfaction.

Don't mistake silence for satisfaction.

As soon as we got feedback on the problems, we bucketed all the negative issues and began to work on making the client experience at SMB better. We didn't run from these problems. We embraced them with open ears and open minds. In fact, we used them as spurs to greater service. Each complaint presented an opportunity to do better. We addressed all the issues our survey uncovered and built a culture of customer happiness at SMB. Not just client "satisfaction" which implies "satisfactory"—in other words, okay, but not great—but client *happiness.*

Three months later, we did the net promoter score surveys again. The change was remarkable. We more than doubled our client satisfaction. We kept working on honing our client experience and the next time we did the survey, the dissatisfaction rate was only 10%.

Today, we continue to roll out quarterly surveys of our clients. Our measurement of customer satisfaction on the NPS surveys is now consistently above 75. To put that in perspective, the average NPS, across 150K organizations, is only 32. The average NPS for a marketing company is zero.

Does this mean we make everyone happy? No! When you're handling people's marketing and teaching them how to grow their law firm when their firm hasn't grown for the past 10 years, inevitably some attorneys we work with are not happy. But, the point is now that we measure that, identify the common causes of unhappiness, and continually work to solve them. This feedback is actually what drives our product improvement initiatives quarterly.

Here's the point. We never would have known we'd had a problem if we didn't measure it. What gets measured gets managed. That's why you need to start tracking your client satisfaction rate *now*. Roll out NPS surveys today.

Quick-Hitting Hack: Curious about how NPS scores are calculated? We could share the math with you, but it's pretty boring. If you geek out about that stuff like Bill does, though, scan this QR code to learn more.

(You'll find all the other bonuses from the book here or you can go to **yourdreamlawfirm.com**.)

Scan this QR Code to Unlock This Bonus

If you don't do these surveys, you're working blind. You won't know what your pain points are, and you won't know how to improve. NPS surveys are one of the most effective tools you can use to lift your firm to a higher level of performance.

Here's why.

Client Happiness Is Everything

We've talked a lot about building more leads through your marketing campaigns in this book, but no marketing effort—no matter how good—can replace the importance of a happy customer. Anything SEO-related will benefit from good reviews. And anything in the Awareness Marketing category relies on you building an appealing brand, which won't happen if you're making your customers angry on a regular basis. Also, let's not ignore the fact that referrals and word-of-mouth is still one of the most common ways for law firms to get clients.

This means client happiness is *everything*. If your clients aren't happy, they're not going to recommend you to others. A happy client, on the other hand, will give you a five-star review and tell their friends how great you are.

Referrals from happy customers are also extremely cost effective! Word-of-mouth doesn't take a dime out of your marketing budget and it's incredibly powerful. You can turn one client into two, three, or more at no cost—*if you make them happy*.

What generates all this goodwill and excellent reviews? *Your firm's client experience process*, which starts the first time a potential client calls your law firm. A large portion of the negative responses to NPS surveys come from the intake process. That happens even *before* the person is even a client!

Think of your client experience process as a flowchart. The first step in the flowchart is that first call to your firm. It has to start the process on a positive note and set the person up for what follows. The last step—well, there *is* no last step. Your relationship with that client can potentially go on forever. At each step, your client must be WOWed by your attention to them and their case.

None of this can be left to chance. You can't just *hope* the client will like you. You can't trust fate to determine the path your client will take on their journey through the complicated process of bringing a case to trial or negotiating a settlement. It's your job to shape their experience as a positive one—preferably, one that causes their jaws to drop in wonder and delight, à la monogrammed chocolates.

Every interaction with a client—from the first call to *years* after the case ends—must contribute to a WOW experience for them. After all, they might talk about their experience with your firm years after they've settled their case. If they had a stellar experience with you, they're likely to refer their friends.

What's the most important thing you can do to guarantee happy clients?

It's not sexy or complicated—but it's also not easy.

Communicate well.

Not only is strong communication necessary for your firm's growth, it's also vital to avoid complaints. According to the American Bar Association, one of the most common reasons for disciplinary action against lawyers is for poor communication.[19] You want more five-star reviews and fewer complaints? Leveling up your communication is a major part of the equation.

Let's break down how to do that.

---

[19] YourABA. 2022. Protect Yourself from Common Disciplinary Complaints. American Bar Association, 7. March. https://www.americanbar.org/news/abanews/publications/youraba/2022/0307/protect-yourself-from-complaints/(accessed: 16 January 2024).

Communication Is Key

"Pssh. C'mon, Bill and Andy. I'm doing good work for my clients. My clients know I value them and that I'm working hard for them. They know my firm has their best interests in mind."

But do they?

One of the biggest myths that lawyers buy into is, "So long as I'm a good lawyer, my clients will be happy and satisfied."

This is not true. Yes, you have to be a good lawyer, but it's not enough. You could be working your heart out, but if you never update your client on the status of their case, or if they don't hear from you for months, what are they going to think? One likely thought: *This lawyer just got my money, and that's all he cares about. He doesn't actually care about me. Otherwise, he'd be communicating with me.*

Yikes. You don't want to make that impression! So instead, *involve* your client in the story of their case. Give them timely and accurate details about what you're doing and why. It's not enough to just send an occasional cryptic email.

Still not convinced? Let's look at a simple example of how mediocre communication can go wrong.

Attorney Tom is a personal injury lawyer who just got a new client: Alice. Attorney Tom determines Alice's case has a value range low of $28K and a high of $40K. He emails the insurance company asking for the case value high of $40K and CC's Alice.

Wow, thinks Alice. *$40K? I can finally do the kitchen remodel I've been wanting to do for years!*

Here's the problem. Attorney Tom never qualified Alice's expectations. He never explained that the final amount she walks away with will likely be less than the case value range high. Imagine her surprise and disappointment when, eight months later, Tom settles the case for $32K—which is what the case is actually worth. Tom might feel pretty pleased with himself. As far as he's concerned, he just won his client a great, big payday.

But is Alice going to have the warm fuzzies about how this all went down if her expectations were geared toward $40K? Absolutely not. She's getting $8K less than she was expecting, and now she has to give up her dream kitchen cabinets. Tom did right by keeping Alice in the loop, but he still fell short in his communication. He should have clearly explained to Alice what that initial demand actually meant and where it was likely to lead. Failing to do so was a failure to communicate well with his client, and Alice is likely to think Tom is either incompetent or just stopped fighting for her. Her final impression is going to be more QuickBooks than Four Seasons.

Here's how David Buckley approaches client communication around the matter of dollar signs, as he shared with us in an email. We've mentioned David Buckley before in our book and—as in this case—his example is nearly always worth copying:

> What do I tell the client about the value of their case?
>
> I NEVER tell them a value.
>
> My conversation goes something like this …

DB: "Hi John. I have finalized your demand, and I have submitted it to the insurance company for their review. I hope to have a response within the next 30 days."

John: "Great. How much are you asking for?"

DB: "I don't make a specific dollar demand. I provide the adjuster with all of the information they need to determine the value of your case. They will then call me with an offer."

John: "But what's my case worth?"

DB: "I can appreciate that you want to know that answer, but my telling you what I think your case is worth at this time serves no useful purpose. You can't do anything practical with that information. All it will do is put a number in your head that will create an expectation."

John: "I just wanted an idea, is all."

DB: "Here's what will happen, John if I give you a number. Let's say I tell you your case is worth 'X'. (I actually say 'X'). That's a number you have stuck in your head. You start thinking about all the things you will do with that money. I then begin negotiating with the adjuster. Things are pointed out in medical records that reduce the value of the case and a 'last best' offer of 'Y' is made. And that last best offer of 'Y' is a great number. But it's less than 'X'. No matter what I do or say. No matter how much I go over why the case came in under 'X'. No matter that 'Y' is the best that you will ever do ... it will always be less than 'X' and you will be disappointed.

"Here's what I can tell you. I am very good at knowing the value of my cases. I know the high and low values of your specific case. I will negotiate with the adjuster to get them to a valuation that is within my range. If their last best offer comes in within my range, I will recommend that you accept the offer. If the last best offer isn't within my range, I will recommend that you reject the offer. But know this. That is the only number that matters. The number that will cause you to make a decision. Giving you a number now is meaningless and it can actually be detrimental to our relationship. Let me do my job and try to get you as much as I can. I will call you as soon as I have a 'last best' and we'll go from there."

David's strategy clearly sets realistic client expectations while reinforcing their trust in him. It's a perfect example of strong client communication.

In sum, lawyer strategy does not always align with client happiness. If you hope to snag a five-star review or a referral, you need to communicate *well* with your clients. Communicating merely what they need to know is not enough. You need to communicate what they *want* to know, plus anything else that would be helpful or reassuring. When I got to my room at the Four Seasons, did I think I *needed* chocolates with my name on them? No. But the fact that they were there made me feel attended to and cared for. In the same way, your communication needs to go above and beyond to care for your clients.

How many excellent reviews and referrals will come solely from working really hard on a case? Probably not too many.

But what if you work really hard on a case *and* maintain an excellent communication process with the client? Those clients will feel cared for throughout the process and eager to rave about you. That's why you should always communicate in a timely, informative, truthful, and caring manner with your clients.

White Glove Experience

Let's think back to the white glove resort experience I described at the beginning of this chapter and draw a few more comparisons.

Your objective as a law firm is to help your clients transition from feeling anxious to feeling like they've been shown a world-class client experience. Remember, most clients are facing life or death situations, and it's scary to be tossed into the legal world with no experience or skill in navigating it. That's an anxiety-inducing place to be. But that also means you can be their hero by building the equivalent of a Four Seasons experience in your law firm by solving their problems and holding their hand.

Give your *full attention* to their needs. Beyond good lawyering, this will require a high degree of compassion, understanding, and tolerance. You'll need to create systems that can scale that demonstration of empathy across all of your client-facing staff so you can deliver a white glove experience to your clients.

How do you create that experience for your client? Start by practicing exaggeration.

Airbnb does this. They challenge their team to come up with a scenario in which the guest booking a room or a house would be compelled to give an *off-the-scale* rating. Like, what would cause a guest to want to give us *ten* out of five stars? Their team responds to the exaggerated prompt with imaginative scenarios:

"What if we flew the guest to their Airbnb in a private jet?"

"And when they get there, a red carpet awaits them, and people applaud!"

"And all their loved ones are there!"

"And every one of them gets their favorite meal!"

The brainstorming goes on until there's no question that any Airbnb guest would be absolutely *WOWed* by such treatment. Mind. Blown.

Then, the brainstorming gets more practical. Obviously, that over-the-top scenario wouldn't work. But the goal is still to go above and beyond "just" a five-star review. They consider … What could Airbnb do to bridge the gap between a five out of five star review and a ten out of five? What are the things they could do that would give a similar feeling to having access to a private jet? By taking their brainstorming to the extreme, Airbnb generates scenarios that, though not on the scale of private jets, nevertheless increase customer satisfaction.

After SMB Team did this brainstorming exercise, we started sending personalized videos to clients right when they signed up and ordering custom gifts for clients within seconds after they gave us any sort of personal news. Most importantly, we designed our core product Elite 360 on what lawyers need—not necessarily what they want or what's popular. The result? Nobody else in the industry can say they merged full-service marketing, coaching, virtual assistants, software, and fractional CFOs the way we did. And there's been a noticeable increase in how happy our clients are to work with us.

We recommend trying this same exercise in your firm. What would completely blow your clients' minds? For instance, maybe your exaggerated client experience envisions picking up your client in a stretch limo for their court date and providing a fitted Armani suit to wear. Your more realistic approach might be providing an Uber Lux for your client to the courthouse. Leading up to the court date, you might arrange a rental of a nice suit if your client doesn't already have one. Once you've gathered a list of astronomically grandiose ideas, start to get practical. What *could* you do, realistically? How could you WOW them with the resources you have?

Needle-Moving Client Experience Strategies

If the question above still causes you to draw a blank, we're going to get you started. The rest of this chapter provides you with strategies that will move the needle on your clients' experience. You'll see client satisfaction on your Net Promoter Score (NPS) surveys jump steadily upward with each new strategy you apply.

Get and Use NPS Software

Do you have a way to measure your client satisfaction? If not—that's your first step. Stop reading this book right now. Seriously, put it down until you've purchased some NPS software from the web.

Once you do, get your first pulse check. Survey all of your clients, both past and present. Repeat the process every three months for as long as you're running your firm.

You will learn things about your firm that you had no idea were true, just like we learned at the start of SMB. You'll see your biggest complaint areas laid bare before your eyes—and that's a *good* thing. These are the areas in which you need to step up and do better. You can use this knowledge to up your game to a white glove experience!

We also recommend using NPS scores to roll out bonuses for your team. Set a standard to reach. For example, if your NPS is 34, tell your team you want to increase that to 50. When you reach your target NPS number, give a flat dollar bonus to everyone on your team.

Once you get there, set another goal. You want to increase your NPS by another ten. When you get there—boom!—another bonus.

This gets *everyone* on the team invested in raising your NPS. It will make them care about your clients' happiness just as much as you do.

One caution here is to make sure you tie the bonuses to a *high survey response rate.* If you send out 100 surveys but only get two responses, that's not an accurate NPS rating. Those two surveys might be so good they boost your NPS to stratospheric levels, even if the rest of your clients actually have a negative impression of your firm. Don't give out bonuses for a high NPS rating if the number is so small as to be inaccurate. You need more than two responses to know for sure if your clients as a whole are happy with your service. We recommend aiming for client responses in the 30% to 40% range.

Which begs the question, "How do you ensure a high rate of response?" A lot of people hate surveys, and many don't answer them. You can overcome this resistance by training your team to phrase survey questions in such a way that they believe answering the survey benefits them.

For example, you could introduce your survey like this: "Thank you so much for being a valued client of ours. Your answers to this survey will be used to help improve your experience with our firm. Every single answer is read by the owner to ensure that your feedback is heard."

Notice how specific that is. You're not giving some vague statement that their answers are very valuable to you. No. It says their responses will be channeled into a set of solutions that will improve their experience going forward. That's how you make it about *them* and not about *you*. And that's how you get people to answer surveys.

As we mentioned, when you start collecting this kind of data, you will get complaints. Some of them may be gut punches. You may be shocked and surprised by what you learn. Just remember that complaints are opportunities to innovate.

Every negative piece of feedback you receive should be looked at as a gift, because it allows you to identify a problem that you can fix, so that potentially hundreds or even thousands of future clients won't experience the same problem. Think of it this way. You need more one-star reviews to get more five-star reviews.

Complaints are opportunities to innovate.

And don't keep this knowledge to yourself! Practice radical transparency with the rest of your team. Have your whole staff read the complaints so they can proactively bring ideas to you about valuable innovations to improve the firm. Their involvement will supercharge the process.

Quick-Hitting Hack: Check out Andy's book *5-Star Attorney* for lots more tips on generating five-star reviews, using one-star reviews to your advantage, and providing your clients with a white-glove experience. To grab a copy of *5-Star Attorney* (and snag all the other bonuses mentioned throughout this book), scan the QR code below or go to **yourdreamlawfirm.com**.

Scan this QR Code to Unlock This Bonus

Expectations Setting

Remember Alice, who expected Attorney Tom to win her a big settlement and was disappointed with what she actually got? The issue there was *poor expectation setting.*

Every time you sign up a new client, you are also signing up years of misinformation. Most people get their ideas about legal work from TV shows and movies. They expect you to act like Tom Cruise from *A Few Good Men*, or Matthew McConaughey from *Lincoln Lawyer*. They might even expect a few hijinks like Saul Goodman would pull from *Better Call Saul*. Your clients may have formed assumptions about legal practice from misleading billboards and TV ads. Rarely do clients fully understand what happens in the course of working a case—especially if this is the first time they're seeking legal help.

There's a lot they don't know. How many times will they have to get on the phone with you? How quickly will they have to provide documentation for the case? How often will they have to see a doctor for issues related to their injury? How much is their case actually worth?

You know the answers to these questions, but your client does not. They might have a completely mistaken idea of what's required from them and from you regarding their case because they don't know the legal process.

That's why it's imperative to strategically set expectations with your clients if you hope to give them a positive experience. As *soon* as your client signs a fee agreement, send them an expectations agreement to sign. This agreement should address everything your client *might likely get upset about*. Such as ...

- The average time it takes to settle a case.
- How medical treatment ties into the valuation of the case.
- What's happening behind the scenes when they're not hearing from you.

- How your initial ask from an insurance company will be higher than the case is worth.

- The email address the client should use for questions and requests.

- How long they can expect to wait before hearing back from you. (Hint: this should be a turnaround of one business day.)

The point here is to give the client clear facts and expectations on how you intend to handle their case. That way, they can't come back later and say, "You didn't tell me I needed to go to the doctor to confirm my whiplash," because you *did* tell them—along with all the other things you told them.

It's also not enough to just do this once. It's your team's job to constantly reset expectations as the case progresses and circumstances change. Don't let this communication get stale and forgotten. Refresh it often and keep the client in the loop on the changes.

Create Proactive Communication Systems

Let's say you respond to your client *only* when they ask you a question or voice a complaint. Would your client call that a white glove experience? Hardly!

Your number one rule is: *Always keep clients updated.* Don't wait for them to contact you. Contact them *first* with relevant and timely information. That's what we call proactive communication.

Don't leave this to chance. Set up a schedule—it can be weekly, biweekly, or monthly—where you email, voice mail, text, and direct message your clients about their case. When you do this regularly, it sends a powerful message to the client. You are committed to their case and are hard at work on it.

Clients need to know they've been heard. Remember the list of our preferences our greeter had at the Four Seasons? That astounding bulleted list showed us the resort was listening to us. They *heard* us.

One form of proactive communication which will create a white glove experience for your clients is thoughtful gift giving. We're not talking about shameless marketing gifts like mugs sporting your face and logo. Your logo is a promotion. Their logo (or name or initials) is a gift. We do this for all the speakers who speak at our events. We give them a custom Yeti mug with their logo, name, or initials on it. It would be easy to slap our own logo on it, but that's far less meaningful. They don't need our logo on it to remember that we gave them the gift. The present will be far more memorable if it's personalized with their logo.

It's even better if you can give a gift that shows you understand your client on a personal level. We once learned that one of our clients was a lifelong Tampa Bay Buccaneers season ticket holder. He and his father went to every game for nearly 20 years! This client had been with us for a number of years and we wanted to do something special to recognize how much we appreciated him. So, we got him a signed Tom Brady Bucs helmet right after they won the Super Bowl. It wasn't cheap—but our client's appreciation was over the moon.

So, consider—what rocks your clients' world? It might be items related to their favorite sports team, their hobbies, their passions, or their families. Make these gifts specific to them and schedule these gifts so they receive them at key milestones in the progress of the case. Alternatively, you could give gifts every three months after signing with you. This sort of attention goes a long way toward creating those Four Seasons vibes.

> **Quick–Hitting Hack:** We highly recommend you invest in Client Relationship Management software (CRM). The right software will help you keep track of things like when to send gifts to clients and when to update them about their case. It's an amazing tool to ensure you're providing your clients with a white glove experience.

In addition to investing in tools like Client Relationship Management software, you can also serve your clients by nurturing a staff culture where your team naturally *wants* to create a white glove experience for all your clients. They need to be excited about listening to client needs and proactively attending to those needs in a creative way.

At SMB, we do this with the morning huddle. This is where we share rave reviews from clients about a gift they got or how one of the team members went above and beyond to deliver first class service. We encourage and applaud each such success. Other team members see these celebrations and are inspired to think of ways *they* can get some of that adulation on the next morning huddle when they read a rave review from a client.

This sort of reporting and applauding works! It's the best way to create a culture where superior service to the client becomes not the exception, but rather routine and expected.

Intangibles

Also, don't forget about the intangible qualities of how your team engages with a client that will impact their experience. What do we mean by this? We'll illustrate.

Scene 1. You go up to the grocery store checker and put down a bag of apples on the conveyor belt. The checker smiles brightly and asks, "Is this all for you today?" You nod and the checker responds cheerfully, "Beautiful." Your day just got a little bit nicer.

Scene 2. You go up to the grocery store checker and put down a bag of apples on the belt. Only *this* checker looks scornfully at the single item and asks you, incredulously, "Is this *all* you're getting?" When you nod, the checker rolls her eyes as though you're completely wasting her time. "Beautiful," she says sarcastically. You leave the store feeling ashamed and upset. What's so bad about buying a bag of apples?

The difference between Scene 1 and Scene 2 is the intangible quality of how the checkers engaged with you, the customer. The first conveyed a cheerful willingness to serve, whereas the second was a sour grumpy pants. We've all encountered service people who do their jobs by the book but accompany it with a side of snark or outright contempt. No one likes that! Be vigilant about not letting this happen in your team. You can implement all of the strategies we've mentioned so far and still come across as an a-hole. Your team can proactively communicate, yet still do it in a completely repellent manner.

This is why every firm needs—in addition to proactive communication—a guide for client communication standards. Train your team so they have a clear understanding about how to gracefully address challenging client situations. What guidance can you offer your team in responding to a client with an unreasonable request, for instance? How should they engage with a client who contacts them too often?

Use training materials like videos and role play practice to familiarize your team with the general principles of communicating with clients. Provide guidance on how communication might differ on the phone, versus on video calls, versus in person. Discuss appropriate attire standards for team members and lead them in role plays going over different phases of the case management process.

Any non-negotiables should be documented in a written guide, so that there's no doubt about the essential standards for client communication. Be aware of how many non-negotiables are in there. The more non-negotiables you have, the more you shift from guiding your team to micromanaging your team. Your team shouldn't have free rein on such an important element of customer interaction, but they should have guidance and standards to reference. No team member should be in the dark about how to handle any client interaction. They should only have to consult the client communication standards to find the appropriate response to every conceivable situation.

Coach your team to respond to clients with a balance of firmness, positivity, and compassion. Let's examine each of these three intangibles.

- **Firmness.** When it comes to legal cases, the client is *not* always right. Show firmness with your clients to demonstrate your expertise in the law. Your recommendations might conflict with their viewpoint, and that's okay. To WOW a client, you don't have to attend to their every whim. Rather, you need to assert your knowledge and tell them clearly what's what, especially if they want to deviate from proven methods of success. We employ firmness in our marketing recommendations to our lawyer clients. For example, we get a lot of lawyers who want to put a certain word on their website. Sometimes, we know that word will adversely affect their SEO. So, we say:"Do you want that word on your website or do you want *results* from your homepage? Because our experience has shown us that word will kill your results." Through communicating a firm recommendation, backed up with relevant information, we're able to demonstrate our expertise and get our clients on board.

- **Positive.** Always keep in mind the state of your client's emotions: law firms are almost always dealing with people who are at a low point in their lives. For that reason, it's vitally important for your team to be shining lights for your clients. No matter how emotional the client is, your team should convey attitudes that are solution-oriented, cheerful, proactive, and appreciative. Clients need to know that when they contact your firm, they're going to leave feeling better, not worse. One of the most important ways to give clients a world-class experience is to have your team visibly smile every time they talk to a client.

- **Compassion.** Pair positivity with compassion, so that clients don't feel bruised by false cheer. That means showing empathy for a client's struggles. Don't let a positive attitude come off as indifference to reality. If a client is crying on the phone, acknowledge their concerns. Show you're listening by paraphrasing your understanding of what they just shared. Show you are there with them by repeating some of their key words and expressing concern. After showing compassion, then you can provide them with direction (firmness) and show them a way forward (positivity.)

These three pillars of client interaction should become second nature to your team. Once again, you can do that by embedding these pillars into the culture of your firm.

At SMB, we have a dedicated client experience and sales training schedule that our team must follow, focusing on the three intangibles above. We also do intensive role-playing so that we're constantly practicing these qualities. Every day, our team members hop on a Zoom call and play the part of a client or a lawyer and have one-on-one interactions. We then analyze those recordings and review them, according to the three intangibles.

Role-playing is extremely effective and is particularly important to do early on. By the time your team is interfacing with real clients, they should already be experts in demonstrating the intangible qualities of cheerful service.

Ending the Client Experience

When the case ends, the client relationship ends—right?

Wrong. So wrong! The end of the case is just the *beginning* of your relationship.

When a case is settled, that's when you explain to the client how you will continue to stay in touch with interactions such as …

- They will continue to hear from you to check in on how they're doing.

- You'll send them a regular newsletter about the goings-on in your firm.

- You'll keep up with them on social media.

- You'll keep them informed about activities your firm is doing in the community.

- You'll send birthday cards and keep up the gift-giving schedule.

- You'll give them a number that only VIP clients get. A hotline they can use to call the firm any time they have a legal problem in the future, or someone they know has a legal problem.

At the end of the conversation, tell your client that you would be *honored* to handle any legal problem they or anyone they know might have in the future.

What does this do? It creates a white glove experience! It tells the client you care about them. You view them as more than a case. You see them as a person, someone your firm desires to continue helping, as needed.

Take it even further! One firm we know rents an amusement park every year and invites all their former and current clients to come have fun. Get your brain thinking like the Four Seasons. How creative can you get with keeping clients in your good graces for 10, 20, 30 years or more? Let your imagination guide you.

"Ending" (and beginning) the client experience with this sort of treatment gets rave reviews, turning a client into a source of quality referrals for years to come. This is the sort of treatment clients crave. They'll respond by boosting your firm with everyone they know. You'll earn their loyalty and enthusiasm in a way that no marketing effort—no matter how good—can possibly match.

Referrals and Good Reviews Depend on All of the Above.

Getting and retaining clients is not a matter of luck. It's a matter of using proven strategies to secure good referrals.

SEO marketing relies on good reviews. Awareness campaigns are built on the backs of happy clients. Good, sustainable, powerful marketing requires good reviews from former or present clients, which is why this chapter is the final, crucial piece in helping you scale your law firm. While you don't want referrals to be your only source of new leads, they're an undeniable component of a strong marketing strategy. In fact, more than half of small businesses, including law firms, report that referrals are their number one new source of business.[20] Those referrals only happen if you provide your clients with a superior, white glove experience.

Will your firm ever be able to create a *perfect* client experience? No. Even the Four Seasons in Costa Rica deals with rainy days. Nothing is perfect. Everything is a work in progress.

Don't let that fact prevent you from growing your firm. Use the data you collect from net promoter score (NPS) surveys to constantly innovate and iterate your clients' experience. You will learn by trial and error. You will make mistakes. Own them, fix them, and keep going, until you can be confident that the vast majority of your clients are walking away happy.

The Ultimate Goal

That's it! You've now absorbed the final recommendations of this book to double your law firm's growth. Learning how to WOW your clients so that they turn into your firm's evangelists.

What's the result of making your clients happy? More happiness for *you* and your employees! It means more clients, which means you get to choose who you work with. It means *right*

---

[20] Press Releases: Customer Engagement a Major Focus of Small Business Technology According to Constant Contact Technology Pulse Survey. *Constant Contact Newsroom.* https://news.constantcontact.com/press-release-customer-engagement-major-focus-small-business-technology-according-constant-contact-t (accessed: 16. January 2024).

fit clients, people who are pleasant to be around. It means you can command a higher case value, which means more revenue. It means you deliver all-star service, which means greater impact. It means you build a firm that's a sellable asset, which means more freedom.

Those are the gifts that come from transforming your law firm, and providing your clients with a white glove experience to seal the deal. Client happiness will enable you to make a life for *yourself* that is happy and fulfilling.

Chapter 12 | Takeaways

1. Net promoter score (NPS), a measurement of client satisfaction, is the fifth KPI we discussed in Chapter 4. Tracking your NPS consistently—and making necessary improvements—is critical for your firm's successful growth.

2. Giving your clients a white glove, "Four Seasons" experience will spur on every other strategy we've described in this book. It will increase your revenue, spur on referrals, inspire reviews, and serve as jet fuel for your marketing. Conversely, if you give your clients a mediocre experience, all the other strategies we've described in this book will be hindered. For that reason, client happiness is everything.

3. Effective, consistent, and positive communication is the single most important factor to ensuring client happiness.

4. Other ways you can move the needle on your clients' experience include getting and *using* NPS software. Establishing clear client expectations. Proactively communicating with your clients. Ensuring your team conveys firmness, positivity, and compassion to your clients. And maintaining contact with clients in a variety of forms, even after a case has been settled.

CONCLUSION

"I bargained with Life for a penny,
   and Life would pay no more,
   However I begged at evening
   When I counted my scanty store;

   Life is a just employer.
   He gives you what you ask,
   But once you have set the wages,
   Why, you must bear the task.

   I worked for a menial's hire,
      Only to learn, dismayed,
   That any wage I had asked of Life,
   Life would have willingly paid"

—Jessie B. Rittenhouse

Imagine being able to take an indefinite vacation, one where you've turned off your cell phone and left your laptop at home because you have total confidence that your team has everything under control.

Imagine being able to go on a date with your spouse without worrying about a client call interrupting the evening.

Imagine spending consistent quality time with your kids, never missing another dance recital or baseball game again.

Imagine living with financial freedom. Walking into Sam's Club and buying anything you want without ruminating over your bank account. Going out to a fancy restaurant and ordering the steak and their best bottle of wine. Purchasing a new car without stressing over the price tag.

Imagine not worrying about money ever again.

Think of a life without fear. No anxieties over the changing economy or inflation. No worries over where your next client will come from. No concerns over making payroll. In this life, you're free to turn down that nightmare lead who walks through the door because you don't have to take every single case. You have the freedom to choose your clients.

And consider impact! With a greater reach, a larger staff, and a world-class firm, imagine seeing countless five-star reviews of people describing the ways you helped them. Think about receiving emails like this one which recently showed up in SMB Team's inbox:

Thank you for the best Quarterly Meeting I have been to with SMB (External)

 Anita Cutrer
to me, Andrew ▾

Thu, Dec 7. 3:56 PM (4 days ago)

Dear Bill and Andy,

I want to thank you for the Q4 seminar. I got more out of this seminar than any other quarterly seminar that I have attended with SMB. Part of this is due to my prior involvement with SMB and the repetition of the concepts. (I might be slow on the uptake.) But there were a lot of new and innovative ideas and information that spoke to me.

One concept in particular that resonates with me is one that Andy brought up and that is that law schools ARE teaching us to be poor. And this continues with our local bar associations and in my case the State Bar of Texas. There is a heavy emphasis on the fact that ours is a PROFESSION and not just a business. The message from them, as I perceive it, is that earning money is secondary to being a lawyer and helping people. The bar associations try to scare lawyers into not aggressively collecting fees and not stopping work when a client is not paying his/her bill. The fear is the grievance committee.

I also wanted to share with you that I have doubled my gross revenues since I started with SMB, but I also realized that because of your program, I have more time for myself. I don't always go into the office at 8:30, mostly I get there at 10:00. This extra time for myself has been invaluable to me personally to get back on my emotional feet. I had a personal tragedy two years ago when my eldest son died and did not have time to take care of myself or deal with my feelings about this at the time because I had to make sure that I billed enough hours to support myself and my other son. Now after being with SMB for over six months, I have an associate attorney and enough paralegals to where my income is not solely dependent on me coming to work and billing hours. I am ready to double my revenue again and I am ready to start putting in the hours needed for that to happen. I am very excited about this.

Anita's message is just one of countless testimonials that we've received in our inboxes, online reviews, and on social media. If you Google us, you can read them for yourself. More law firm owners than we can count attest to the explosive growth they've experienced as a result of implementing the Law Firm Growth Accelerator—and share about the increased freedom and impact that came with it.

All of this is possible for you. We've seen these transformed realities unfold in law firms time and time again. In fact, SMB Team is living proof of the efficacy of these concepts. In 2023, SMB Team's companies grew to $34.7M in annual recurring revenue and collected $25.8M with over 100 full time W2 employees. In 2024, our goal is to be at $85M in annual recurring revenue, with $51M collected, putting our company's enterprise value at $158M. How do we execute that level of growth? We've applied and continued to apply every single one of the concepts in this book. We don't just preach it. We live it.

And in this book, we've given you the proven road map to execute your firm's exponential growth.

When you commit yourself to doing the work involved in climbing the Lawyer Legacy Staircase, you commit yourself to a future with more *money*, more *freedom*, and more *impact*. It's a future where you've evolved your identity into that of a law firm owner, a freedom entrepreneur—even a wealth multiplier.

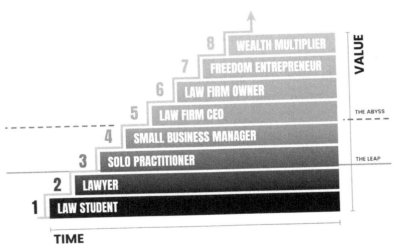

LAWYER LEGACY STAIRCASE

Make no mistake. You do need to commit to do the work. You started this climb as a lawyer, but that's not where your journey ends. You're now an entrepreneur—a business owner who happens to be a lawyer. If you want to keep climbing the Lawyer Legacy Staircase until you're a Law Firm Owner or a step above, you need to act like what you want to become. You have to make decisions like a Law Firm Owner. You have to invest like a Law Firm Owner. You have to do the sorts of things a Law Firm Owner does.

Look at it from the perspective of becoming a professional athlete. Do you think a professional athlete becomes a professional athlete and only then starts doing the things a pro baller does? Do they begin a regimen of eating well, playing seven days a week, and hiring a performance coach only after they get their professional athlete contract? No. They do all the things that a professional athlete does before they ever reach the big leagues, and it's because they do the things a professional athlete does that they actually become a professional athlete!

The same is true for you. You can't wait to make the decisions of a Law Firm Owner until you're a Law Firm Owner. You need to start acting like a Law Firm Owner now. And by making the decisions of a Law Firm Owner, you will become a Law Firm Owner.

We've asked you to make some very scary decisions in this book—decisions that will require your commitment and courage. We've asked you to hire A-players before you're ready. We've asked you to commit to spending 20% of your expected revenue on marketing, 40% of your expected revenue on payroll, and 10% of your expected revenue on getting answers. We've asked you to revamp your operations, marketing, and client services. That's a lot. You may feel hesitant to do any of it.

But ask yourself, *What would a Law Firm Owner do?* And conversely, what would a Solo Practitioner do? A Solo Practitioner would probably be scared and not do any of this. If they make that choice, they'll always remain a Solo Practitioner. But what would a Law Firm Owner do? They would invest before they're ready, hire A-players before they're ready, make marketing videos before they're ready, and so on.

That's how you climb the staircase. Step into the identity you want to claim for yourself. Act like the person you want to become.

And after reading this book, you know the specific decisions and action required. You've learned how to implement the Law Firm Growth Acceleration Model. Establish clear goals for profits, create a foundation of lead abundance, level up your intake, and lead a self-managing team.

LAW FIRM GROWTH ACCELERATION MODEL

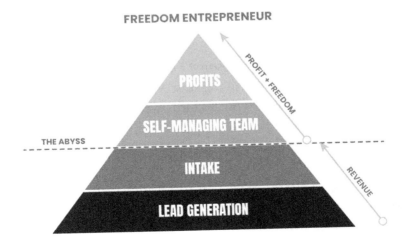

It's this proven framework that leads to your firm's increase in revenue, profit, and freedom, helping you step into the identity you've always wanted and live the life of your dreams.

But none of that happens unless you execute.

If you choose to climb that staircase, then get specific. What action will you take next?

What strategy in this book can you execute on within the next 24 hours?

We're going to jog your memory with a high-level summary of the chapters you just read. As you review each one, think about the first step you need to take to climb the Lawyer Legacy Staircase. Get out a highlighter and mark up this book. Or pull out a piece of paper and write it down. Create a new document on your computer and type it up. Somehow, in some form, document what you're going to start executing on in the next 24 hours so that your dreams can become reality.

We first taught you to **Plan Your Profit,** identifying where you want to go and how to reverse engineer your dreams into reality.

- **Chapter 1: Your Compass Point.** You learned how to think of yourself as a business owner rather than a lawyer, then mapped out your dream life, identifying *where* you wanted to take your firm and *why*. We spelled out reasons you may be holding yourself back, enabling you to overcome those mental hang ups and climb to the next stair.

- **Chapter 2: The Lawyer Legacy Staircase.** We explained how you will evolve your identity in this staircase climb, breaking down the key steps that will take you from Step 3, Solo Practitioner, all the way to Step 6, Law Firm Owner—and then beyond. You also became familiar with the Four C's of change which begin with your *commitment* to action and then the *courage* to follow through.

- **Chapter 3: Plan and Execute Your Law Firm Growth Strategy.** Time for brass tacks. This chapter helped you develop your firm's Vivid Vision and create an Annual Plan that will launch you into accelerated growth. We also taught you the 20/40/10 budgeting rule: 20% for marketing, 40% for payroll, and 10% for getting answers.

- **Chapter 4: Golden Numbers and Great Big Rocks.** In Chapter 4, you busted out your calculator. You learned to identify and calculate the all-important five KPIs to strategically build your law firm's accelerated growth: lead volume, conversion rate, average case value, profit metrics, and net promoter score. Then we explained how to set your firm's Quarterly Boulders to inspire, motivate, and direct your team—turning your firm into a rocket ship.

In Part 2 of the book, we discussed **Growing Your Firm.** Generating lead abundance, forming your marketing strategy, and leveling up your intake.

- **Chapter 5: The New Way of Marketing a Law Firm.** No more "hope and pray" marketing for you.

508

You learned how to provide potential clients with *real value* in your marketing. We also explained how to be strategic in your marketing regarding the *when* (four stages of marketing), *who* (niche down), *where* (fish where the marlins are), and *how* (business strategy > marketing strategy).

- **Chapter 6: The Eleven Commandments of Marketing.** You toured through four stations of a proverbial marketing kitchen, building your understanding of fundamental marketing principles. First, you learned how to *lay the groundwork* for effective marketing copy, then you learned compelling ways to make *the pitch*. From there, we taught you principles to ensure a positive *afterglow,* and we wrapped up by reviewing *global marketing principles*.

- **Chapter 7: Demand Marketing.** This chapter taught you how to get your firm on page one of Google, the most frequently searched website in the world. You can *buy your way in,* using a short term ads-driven strategy, and *build your way in*, enhancing your SEO and capitalizing on keywords to promote your visibility.

- **Chapter 8: Awareness Marketing.** Awareness Marketing layers on top of Demand Marketing as you proactively build awareness about your firm in potential clients who don't yet know about you, using a social media strategy. Using a combined approach of ads, organic marketing, and videos, you learned how to help potential clients *Know, Like, and Trust You.*

- **Chapter 9: Intake & Sales.** With an abundance of new leads, this chapter taught you how to process and capitalize on them. The number one intake goal is to convert your "right fit" clients. The number one intake principle is to follow up relentlessly. We broke down strategies to create a great first impression, weed out unqualified leads, identify "right fit" clients, relentlessly follow up, and ensure your dream clients know, like, and trust you.

Part 3 turned the focus to effectively leading the people making it all happen, creating a **Self-Managing Team.** These chapters taught you how to recruit and lead a team of A-players and deliver a world-class experience to your clients.

- **Chapter 10: Hiring A-Players.** You need stellar people on your team if you're going to accelerate your law firm's growth. This chapter taught you how to hire all-stars. *Attract* great recruits (culture is critical), *win them over* using job ads and interviews, and do the *hiring math* so that you know how much to pay them and hold them accountable to their goals.

- **Chapter 11: ~~Managing~~ Leading A-Players.** You might have re-thought your leadership style during this chapter, because truly great team members will shrivel under micro-management, but level up when they're effectively led. We talked about creating a people-focused firm, using culture, clarity, and effective systems to ensure your A-players perform at their best. We also taught you how to run meetings effectively so that your teams get the information they need without wasting time.

- **Chapter 12: How to WOW Your Clients.** This final chapter focused its attention on how to dazzle your clients with a world-class experience so that they can't shut up about how great you are. You learned how to enhance your client communication, provide them with white-glove treatment, and generate "needle-moving" client experiences that will lead to countless five-star reviews and referrals.

We've given you this chapter breakdown because each one of those chapters gives you strategies you can execute on. Pick one thing from each chapter, then identify the strategy you want to start implementing immediately. Once that's in motion, tick the next one off your list. After you've completed that first set, go deeper into each chapter. Ask yourself, what's another thing I can execute on within 24 hours?

Use this book as an information buffet. You can come back to the buffet as many times as you want, free of charge. This book is not intended to be read and shelved. Use this book as a reference tool. These principles, strategies, and tools are meant to serve you over and over and over again.

Taking action immediately is the strategy that has enabled us both to achieve such success in our own lives. We learn as we go, jumping out of the plane and building the parachute on the way down. We don't *wait* to have all the information we need before getting started. We learn by actually executing.

Just recently, for instance, our sales team was struggling. We bought books on how to lead a sales team effectively, read them over the weekend, took notes, and by Monday, we were implementing changes. We rolled out a new plan *immediately*.

Don't get stuck in analysis paralysis! Now is the time to *move*. Books are a huge piece of any "freedom entrepreneur's" recipe for success, but **books are meaningless without ACTION.**

When Bill was 22 years old, he read *Think and Grow Rich*. The book told him to create a major definite purpose statement and recite that purpose statement out loud, every single day, for the rest of his life. He's done that every single day for the past decade, and he has turned that purpose statement into reality. His anxiety went away, his finances transformed, and his whole life changed. That had everything to do with the fact that the book told him what to do, and he did it immediately. He worked to form necessary habits and stuck with them long enough until things were working right.

Before Andy created a massive YouTube library, he read the book *Expert Secrets* by Russell Brunson. The day he finished the book, he bought a video camera. Ironically, the action then lagged. He waited six months before making his first video because it was scary to do something new. Finally, his desire to make an impact outweighed his excuses, and he made his first video. He resolved to suck long enough to get good at something, and *1,600+* videos later, he now has the freedom, impact, and profit that he used to only dream about. That came when he stopped making excuses and started making reality.

No, it's not easy. None of this success will come overnight. There have been days where we've asked ourselves,

"Is this working? Should we keep doing this?" There have been nights of pacing in the kitchen while our families are asleep as we continually remind ourselves of the goals that drive us.

This is not easy, but it's those days and nights that will make you a champion. Pushing through the challenges will forge you, enabling your success story, one where people praise you in public for what you do in private. Give yourself time for this transformation to happen and *keep taking next steps*. Continue to execute. Continue to push yourself and your firm up that stairway.

The one way to guarantee your success is to simply not quit.

Make Your Days Count

The average person has around 30K days to live. Pull out your calculator one more time and do the math. How many days are already behind you? What percentage of your life do you have left to live?

Have you used up 60%? 70%? 75%?

Now, ask yourself ...

What am I going to do with my remaining time?

You could spend that time glued to a law firm that you can't escape. You could keep apologizing to your family for the time you *can't* spend with them, never taking a vacation, working for clients that you can't stand.

513

Or …

Do you want something different?

At this point, you have a choice. You can go back and do what you've always done, and get what you've always gotten.

Or you can use a proven system—one which so many other lawyers before you have already used to change their lives—to get more impact, profit, and freedom. You can be a success story and leave a legacy that makes your family and friends proud.

You have a choice. All you have to do is say YES, then start implementing. Stop tolerating what you're experiencing now as good enough. Get yourself more freedom. Build your firm's impact. Go get rich.

Start executing today.

That's how you live the life of your dreams!

ABOUT THE AUTHORS

Bill Hauser

Bill Hauser is CEO of SMB Team. Founded by Bill in 2018, SMB Team works with 400 of the fastest-growing law firms in North America. With the power of the innovative Law Firm Growth Acceleration Model, the average law firm who works with SMB Team grew their revenues by 81% last year.

Due to their unique approach to digital marketing rooted in "signed case" data, sales and intake training, virtual assistants, Fractional CFOs and management coaching, INC 5000 ranked SMB Team in the top 1000 fastest-growing private companies in the entire United States in 2022 and 2023 (#729 and #641 respectively).

Due to the impact SMB Team was having on its clients and employees (and a 915% three-year growth rate), Bill was chosen by Ernst & Young as recipient of the Entrepreneur Of The Year® Greater Philadelphia Award.

Bill also hosts the largest legal industry event series, where he has interviewed names like: Alex Rodriguez, Magic Johnson, Kevin O'Leary, Gary Vaynerchuk, Daymond John, Jocko Willink, Emmitt Smith, Brian Tracy, Patrick Bet David, Ed Mylett, Jordan Belfort, Grant Cardone, James Clear, Jillian Michaels, Kevin Harrington, Verne Harnish, Dan Sullivan, Jay Abraham, Dr. Robert Cialdini, Michael Gerber, Evan Carmichael, and dozens of the largest revenue law firm owners in North America.

After his family went bankrupt in the 2008 recession, Bill was motivated to change his career path and embrace business so he could control his financial destiny. Bill has now dedicated his entire life to helping his clients build "recession-proof" businesses as he builds his own recession-proof business (the business he wishes his family had in 2008).

With Bill's wife Emily, daughter Camille, and dog Jade, Bill is the only man in the house—always surrounded by his three amazing ladies! Follow Bill on any social media platform to see all of the content he puts out on a weekly basis.

Andrew Stickel

Andrew Stickel has been helping attorneys grow their practices for over a decade. His first agency, Social Firestarter, was founded in 2012. In 2022, he merged forces with SMB Team. Since then, they have scaled to the #1 Fastest Growing Law Firm Coaching & Marketing Company, through which he has impacted the lives of thousands of lawyers across the country.

Andrew is the author of two best-selling books for attorneys: *How to Get More Law Firm Clients Without Losing Time and Money or Getting Screwed by a Marketing Company* and *5-Star Attorney*. These influential books have further amplified his impact on the legal community, providing actionable insights for lawyers seeking growth and success.

Additionally, he has created over 1,600 YouTube videos offering practical advice and strategies for law firm growth. His expansive library of content has been an invaluable resource for attorneys seeking to navigate the complexities of managing and expanding their practices.

Through these endeavors, Andrew has helped thousands of lawyers not just grow their firms, but fundamentally change their lives. His mission is to empower attorneys to excel in their personal and professional lives nationwide, guiding them to grow their practices, secure more clients, and optimize their time.

As a husband and father of three, Andrew emphasizes the importance of finding success both in work and at home. He's a firm believer that lawyers can and should strive for excellence in every facet of their lives.

ACKNOWLEDGMENTS

From Bill Hauser

Thank you to everyone who made this book possible.

To my team at SMB Team. If we didn't have such an amazing team, Andy and I wouldn't have been able to step away from the business to write this book. Thank you SO MUCH, Team, for consistently going above and beyond and being a group of people I can always put my trust in.

To my clients at SMB Team. Thank you to the hundreds of attorneys who are clients of SMB Team. I always say, without motivated law firm owners, our business would not be possible. Thank you for trying out a completely new business model with me. Thank you for being growth-minded. Thank you for putting your trust in me. Thank you for paying for the book, too! Without you being a client, we wouldn't have been able to invest the hundreds of thousands of dollars it took to write this book.

To Jen, my executive assistant. Thank you for putting your trust in me. I know in the past, you have been the assistant to some big-name CEOs. I don't take it lightly that you took a chance on some lunatic like me. You have seriously revolutionized many parts of our business and also my personal levels of contribution to our company and our mission. Thank you.

Thank you Brandon for entering this learning journey with me, which made up most of the lessons in this book. Your ability to always bounce back from adversity is amazing.

Lastly, thank you to YOU—the reader. I know running a law firm is busy. But, you're investing your time in something that 99% of lawyers never focus on: the BUSINESS of law. I know this book is long, but I promise you—if you drill down, read, and implement what you learn—you will emerge as the market-dominating force and have a transformational impact on your market.

From Andrew Stickel

This book, a journey in itself, would not have reached its destination without the unwavering support and invaluable contributions of several key individuals.

First and foremost, I extend my deepest gratitude to Emmy Anderson, whose exceptional organizational skills and daily support have been the backbone of this project and my everyday life. You have kept me on track through the chaos, ensuring that each day was a step closer to completion.

To our clients, I am deeply grateful for your trust in me with your business and, more importantly, your livelihoods. Your faith in our work has been a source of motivation and inspiration, driving me to strive for excellence continually.

I cannot express enough gratitude to our team. Day in and day out, you work tirelessly for our clients, changing lives with your dedication and expertise. Every day you demonstrate what it means to "be the bar," exemplifying excellence and profoundly impacting the lives of our clients. Your unwavering commitment is a vital part of making our work meaningful and effective. This book is as much a result of your hard work as it is ours, and I am incredibly proud to be part of such a committed and impactful team.

Lastly, I want to thank you, the reader. In a world brimming with endless reading options, you chose this book. Your decision to invest your time in these pages is deeply appreciated. I hope this book not only enlightens you but also brings positive changes to your life and the lives of your family. Your engagement is the ultimate reward for our collective efforts.

From Andrew and Bill

A special thanks to Greta Myers, whose expertise brought the pages of this book to life. Greta, your ability to weave words into impactful narratives has been remarkable. This book would not be what it is without your talent and dedication.

Thank you, Lori Lynn, for your expert editing. Your precision and dedication not only enhanced this book but also met a tight deadline, making complex ideas clear and engaging.

Our gratitude also goes to Shanda Trofe for her exceptional book cover and layout design. Shanda, your creativity and meticulousness, under a tight deadline, have perfectly captured and presented our message.

GET MORE SUPPORT FROM SMB TEAM

The blueprint revealed in this book is how law firm owners around the world are doubling their revenues and changing their lives. It's a lot to take in. Which means there's one question you need to ask yourself ...

Do you have *time* to implement each part of this Growth Model?

Probably not. We bet you have a *ton* of client calls, court appearances, and meetings on your calendar this week already. Your time is scarce ... and you need to spend it wisely.

That's why shortcuts are so valuable.

Since you're obviously committed to growing your firm, we've decided to do something special for you. Consider it a final parting gift from us before you close this book.

We'd like to offer you a no-cost Strategy Session with one of our in-house Growth Specialists to implement the Law Firm Growth Acceleration Model.

But, we need to give you fair warning ...

We can only do this for a limited number of attorneys. Why? REAL research and time go into each one of these Strategy Sessions from our Growth Specialists, who are real people. This isn't a quick overview of your law firm's website with generic strategies on how to grow your firm from an AI bot. It's a specific blueprint valued at $499, with *your* direct next steps outlined to start ascending the Lawyer Legacy Staircase. It includes:

- A customized marketing strategy to show you the fastest way to get more qualified leads for your practice.

- A direct comparison of how you stack up against your top competitors—*plus* individualized strategies to beat them.

- An analysis of your law firm's intake processes.

- Resources to help you change your law firm's operations so you maximize profits and efficiency.

- An analysis of your team, as well as help identifying the bottlenecks of your law firm.

- A personal 1-on-1 strategy session with your Growth Specialist where they go over each detail of your Growth Plan so you get complete clarity.

Oh, yes, and for that unspoken question in your head? It's *not* a glorified pitch session where you're blindsided with a sales presentation at the end. It's a thoughtful analysis of your firm's digital marketing strategy, your intake system, and your business model—everything from beginning to end—to find immediate areas of improvement for your practice.

As you can see from the Google reviews below, you'll get lots of value, and our team will show you *exactly* how to grow your firm:

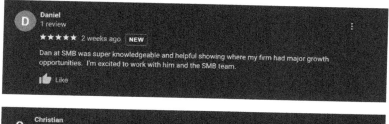

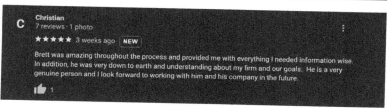

You don't have to figure this out alone. Running your practice is already hard enough without having to add on the concepts from this book to your plate.

If you're ready for your personalized plan to ascend the Lawyer Legacy Staircase so you can provide the life for your family that others only dream of, our team is here to help.

Scan the QR code below to set up a time to receive your customized Strategy Session and Growth Plan:

yourdreamlawfirm.com/custom–plan